DEAD GIVEAWAY

Murder Avenged
from the Grave

Donald Thomas

For Patrick and Audrey

Acknowledgments

In writing this book, I have incurred several debts of gratitude, to the British Library; Cardiff City Library; the London Library; the library of Rhodes House, Oxford; to Michael Thomas of A M Heath and to David Roberts of Michael O'Mara Books.

First published in 1993 by
Michael O'Mara Books Limited
9 Lion Yard, Tremadoc Road, London SW4 7NQ

A CIP catalogue record for this book is available from the British Library

ISBN 1-85479-172-9

Typeset by Florencetype Limited, Kewstoke, Avon
Printed in England by Clays Ltd, St Ives plc

Contents

INTRODUCTION

Getting Away with Murder

On Sunday 5 November 1961, three pot-holers were exploring the excavations of an abandoned lead mine at Brandy Cove on the Bristol Channel coast of south Wales near Swansea. They had planned the descent of an old airshaft, which began as a hole in the ground on the clifftop, long overgrown, and ended in an underground chamber fifty feet below. In this dank underground vault, remote from the sounds of the upper world, their lamps played upon earth and rocks that no one had seen for half a century. Some of the rocks were the size of boulders and it was behind one of these that the the first lamplight showed a scattering of bones. It was possible that an animal had fallen down here, of course. But the bones were in three groups. One of the groups contained a human skull.

Beside the bones there were two rings on the earth floor and some decayed fragments of sacking. It was easy enough to determine that this was a woman's skeleton and that she had been dead for a very, very long time. But who was she? When and how had she died?

The two rings dated from the early years of the twentieth century, so she was presumably still alive then. The South Wales police went back to the files of missing persons for that time. One such person had had a good deal of publicity.

Her name was Mamie Stuart, a chorus girl at sixteen in 1909, who had gone missing in 1919. 'Where is Mamie?' the press headlines of the day demanded, politely describing the

iv

girl as having 'a roving disposition'. At twenty-four she had married George Shotten, a marine surveyor from the little seaside town of Penarth, just west of Cardiff. To begin with, in 1961, where was George Shotten?

The police could find very few witnesses to the events of forty-two years earlier. There was an elderly woman who identified the two rings as being those she had seen Mamie Stuart wear. A long-retired postman recalled how he had seen George Shotten one day in 1919, outside the semi-detached house where the couple lived in Swansea. Shotten had been carrying a heavily laden sack from the house to a van and, when he saw the postman, said that the brass buttons and uniform had given him a fright because they looked so like a policeman's.

Fortunately for the forensic scientists, Mamie Stuart was in the business of having pin-up photographs taken of herself for theatrical publicity. These were now projected against photographs of the skull and it was concluded that they matched. As it happened, this technique was later regarded with scepticism when it appeared to produce a miscarriage of justice at the trial of the concentration camp guard Ivan Demjanjuk, as 'Ivan the Terrible', which began in Israel in 1988. In Mamie Stuart's case, however, there was no reason to think the scientists had got it wrong.

In 1920 the police had been called to the Grosvenor Hotel in Swansea, where a suitcase had been left months before, containing Mamie Stuart's clothes and personal effects. The police went to the house where she had lived with George Shotten, searched the premises and dug up the garden. Nothing was found. She had run off from Shotten as she had run off from her parents ten years earlier. There were certainly men apart from Shotten with whom she had sexual relationships. Indeed, Shotten had begun to find her cold as well as unfaithful.

Public curiosity about the couple revived briefly in 1920 when Shotten was convicted of bigamy and sentenced to eighteen months in prison. He already had a wife and family near Swansea when he married the now vanished Mamie.

After the bigamy case, however, the authorities lost interest in him.

In 1961 after the discovery at Brandy Cove, that interest returned. There was a nationwide hunt for George Shotten as the murderer of Mamie Stuart, the chorus girl of 1919. It took several weeks but the police ran him to earth at last. George Shotten was lying in an unmarked grave in the vast necropolis of Bristol's Arnos Vale cemetery, a hundred miles from where Mamie Stuart had been found. He had died in poverty, of natural causes at the age of seventy-eight, three years earlier in 1958. Had his secret been known, there seems no doubt whatever that he would have been tried and hanged in 1920. Though the police were able to close the case, George Shotten was a man who got away with murder in the most public manner.

From a deserted lead mine on the Welsh coast to a fashionable house at 404 Alvarado Street, Los Angeles, might seem a considerable jump, though the gap in time was only two years. On 2 February 1922, the occupant was found dead on his study floor, shot in the back by a .38-calibre pistol. His name was William Desmond Taylor, director at Paramount and elsewhere of such hits as *Huckleberry Finn*, *Tom Sawyer*, *Davy Crockett* and *Captain Kidd Jr*. Among his leading ladies were Mabel Normand and Mary Minter.

Unlike Mamie Stuart, William Desmond Taylor's death was news from the start. His name was instantly linked with bootleg liquor, drugs, pornography, boys, and Mary Minter among others. A passionate letter of Mary Minter's was said to have been folded into a copy of *White Stains* by Aleister Crowley, the black magician whose name reeked with rumours of devil-worship, torture, murder, child-sacrifice, sodomy and slavery, centred on his 'abbey' at Cefalù in Sicily.

It was strong stuff but it seemed to be of little assistance to the Los Angeles Police Department. Everyone knew Taylor had been murdered, no one knew who had done it. Despite the publicity, Taylor's killer was to get away with it in much the same manner as George Shotten. More than forty years passed before the film director King Vidor turned his

INTRODUCTION

attention to the case. The story which he unearthed, though keeping it secret, involved Mabel Normand leaving the Taylor house and Mary Minter emerging from the bedroom just as her possessive and neurotic mother Charlotte Shelby arrived. If Charlotte Shelby shot dead William Taylor, it would perhaps explain why she afterwards made regular payments to the man who gave her an alibi and why her other daughter, Margaret, who threatened to reveal Charlotte Shelby's guilt, was committed by her mother to the psychopathic ward of a mental hospital.

The District Attorney, Thomas Woolvine, was dead by the time that King Vidor started his investigation. His successor, Buron Fitts, shot himself through the temple in 1973 as Vidor pursued his inquiry. But long before that inquiry had begun, Charlotte Shelby had died in 1957. Mary Minter lived on in Malibu until 1984, a fading star of the silent screen with an air of 'Norma Desmond' from *Sunset Boulevard*. By the time that the facts were published, the murderer of William Desmond Taylor was as far beyond justice as George Shotten in Arnos Vale.

The most complete escape from a murder charge is where no one knows that a murder has taken place. As we shall see in the cases which follow, only the murderer's insistence proved that the 'Lambeth Poisoner' killed Matilda Clover. Again, had it not been for a six-inch fluke of excavation in 1989, her friends and family might still imagine that Karen Price, 'The Body in the Carpet', had grown up and was living with a family of her own.

The cases in this collection describe defendants, some in England, some in the United States and some even with a foot either side of the Atlantic, who never thought they would face justice, yet were caught in the end. Some of them had lived guiltless of any other crime for years after committing murder. One or two were highly thought of by those who knew them. On which side do our sympathies lie, as a trick of fate from the past summons them to justice? Crimes like those of the 'Lambeth Poisoner' or the racketeers of Palm Beach are planned and executed with cold-blooded savagery. At the other extreme murder is, if not accidental, something that a few minutes beforehand the accused had no idea was going to happen. So, according to eyewitness evidence given in the 'Body in the Carpet' case, Alan Charlton lost his temper and hit Karen Price with his fist. Then he said, 'God, she's dead!' Neither he, nor his co-defendant Idris Ali, planned murder. They had nothing to gain from killing the girl and, as it proved, everything to lose. Though not blameless, they were to some extent victims of circumstance as much as she. They attract a sympathy which few people would feel, in the following cases, for the killers of Matilda Clover or Gale Benson, Judge Chillingworth or Millie Jackson.

The safest way of getting away with murder is to let an innocent party be convicted and let the police files close. Even if the innocent man or woman should be released, the odds are against the true murderer being caught after years of delay. In the case of Paul and Wayne Darvell, released in 1992 after serving six years for the murder of Sandra Phillips, a Swansea sex-shop manageress, the promised re-opening of the file to track down the true killer gave birth only to a long silence.

An even more controversial case of this kind followed the 1988 murder of a twenty-year-old prostitute, Lynett White, in the so-called 'Tiger Bay' of Cardiff dockland. 'At the end of the day, the jury were left with so many contradictions, where would they find the truth?' Stuart Hutton, solicitor for one of the accused, pronounced this epitaph on the longest and most expensive murder trial in British legal history. On 22 November 1990, Tony Parris, Stephen Miller and Yusef Abdulahi were gaoled for life for the murder of Lynett White. She was stabbed to death in a flat off the main stem of dockland, Bute Street, in the small hours of 14 February 1988. Police issued a photofit of a white man, seen outside the flat at the time of the murder, agitated and with her blood on his hands. Chief Superintendent John Williams, on BBC Television's 'Crimewatch', appealed for that man to be found. The suspect was 'bleeding himself, he's also got blood on him from the deceased.'

INTRODUCTION

After months of inconclusive inquiries, the police arrested eight men – none of them white – and charged five with murder. Three were convicted: Tony Parris, Stephen Miller, and Yusef Abdulahi. The chief witnesses were two prostitutes who claimed to have heard Lynett White's screams, to have gone to her flat and then also been made by the accused to stab the body. When the body was found, there were some fifty stab wounds and the throat had been cut with such violence that the victim was almost decapitated. Yet sound-tests now reveal that screams in one flat could barely be heard in the other, on the far side of the street. DNA testing of blood in the room, almost certainly from the assailant, does not match that of deceased, accused or witnesses. Abdulahi's claim to have been working all night on a ship in Barry Dock, eight miles away, is supported by witnesses. Tony Parris's alibi of working until two hours after the murder at the Casablanca Club is also supported by witnesses.

Apart from the two prostitutes, the prosecution case rests on a confession to the murder by Stephen Miller. But during hours of questioning he denied being in Lynett White's room on the night of her death. He denied it three hundred times under interrogation. Miller's IQ is a little above subnormal. His interrogation was long and what the appeal court judges called 'oppressive'. As prostitutes make the worst witnesses, so those of under-average intelligence are readiest in such circumstances to put an end to their ordeal by telling the police what the police want to hear.

On 10 December 1992, the Court of Appeal quashed the convictions of the three men. The most troubling development, however, is the death of Geraldine Palk, a Cardiff office worker, in a similar stabbing a few miles away. It happened a month after the three men accused in the Lynett White case had gone to prison for life. Was it coincidence? The South Wales constabulary thought so. The press headlines reported, 'Cardiff Police Slam "Ripper Theory".' This 'slamming' dismissed the suggestion that the killer of Lynett White was still a free man, while three others served a sentence for him.

So far as the Lynett White case is now concerned, the position was made clear on Channel 4's 'Black Bag' programme on 14 January 1993 by Assistant Chief Constable Robert Evans of the South Wales Police. 'We have no plans to embark upon another investigation. But if there's anybody out there with information which could throw some further light on the events of 13–14 February 1988, which led to the death of Lynett, we would welcome hearing from them.'

The cases which follow describe the apprehension of murderers who went free for months or years, some believing they were beyond risk by their own skill or good fortune, others by the lapse of time. In one case, however, there is a possibility that the man who actually committed the murder is still at liberty, twenty-five years after the crime. Unless, like George Shotten, death may have claimed him in the meantime.

In the case of 'The Body in the Carpet', the two defendants found guilty of the murder of Karen Price have both appealed against their convictions. Whatever the outcome of that, the last days of Karen Price were witnessed by a number of her contemporaries who were innocently involved in the events. One of her friends, then thirteen years old, was present when Karen Price died. No public interest would be served by identifying such people and they are referred to by their first names only. An exception is the innocent witness of Karen Price's death, who is referred to as 'Mandy'. That was not her real name and, indeed, no one of that name was involved in the case.

ONE

The Gentleman from Chicago and the Voice from the Grave (1881–92)

I

The 'Lambeth Murders' of 1891–2 constitute one of the more bizarre series of crimes ever to span the Atlantic Ocean. Their story touched the brash commercial society of Chicago in the years before the city's World's Fair, the two hundred brothels, gambling saloons and dance halls of the Levee behind the elegant buildings of Lakeshore Drive and the commercial grandeur of La Salle Street. It reached to the darkest cells of the state penitentiary at Joliet, Illinois, where 1,500 of America's most feared criminals were held in conditions of medieval barbarity. On the European side of the Atlantic, the killings intensified a scandal in the politics and aristocracy of Oscar Wilde's London, which ended in a Trial by Peers before the House of Lords. Their most macabre drama was enacted in the din and glitter of London after dark at the high point of Empire and self-confidence. It was a world of rowdy music-halls, street-fights between scarlet-clad soldiers of the Queen, and the brightly-lit entertainments of the gin palace or the more decorous pleasures of the carriage-trade. Yet the new city of the plain in which the killing began was in many ways a more remarkable place than the great capital of empire in which it ended.

Before justice was done, the shadow-man of the crowded streets almost confessed to being the most wanted killer in criminal history. 'I am Jack . . . .' he said. He was dead before he could complete the sentence.

On 26 September 1833, seventy-six Indian chiefs assembled on the banks of a muddy river whose few shoreline buildings stood on the next best thing to a swamp. At the backs of their leaders were several thousand tribesmen. In front of them stood about fifty settlers, hundreds of miles from armed assistance. But the peaceable Indians made their marks on a treaty. In exchange for several consignments of consumer goods, they moved off west of the Mississippi.

Fifty years later, the land where the settlers and the Indians had stood contained half a million people. Ten years later, it held one million. The newcomers were principally Germans, Irish and English, in order of numbers. The new city of Chicago listed its principal industries as hog-packing, beef-packing, brewing and distilling, the manufacture of iron and steel, wood, brick, leather, chemicals, boots and shoes, cigars and tobacco. The list might also have included the George M Pullman 'Pullman car' and the 'Mickey Finn Special', made up from snuff sprinkled on raw alcohol. Chicago retained the energy and self-confidence of a frontier settlement. It had, literally, raised itself up, using 6,000 jackscrews simultaneously to lift the main buildings several feet above the mud of Lake Michigan. Then it had rebuilt itself after the fire of 1871, which left the streets and buildings of the shoreline looking like Berlin in 1945.

Surrounded by prairie grass and flowers in summer or snow in the winter, Chicago represented wealth, sophistication, crime and vice. As early as 1860 it played host to the Prince of Wales, later Edward VII, the first British monarch to have crossed the Atlantic. It saw Abraham Lincoln nominated at the Republican convention later in that year. At the upper level of its social strata, it became a city of society hostesses, racing at Washington Park and galas at Crosby's Opera House.

Like all frontier towns, Chicago numbered drink and sex among its problems. The first settlement contained too many men and too few women, opening the way for a lucrative brothel trade. This took root at first on Chicago's North Shore and moved south, after the great fire, to the long axial streets which ran inland round the Grand Central Railroad Depot.

Chicago was a national hub for rail travel, east to west and north to south.

The city had no need of Al Capone to teach it the ways of crime. Some of his unsuccessful predecessors went to the Illinois State Penitentiary at Joliet. Some were 'Jerked to Jesus', as the *Chicago Times* described death by hanging. Scientific ingenuity had tried to improve on the gallows 'drop'. Why not hang the condemned man by jerking him off his feet, the rope running over pulleys? It was a mechanical failure. When the jerk was too light, the culprit was left to choke to death. With a too vigorous jerk, the head was pulled off. Though the clients were in no position to complain, the experiment was abandoned.

Crime and vice enjoyed a central location in Madison Street. Madison Street ran inland east to west, and was the municipal division of north and south Chicago. It grew into a busy, shabby thoroughfare with electric trams, stores, cheap hotels with iron fire-ladders and houses where few questions were asked. Its bars introduced 'waiter-girls' for added appeal, though warning the clients that handling the girls 'interferes with the discharge of their duties'. With little disturbance by the authorities, the vice trade published its own guide, the *Sporting and Club House Directory*. Each brothel in the *Directory* gave its address, the name of the madame, the number of girls and a promise of cleanliness combined with confidentiality. Some houses, like Annie Anderson's at 445 South Clark Street, had only half a dozen girls, though hers was 'safe and one of the jolliest houses in Chicago'. Carrie Watson, in the same street, had twenty girls, a pool room, and a 'Mikado' room whose walls and ceilings were covered with 'solid French plate mirrors'. For the enthusiast who wanted more, there were also several Chicago newspapers which advertised girls and brothels, 'pox-doctors' who treated impotence or venereal disease by post, and pornographers who offered sets of photographs showing either nudity or 'Special Subjects'.

But even in this 'jolly' world, death would intervene from time to time. Occasionally, it was a matter for the police. On a hot August day in 1880, they were called to 434 West Madison Street. It was one of a shabby row of bow-windowed houses, demolished a hundred years later. During 1880, Mrs Adell Gridley lived in the back rooms and let out the front as offices. On 23 August, a body had been discovered on the premises. It was that of a young Canadian, Julia Faulkner. How her body came to be there or how she had died was not clear. The strangest part was the discovery that the premises were a doctor's consulting rooms.

Dr Thomas Cream was thirty years old and a Scotsman by birth, one of several thousand from that country who had come to Chicago in the past few years. He had no criminal record and could not say who had put the dead girl in his office. The police investigated a little further. Dr Cream proved to be one of those medical men whose income came from brothels and sexual maladies. From time to time, a girl in one of the houses would get pregnant from all the jollity. A good abortionist was needed and this was Dr Cream's speciality. When Julia Faulkner's body was examined, there was no doubt that she had died as the result of a botched abortion.

The brothel from which she came was run by a coloured woman who was variously known as 'Sally Bowman' and 'Black Bitch Sal'. But who had tried to abort the dead girl? Dr Cream? Sal? Or both? The suspicion was that Dr Cream had performed the operation in Bowman's house and then left. When the girl died there, the mistress dumped her remains at the consulting rooms, as if returning damaged goods.

Dr Cream and the woman were indicted for murder. But the Scots physician defended himself against charges of abortion and murder with quiet skill. It was by no means clear what his part in the girl's death had been. The principal witness against him was Sally Bowman, co-accused. Her reputation was bad and her motive for telling lies against him was strong. Dr Cream showed to advantage when compared with her. As the *Chicago Tribune* was shortly to say of him, 'The doctor told a very straightforward story, and talked very intelligently.' There was no substantial case against him in court and he was acquitted.

All the same, it appeared that Dr Cream was having a run of bad luck. In December 1880, another of his patients, Mary Stack, died. It seemed she had been an associate of Julia Faulkner. Dr Cream's response to the tragedy was to confront the druggist, Frank Pyatt, and accuse him of having bungled the prescription by putting too large a dose in each capsule. He continued to harass Pyatt for some months, until the accusations exchanged between them were overtaken by more serious charges.

Among Dr Cream's patients was Joseph Martin, an immigrant from England. Martin lived on West 13th Street, just south of Madison and close to the city centre, where he prepared furs for the retail trade. Times were hard just then. Dr Cream's latest bill had not been paid. Instead of the usual reminder, Mr Martin received a personal and extremely abusive note from his medical man. Unless Dr Cream's bill was paid at once, he would tell the world that Mr Martin's illness was venereal disease, by which his wife and children were also affected. Mrs Martin was outraged and said so. Mr Martin received a second and a third note from the doctor, written in fine frontier style.

> *You had better learn that low, vulgar vixen woman of yours*
> *to keep a civil tongue in her head, and not talk about others.*
> *Two can play that game. Remember the bastard child you*
> *left in England.*

As bastardy was added to the pox, Mr Martin went to the police. Dr Cream was arrested on charges of sending scurrilous material through the post. He was bailed to await trial, the money being put up by a lady friend, Mrs Mary M'Clellan of 13th Street. The *Chicago Tribune* swore that Dr Cream had 'blasted the good name' of Martin's wife and children. 'Even hanging would be too good for him should he be proved guilty,' the paper added on 19 June 1881. But this case was leapfrogged in its turn by something far more dramatic.

Dr Cream needed women in variety and frequently. Whether his services to the vice trade were the cause or consequence of this frailty remained to be established. He made no secret of it, however, and carried an impressive collection of pornographic photographs, entertaining his male companions with it. By June 1881, his attention was fixed upon Julia Stott, the thirty-five-year-old wife of a sixty-one-year-old station agent, Daniel Stott, on the Chicago and North-Western Railway at Garden Prairie, Illinois. Cream had a number of patients in that area of Boone County, round the little county town of Belvidere. Julia Stott, described by the *Chicago Tribune* as 'very delicate-looking and very plain-spoken', was not his patient, though her husband was. She visited Chicago regularly to collect prescriptions and have them made up.

On her very first visit, as she was soon telling the court, Dr Cream began giving her the vigorous exercise on his consulting-room couch that Mr Stott seemed unable to provide in the marriage bed. The doctor was also rather more adventurous and advanced in his techniques of making love than anything Julia Stott had encountered before. Nor was it a matter of a transient passion. Dr Cream took her across to Mrs Viry's millinery store at 235 Madison Street and commanded the clothes she should wear for their passionate encounters. That she should have the right underwear seemed very important to him and Mrs Viry recalled that he was particular about it, down to the very 'trimmings'. He rather indiscreetly told ten-year-old Amy Revell Stott that he loved her mother and would like her as his own. Something in his manner suggested that he would also like Amy as his own, when she had grown up a little. For the moment, when her mother brought Amy to Chicago on her shopping trips, the little girl sat and waited in another room while adult passion was satisfied.

In an age before air-conditioning, afternoons of sweltering passion on the doctor's couch above the dust and din of Madison Street were followed by a scamper to catch the homeward train at the Chicago and North-Western Railroad Depot. Delicate-looking Mrs Stott would board the train for Garden Prairie, sixty-five miles to the north-west in Boone

County. The pair made little attempt at secrecy. Frank Nordstrand, a brakeman on the train, saw them together in compromising circumstances at the Wells Street depot 'about half a dozen times' in a few weeks.

Dr Cream was treating Daniel Stott for epilepsy at the same time as he was threatening to reveal the Martin family's venereal diseases. Even before he was arrested on 18 June for the letters sent through the post to Joseph Martin, there was a more sinister event in the little town of Garden Prairie. On 11 June 1881 Julia Stott had made one of her usual visits to West Madison Street. Dr Cream had written a prescription for Daniel Stott. Mrs Stott had it made up nearby at Buck & Rayner's drug store. She took the medicine home and gave it to her husband. In twenty minutes he was dead.

Now it was Buck & Rayner who were accused of homicidal incompetence. Dr Cream wrote to the coroner of Boone County, Dr F S Whiteman, alleging that Stott had been poisoned. When this achieved nothing, telegrams followed the letters. At last, Dr Whiteman ordered the body of Daniel Stott to be disinterred. He cut the stomach out and sent it to Professor Walter S Haines of Chicago's Rush Medical College. Professor Haines reported the presence of enough strychnine to kill three people.

Dr Cream asked Julia Stott to grant him power of attorney to prosecute Buck & Rayner. He had given her the prescription without telling her which druggist to go to. Mrs Stott had gone there, travelled straight home and given it to her husband with fatal results. The blame lay squarely on the druggist. Julia Stott refused to give him power of attorney. Instead, she told a different story. Dr Cream had instructed her to go to Buck & Rayner and then come back to him with the medicine. While they were together, she thought 'he put something in it'. Then she went home and gave it to her husband.

Sexual passion now gave way to mutual accusation. Julia Stott not only regarded herself as having been used by her lover to satisfy mere sexual appetite but also began to view his affection for her daughter Amy in a less than favourable light. The police of Boone County decided to arrest both Dr Cream and Mrs Stott. They got Mrs Stott easily enough but the consulting rooms of the quietly-spoken Scottish doctor at 434 West Madison Street were abandoned. Dr Cream had gone, perhaps back to his native Glasgow. Sheriff A T Ames of Boone County was the bloodhound on the scent. For almost six weeks nothing was heard. Then, on 27 July, he found Dr Cream across the border at Belle River, Canada. The doctor made light of having skipped bail on the charges of sending scurrilous cards by the postal service. As for the murder charge, it was so absurd that he agreed to come back to Boone County without waiting for extradition proceedings.

On 20 September the four-day murder trial opened in the Italianate courthouse of Belvidere, a handsome and prosperous settlement, less than ten miles west of Garden Prairie. It was a moment of fame for the little town. The State's Attorney A W Coon led for the prosecution with Senator Charles E Fuller, son of Allen C Fuller, a Civil War general who had been the town's founding father. Cream was defended by Colonel the Hon. D W Munn of Chicago, another Civil War veteran turned lawyer who had seen service in the 126th Illinois Volunteers and the 1st Alabama Cavalry. After the war he edited the *Daily News* at Cairo, Illinois and sat in the State Senate.

Colonel Munn put the case for his present client in 'a very brilliant, able, and eloquent argument'. The *Chicago Tribune* added that if the defendant were to be convicted, 'it is not the fault of Col. Munn'. If the doctor told the truth in his evidence, Daniel Stott died either by the incompetence of the druggist or the malice of Julia Stott. He even denied that he had had any sexual relationship with the woman. But the evidence was against him on this, from the brakeman, the milliner and little Amy. Once that was established, his innocence appeared tarnished. All the same, the *Tribune* reported, the defendant had been a calm and impressive witness, putting his case with logic and persuasiveness. 'The general impression of the people of this county is that the jury will not agree on a verdict.'

But the county was wrong. The jury retired in the afternoon and brought in a verdict of guilty next morning. Perhaps it was some doubt over the extent of Cream's responsibility which persuaded the jurors to fix the sentence at life imprisonment rather than the gallows. Cream appealed against his conviction but Sheriff Ames had done a little investigating in Canada. Dr Cream was quite well known in that country, though he had come from Glasgow, indeed he had a medical degree from McGill University in Montreal. While a student, he had insured his possessions for $1000 and shortly afterwards there had been a fire in his rooms, in which he claimed that his property had been destroyed. The Commercial Union Insurance Company of Montreal had resisted the claim at first but eventually agreed to pay him a third of the sum.

He had impregnated Flora Eliza Brooks, daughter of a hotel proprietor near Quebec. She suffered an abortion under sinister circumstances. Her father sought out Dr Cream and enforced a marriage at gunpoint. Young Mrs Cream died of tuberculosis the following year. The widower set up a practice in London, Ontario. Shortly afterwards, a young chambermaid died from the administration of chloroform. It seemed that she had committed suicide but she had done so after going to Dr Cream for an abortion. Several doctors pointed out to the inquest the impossibility of her having committed suicide in the circumstances described. The coroner's jury returned an open verdict and Dr Cream left hastily for Chicago.

There was no reason for the Belvidere court to show further clemency and the *Chicago Tribune* warned Dr Cream that a jury at a retrial might well opt for the death sentence. He had best serve his time and keep his mouth shut. On 19 October 1881 Sheriff Ames escorted the prisoner to Joliet, some thirty miles south-west of Chicago. The Illinois State Penitentiary was a massive building with the look of a nineteenth-century factory built in the style of a medieval fortress. By 1986 the regime was liberal enough for the inmates to enjoy a visiting performance by female mud-wrestlers, half naked in skintight leotards. A century earlier, it was spartan and brutal. The authorities turned a blind eye to such unofficial punishments as 'The Humming Bird', for which the guards tied a difficult convict in a tin bath of cold water, connected him to the electricity supply, threw the switch and left him to suffer – and sometimes die. The guards boasted that they could make the man's very bones hum with the electric current, as well as the tin bath.

In one of the 900 cells, dressed in a convict 'Zebra suit'. Dr Cream would live out his days. The cell would be eight feet long by four feet wide, containing only an iron-framed bunk with a husk mattress and straw pillow, a dish and a bucket into which he would relieve himself and which he must 'slop out' when told to. Here he would live and very probably die. His cell-block companions in misery included Stiff-Necked Tom, Memphis Bill, Gopher Jim, Lame Sam, Speckled Ed, Bill the Knuck, Chicago Jack and Piano Charley. Here he would eat his 'slum-gulleon'. As for escape, few tried it and almost none succeeded. The forty-foot walls were patrolled by guards with Winchester repeaters under their arms, capable of firing sixteen rounds without reloading. As for his natural passions, it was hard to imagine that prisoner No. 4374, as he now became, would turn from dreams of Mrs Stott and the promise of little Amy to the all-male sex life of the prison, where a man was a jocker or a punk, according to whether he was the dominant or submissive partner.

The world forgot this strange and lethal Scotsman after the autumn of 1881. Julia Stott was discharged from the case on 1 November, much to the chagrin of her lover, and disappeared. Dr Cream tried, in vain, to hire Pinkerton's to find her so that her guilt might be further investigated. Behind the walls of Joliet, he was left to his own troubled thoughts.

Despite his annihilation of three or four people, Dr Cream was by no means the most spectacular Chicago killer of the age. His most common problem had been women or male rivals and how to get rid of them when they posed difficulties. Poison was effective but it had not made for a particularly dramatic trial in 1881. At least in 1881 the citizens of Chicago felt secure from the activities of that Scottish healer of the sick who had practised his curious arts for two years at 434 West Madison Street.

CHAPTER ONE

II

Four thousand miles from Chicago, Chief Detective-Inspector Tunbridge led a life of monastic calm by comparison with that of West Madison Street. A rather bland-looking man with a heavy moustache and clean-shaven chin, he had shown formidable intelligence as a criminal investigator at Scotland Yard. Now he looked forward, with quiet confidence, to a senior appointment. Tunbridge was the Top People's policeman. When a successful businessman or a peer of the realm needed the assistance of a constable, he did not visit his nearest police station. Instead, he sent his solicitor to communicate with John Tunbridge in Whitehall.

Every morning at 9am Chief Inspector Tunbridge would mount the high counting-house stool at his desk in the Criminal Investigation Division. His colleagues noticed that his hair always retained its scrupulously fine parting, his necktie was dead centre between the butterfly wings of his starched white collar, his moustache-ends were waxed and twisted neatly upwards. Tunbridge was a keen gardener and, from time to time, would present flowers or vegetables to his officers. The precincts of the Victorian Parliament buildings, the medieval pastiche of the Palace of Westminster and the baronial style of Scotland Yard made an agreeable place of work. Other men trudged the streets or ferreted out villainy in noisy slums and rancid lodging houses. John Tunbridge looked out on a Canaletto view of the graceful buildings of Whitehall, the broad sparkle of the river and its handsome bridges.

Yet, in October 1891 Inspector Tunbridge first encountered an antagonist who was to cause him more trouble than all his other criminal investigations combined. He needed the assistance of the Special Branch, not to mention the humble plodding constabulary of the London divisions, to catch a particularly dangerous killer. Tunbridge was well used to dealing with criminals of the common type. He was about to discover that a truly deranged but intelligent murderer might be impossible to track down.

The nightmare began in the shabby streets of Lambeth, just across the river from Tunbridge's office and the Houses of Parliament. Waterloo Road, running south from the bridge past the South Western Railway terminus, was a match for Chicago's Madison Street. It was another commercial thoroughfare. The shabby terraces running off it were one of London's rougher districts, dragged down by the coming of the railway terminus twenty years before. With its tenements and warehouses, the din of engines and waggons, there was little peace in the Waterloo Road by day or night.

On the evening of Tuesday 13 October 1891, Jimmy Styles, a barrow-boy of East Street, was drinking with other coster-mongers and their girls in the Wellington public house opposite the station. There were more public houses in the Waterloo Road than in most parts of the city. Within a minute's walk, there were the Wellington and the Lord Hill opposite the station and the York Hotel up towards the river bridge. The October evening was dark and wet, gaslight flaring and shining from the pavements, pillars of flame-lit steam rising from the engines of the trains as they pulled out of the terminus in a muffled thundering towards Southampton or Exeter. In the street itself, there were 'toffs' in silk hats who had come over the bridge to look for the pleasures they missed at home. Girls from the terraced houses, long dresses dragging in the wet, were heading north to the promenade bars of the music halls, Gatti's, the Royal, the Oxford or the Empire. Some went for pleasure and many on business.

At quarter to eight, Styles left the other barrow-boys and their girls, stepping out on to the pavement by the public bar of the Wellington for a breath of air. At first he saw nothing out of the ordinary in the crowds. The girl of eighteen or nineteen who was clinging to the wall by the bar of the Lord Hill was just one more who had got drunk early. As Styles watched her, she uttered a wild cry. The sound was not uncommon when one of the street-girls began to suffer the 'horrors' after a bout of daily and nightly drinking. This one was staggering and her face was twitching, almost as if she was not conscious of where she was. Jimmy Styles knew her vaguely as one of the street-girls run by Fred Linnell. Her name was Ellen Donworth, or 'Ellen Linnell', as she sometimes called herself, and she was still pretty enough to catch the eye in her late teens. She clung to the wall and screamed — and then screamed again.

One or two people looked at her. She also seemed to them another habitual drunkard among the young women of the streets, just one more 'fit of the horrors', doing the 'Lambeth Walk' down the Waterloo Road. Then she fell to the paving, doubled up and writhing. Jimmy Styles had seen and heard dozens of men and women the worse for drink. He had never heard one scream or seen one writhe like this. When someone tried to help her or lift her, she would fight them off and begged to be left face-down, pressing herself prone on the pavement with all her strength.

Styles made his way across to her between horses and carriages. When he got to her, she was 'shivering and trembling'. Between spasms of shrieking and moaning, she gasped out a story of some kind. 'A tall gentleman with cross-eyes, a silk hat, and bushy whiskers . . . gave me a drink twice . . . out of a bottle with white stuff in it.' He was one of her clients and he had promised that the drink was something to make her feel eager for sex.

Styles asked her where she lived and she told him that she lodged at 8 Duke Street, off the Westminster Bridge Road. Then the spasms of agony began and she could not bear to be moved nor touched. Though the seat of the pain was in her stomach, she swore that she was in pain 'all over'. Those who stood round her agreed that the best thing was to get her home, if necessary on a shutter. This was a world without ambulances or emergency medical aid. But every time they tried to move her, the spasms began again, with her back arched and rigid, the pain intense. So they let her lie there and she seemed to feel easier by pressing her stomach hard on the paving. In the end, there was nothing for it. Though she screamed out in agony and her body went rigid in its spasm, they lifted her. The makeshift stretcher-bearers moved off down the Waterloo Road, past the Artisans Café and Coffee

House on the corner of Morpeth Place, towards Duke Street.

Ellen Donworth was no better when they got her home and put her to bed. It was hard to straighten her out and, when the spasms came again, it took several of the witnesses to hold her down. Someone ran to the South London Medical Institute to get help. John Johnson, a doctor's assistant, hurried to the little house in Duke Street. He found several people still holding her down on the bed. When Johnson questioned her, she described 'a tall, dark, cross-eyed fellow', who had given her something to drink from a bottle. He was the same man who had written her letters. Where were the letters? She had taken them with her and given them back to him. He insisted on that as a condition of paying her. It was not uncommon. Few respectable middle-class clients wanted their notes of assignation left in the hands of a prostitute.

Then Ellen Donworth gasped out that she believed she was dying. The spasms began once more and Johnson had not the least doubt that she was in tetanic convulsions. 'I considered her very bad. In fact, she was in a dying state, and I ordered her to be taken to the hospital.'

Before she was removed, there was another arrival in the little room at Duke Street. Inspector George Harvey of 'L' Division, Metropolitan Police had been alerted to the drama, probably by the South London Medical Institute. He had come straight from the divisional police headquarters in Kennington Lane, South Lambeth. Harvey was a man with a kindly look and a curly beard, suggesting a schoolmaster or a doctor rather than a detective. Quietly and patiently, he encouraged the frightened and tormented girl to tell her story.

He could get little from Ellen Donworth except that the man who had given her the drink had also written two letters to her, arranging to meet her, letters which she returned to him when they met. There was no other evidence of his identity. She was then taken to St Thomas's Hospital, a little distance away on the south bank of the river by Westminster Bridge. But the victim of 'Satan in a Silk Hat', as the penny papers called him, was dead on arrival. Dr Thomas Kelloch, the house physician, reported, 'She was dead when I saw her. There was nothing external to account for death. I afterwards examined her. I found nothing at all to account for death.' Subsequently, Dr Kelloch examined the contents of the girl's stomach. In the stomach alone, he found quarter of a grain of strychnine. She had been given enough to kill two or three people.

'Her death caused a fearful sensation in South Lambeth,' Inspector Harvey recalled. There was good reason for that. So long as there was an unidentified homicidal lunatic at large with a supply of strychnine, little could be done to prevent the powder being slipped into a drink or into food. It was plain that Ellen Donworth had been deliberately put to death and more than probable that her killer had lurked in the shadows of the Waterloo Road to enjoy himself listening to her screams. Yet more sinister, morphia had been added to the strychnine, in the hope of prolonging the girl's last hours, so that the man's entertainment should not end too abruptly. The great Victorian poisoners like Palmer of Rugeley and Dr Lamson had been motivated by simple hope of financial gain. This was different. Ellen Donworth at nineteen had been murdered for pleasure, for the excitement of hearing her as if under the attentions of a butcher's knife. Had this been advertised in Lambeth, it would not have taken much for what Harvey politely described as 'sensation' among the street-girls to turn into panic.

The man must be found. Harvey thought he had found him, almost at once. His name was Slater, a travelling salesman for a firm of jewellers. 'He was a tall man with drooping shoulders and straggly beard. There was a general worn-out appearance about him. He was not stout. His age would be about forty or forty-five. One of his eyes had been injured and that gave him a rather peculiar look.' It was not likely that Slater could have got hold of strychnine in medical form but it was also used as a pesticide. He was known to pester women and was, indeed, on remand on various charges when Ellen Donworth died. Inspector Harvey, or rather the prosecutors of the Treasury Solicitor's Department, liked the look of Mr Slater for the part. But then witnesses failed to identify him and it became clear he could not have been with Ellen Donworth between 6pm and 8pm on 13 October. Reluctantly, 'L' Division released him from the cells and Mr Slater moved to higher ground at Clerkenwell.

Harvey's men inquired from door to door in the Lambeth streets without finding a single lead. Two days after her death, an inquest had been opened on Ellen Donworth. The jury brought in a verdict on 22 October of death from poisoning by a person unknown. True, there were other girls who thought this might be the same man as the one who called himself 'Fred' and wore a tall silk hat. But it was estimated that, at this time, there were about 40,000 men in London wearing tall silk hats and a lot more who were called 'Fred', supposing that he had given his true name.

Seeing that the police could find no lead, it seemed that someone was prepared to help them. As the inquest on Ellen Donworth ended, a letter arrived at the coroner's office.

To G P Wyatt, Esq.,   *London, 19th October, 1918*
Deputy Coroner,
East Surrey.

I am writing to say that if you and your satellites fail to bring the murderer of Ellen Donworth, alias Ellen Linnell, late of 8 Duke Street, Westminster Bridge Road, to justice, that I am willing to give you such assistance as will bring the murderer to justice, provided your Government is willing to pay me £300,000 for my services. No pay if not successful.

A O'BRIEN, Detective

The use of a second name by the dead girl, as Alfred Linnell's common-law wife, suggested that the author of the letter might have some personal knowledge of her. The style also had the ring of unspoilt lunacy. Most chilling was the similarity of its style to those notes received by the police from Jack the Ripper, three years earlier. And Jack, whoever he might be, was officially still at large.

The police were not alone in their troubles. Across the river, in the wide Victorian boulevard of the Strand, stood the main offices of W H Smith, the largest, most successful and most respectable of the nation's booksellers. The original W H Smith, who had died that year, had entered Conservative politics and had been successively First Lord of the Admiralty, First Lord of the Treasury and Leader of the House of Commons, while Lord Salisbury remained Prime Minister in the House of Lords.

A fortnight after the coroner received his offer from 'A O'Brien, Detective', Alfred Dyke Acland of W H Smith opened a letter addressed to the head of the firm, Frederick Smith.

> *On Tuesday night, 13th October (last month) a girl named Ellen Donworth, but sometimes calling herself Ellen Linnell, who lived at 8 Duke Street, Westminster Bridge Road, was poisoned with strychnine. After her death, among her effects were found two letters, incriminating you, which, if they ever become public property, will surely convict you of the crime . . .*

Acland read the letter with mingled disbelief and consternation. It was not a demand for money but an offer of professional services.

> *My object in writing is to ask if you will retain me at once as your counsellor and legal adviser. If you employ me at once to act for you in this matter, I will save you from all exposure and shame in the matter; but if you wait till arrested before retaining me, then I cannot act for you, as no lawyer can save you after the authorities get hold of those two letters.*

The offer was signed by 'H Bayne', a barrister. If Smith wished to retain him, then he must write a message saying, 'Fred Smith wishes to see Mr Bayne, the barrister, at once', and paste this in one of his shop windows in the Strand. But that was not quite all. A letter was enclosed, apparently written to Ellen Donworth as a warning against Frederick Smith. It suggested that Smith was afraid he had made her pregnant and was preparing a mixture which he promised her would bring on menstruation but which, in truth, had killed her.

Miss Ellen Linnell,

I wrote and warned you once before that Frederick Smith of W H Smith & Son, was going to poison you, and I am writing now to say that if you take any of the medicine he gave you for the purpose of bringing on your courses you will die. I saw Frederick Smith prepare the medicine he gave you, and I saw him put enough strychnine in the medicine he gave you for to kill a horse. If you take any of it you will die. (Signed) H M B.

To complete the madness of this, it appeared that H Bayne was also 'H M B' and that Bayne was inviting Smith to pay him money as protection from Bayne himself. Acland handed both letters to the firm's solicitors, who forwarded them to Scotland Yard. This was a confidential matter involving the higher strata of Victorian society and not for the eyes of Inspector Harvey and the foot soldiery down at Kennington Lane. Chief Inspector Tunbridge asked Frederick Smith to put the stipulated notice in his Strand window. This was done but with no result. At the same time, 'H Bayne' evidently thought that by slinging enough mud at the unfortunate bookseller, he could make some of it stick. Horace Smith, the Clerkenwell magistrate, now received a letter saying that there was 'enough evidence to hang Mr Frederick Smith', and that someone would 'make it hot for the police' if they took no action.

It was preposterous, of course. Then there was another complaint from one of the most notorious young Englishwomen of her day. Her name was Mabel Edith, Countess Russell, and she was living at the Savoy Hotel. Her contribution added a still more surreal dimension to the murder inquiry.

Lady Russell had received a letter about her estranged husband. They were a controversial young couple, he the

CHAPTER ONE

grandson of Earl Russell, the former Prime Minister, she the
daughter of the divorced and dubious Lady Selina Scott,
whose sister still worked as a 'masseuse' in an establishment
off Leicester Square, which also sold rubber goods and erotic
books, written in English but printed in Paris. As Lady Scott
wrote to Lady Cardigan, young Frank Russell was second
best as a son-in-law. She had hoped her daughter would
marry 'a rich American gentleman to help me through all my
expenses'. Lord Russell was now twenty-six years old. He had
been sent down from Oxford by the Master of Balliol for
'disgusting conduct' towards another undergraduate. In 1890
he was married to Mabel Edith in a society wedding at St
Peter's, Eaton Square. The marriage foundered after a few
months among accusations of domestic violence and sodomy
as well as dark hints of bestiality. All this was now coming to
light in the public entertainment of *Russell* v. *Russell* which
opened at the Law Courts in December 1891 with Mabel Edith
petitioning for a judicial separation. The marriage was to last,
unwanted by anyone, for another ten years, by which time
Lady Scott had been gaoled for criminal libel. Earl Russell had
also been gaoled, though in his case it was by his peers, after
a full-dress medieval trial in the House of Lords in 1901, on
charges of bigamy committed in Reno, Nevada.

As Tunbridge pondered the anonymous letters, he heard
from young Lady Russell's solicitor, George Lewis. Her lady-
ship had been sent a letter informing her that Lord Russell
was the Lambeth poisoner. Unfortunately, in what her
husband called her 'flighty' way, she had lost the letter. As
December approached and just down the Strand from the
Savoy Hotel her lawsuit began, she had other things on her
mind. But the letter had existed. She had shown it to George
Lewis, and he confirmed the fact. If Lord Russell could be
shown to be the Lambeth poisoner, she would get her judicial
separation effortlessly.

It seemed as if the letter to Lady Russell was the work of 'A
O'Brien' or 'H Bayne'. But hers was not quite the case of
Frederick Smith. Lord Russell had, by any description, a bad
reputation. He was destined for prison and scandal. (He was

also destined to be Under-Secretary of State for India in the Ramsay MacDonald government of 1931.) He seemed a much more likely candidate for a crime with sexual overtones than Frederick Smith would ever be.

Chief Inspector Tunbridge questioned Lady Russell and had no doubt that she was telling the truth about the letter. Her correspondent had been quite positive. Lord Russell was the Lambeth poisoner whose lechery was causing prostitutes to die in agony. He it was who had done to death Matilda Clover, for example. Tunbridge explained that the girl in Lambeth was Ellen Donworth, not Matilda Clover. Lady Russell and George Lewis were certain that the girl named in the letter was Matilda Clover. Tunbridge said that, so far as the police were concerned, no one called Matilda Clover had died, let alone been murdered. There was no evidence that she ever existed. That seemed like the end of it. Scotland Yard could hardly be expected to open a murder file each time a lunatic or mischief-maker claimed a non-existent person had been murdered.

Shortly after this, another letter was brought to Tunbrldge. It had been sent to an eminent London doctor, William Broadbent of Seymour Street, Portman Square, from an otherwise unknown correspondent, 'M Malone', who accused Dr Broadbent of the Lambeth poisoning. 'Evidence was found which showed that you not only gave her the medicine which caused her death but that you had been hired for the purpose of poisoning her.' Yet all was not lost for the fashionable physician of Portman Square. 'Now, sir, if you want the evidence for £2,500, just put a personal in the *Daily Chronicle*, saying that you will pay £2,500 for his services, and I will send a party to settle the matter.'

But this was not a letter about the death of Ellen Donworth. The girl named was once again Matilda Clover. 'M Malone' gave her address as 27 Lambeth Road and her date of death as 20 October, one week after Ellen Donworth.

Then the letters stopped. Tunbridge submitted those in his possession to an expert in handwriting, Walter de Grey Birch of the British Museum. This examination confirmed that they had been written by various people and that some of the handwriting was female. The possibility of a gang of psychopaths working together went against all experience.

Tunbridge was convinced by now that this was at best a hoax and at worst an attempt at blackmail. He saw no reason to trouble Inspector Harvey and the Lambeth division nor to send an officer to check the allegations. Had he done so, he would have discovered that there was a Matilda Clover living at 27 Lambeth Road, near St Thomas's Hospital, and that she had died on 20 October 1891 at the age of twenty-seven.

III

John Tunbridge's mind went back to Mr Slater, molester of young women in Lambeth, now living in Clerkenwell. A goodly number of people with grudges to work off against the police might have amused themselves by sending the notes of 'A O'Brien', 'H Bayne', or 'M Malone'. The magistrate in Clerkenwell, where Slater now lived, had received one of the letters. Slater had a grudge against the police and had perhaps decided that a few malicious notes would make the lives of the force more difficult. Was it significant that the letters ceased as Slater went to trial?

Tunbridge hesitated. It might still be blackmail, though he doubted it. He agreed to put an advertisement in the *Daily Chronicle* on 3 December on behalf of Dr Broadbent, as 'M Malone' had demanded. Then Tunbridge went home to his gardening. 'The letter was looked upon as a letter from an insane person,' he explained, 'Other letters had been received of a similar character, and inquiries had been made and no one had turned up in relation to them.' The inquiries did not extend to knocking on the door of 27 Lambeth Road and asking if Matilda Clover lived there, within half a mile of Tunbridge's office.

Nothing came of the newspaper advertisement. For the time being, Tunbridge agreed to put a man outside Dr Broadbent's house in the expensive calm of Portman Square. Nothing came of that either and the man was withdrawn. Yet

Dr Broadbent and Miss Clover had been very differently treated by Scotland Yard. It seemed that an eminent medical man in Portman Square, threatened by a foolish letter, counted for more than a woman in the Lambeth Road who was said to have been put to the most agonising death. Chief Inspector Tunbridge was subsequently and unsympathetically questioned as to why he had not even bothered to send an officer round to the house where Matilda Clover lived and died.

'Here is a real person,' said Sir Henry Hawkins, the trial judge, irritably, 'who actually lived at 27 Lambeth Road, and it is said that this person was poisoned by strychnine. This information comes to Scotland Yard, within a quarter of an hour's walk of the place. How comes it that no one took the trouble to make an inquiry at Lambeth Road?'

'Well, it was not done,' said Tunbridge airily.

Hawkins persisted. 'I cannot see why it should have been thought of more importance to watch Dr Broadbent's house than to make this inquiry.'

'It was thought from the tone of the letter,' Tunbridge insisted, 'that it was an attempt to extort money.'

This made nonsense of his first suggestion that it was regarded simply as the work of a lunatic who never tried to collect the money. Hawkins asked whether, if the blackmailer had been caught, Scotland Yard would then have investigated the possibility that Matilda Clover had been murdered.

'I presume so,' Tunbridge said, as though it did not directly concern him.

'I should presume not,' Hawkins snapped at him.

27 Lambeth Road was not the only place within a short walk across the river from Scotland Yard. So was 'L' Division of the Metropolitan Police in Kennington Lane. Inspector Harvey, leading the divisional inquiry into Ellen Donworth's death, was told nothing of the lunatic letters. Naturally Frederick Smith, Lady Russell, Coroner Wyatt and Dr Broadbent had gone straight to the top with their complaints of being threatened, to Scotland Yard. And there their information remained for more than five months. As Sergeant Ward and his

Lambeth constables inquired door to door or asked questions among the girls of the streets, neither they nor Inspector Harvey had any idea that the person who had presumably killed Ellen Donworth was also claiming to have poisoned Matilda Clover. And Matilda Clover was certainly dead and buried. What was worse, no one need even have walked the short distance from Scotland Yard to 'L' Division. Employing the latest technology to combat crime, the Yard had a telegraphic wire to every divisional headquarters in the London area. On this occasion, no one bothered to use it.

The murder inquiry was at an impasse. Perhaps it was over. In Lambeth Inspector Harvey had no one in his sights, not even Mr Slater with his casually sadistic penchants and his pestering of the local young women.

The opinion across the river at Scotland Yard was still that there were two crimes outstanding. One was the murder of Ellen Donworth, which 'L' Division was methodically investigating among the lower orders of Lambeth. The other was a blackmail plot against some Very Important People in Victorian society with even more important lawyers. Without question, the letters were regarded as the work of someone other than the murderer. In any case, after the letter accusing Dr Broadbent of having been hired to murder Matilda Clover by poison, the correspondence ceased. South of the river, as the melodrama of Ellen Donworth became yesterday's news and then last month's news, there was no more murder and no further sighting of the absurd 'Fred' in his black silk hat.

Perhaps the killer had committed suicide, as Jack the Ripper was thought to have done by Scotland Yard, whose chief commissioner named the killer as Montague Druitt, a barrister. Yet the Lambeth letters sounded too devilish and self-confident for a suicide. Moreover, they had been written by several people. That was one reason why Tunbridge thought they were not the work of Ellen Donworth's killer. The opening months of 1892 passed without a letter or incident of any kind in the case. Instead, the public was titillated by accounts of the Russell matrimonial dispute in the Law Courts of the

Strand with its stories of strange people going bump in the night. Other forms of theatre did good business as well, Oscar Wilde's new play *Lady Windermere's Fan* and *Widowers' Houses* by the music critic of *The World*, George Bernard Shaw. Rudyard Kipling's *Barrack Room Ballads* covered the bookstalls. Lottie Collins first sang 'Ta-ra-ra-boom-de-ay' on the music-hall stage.

By April the minds of most people turned towards a pair of elections, in England where Mr Gladstone was trying to unseat Lord Salisbury and in the United States, where Grover Cleveland and the Democrats seemed to be ahead. The immediate news was of a severe earthquake in California. Yet in the well-upholstered comfort of London's Metropole Hotel in Northumberland Avenue, scarcely a stone's throw from Scotland Yard, there was more immediate consternation among the guests who received a printed notice.

ELLEN DONWORTH'S DEATH

To the Guests,

of the Metropole Hotel

Ladies and Gentlemen,

I hereby notify and warn you that the person who poisoned Ellen Donworth on the 13th last October is today in the employ of the Metropole Hotel and that your lives are in danger as long as you remain in this Hotel.

Yours respectfully,
W H MURRAY.

London   April   1892

This was no handwritten joke but a handsomely-printed circular distributed in a large number of copies. The thought of a sinister chef, stirring strychnine into the consommé was enough to start a general exodus from this estimable hotel. W H Murray, whoever he was, certainly sounded like the voice of authority. Scotland Yard was almost next door. Was he an official there? He seemed like a man who knew what he was talking about. But time passed and no one died of the consommé. The guests who had panicked returned, rather self-consciously, to the dining-room and guessed that they had been had. But when they picked up their newspapers next day, they saw that farce had once again turned to horror.

Police Constable George Cumley was not a man to whom a pretty young countess or a captain of commerce like Frederick Smith would turn for assistance. He was 'PC Plod' in his tall helmet and cape, carrying his bull's-eye lantern and truncheon like a medieval watchman. During the second week of April Cumley was on night duty, patrolling his beat south of the Thames and going off duty at six every morning. Just before two o'clock on the morning of 11 April, Cumley turned east from Waterloo Road, near the bridge, and made his way steadily down Stamford Street. It was a long street of terraced houses and commercial buildings which came out by Southwark Cathedral and London Bridge. When he was about thirty-five feet from the pavement door of Number 118, which backed on to the wharves and lanes of the riverside, the door opened and a man was let out by a girl. He was later to recognize the girl as Emma Shrivell, eighteen years old.

Cumley was not the stuff of future chief inspectors but he could memorize the face and figure of a man. 'He was about five feet nine inches or five feet ten inches in height, and about forty-five to fifty years of age. He was dressed in a dark over-coat with a silk high-hat. As he turned by the street door, I saw by the reflection of the street lamp that he had glasses. He had a moustache, no whiskers.' Cumley knew well enough what the man had been doing in the house. Several girls lodged there, picking up men in bars or music halls and bringing them back to this place of business. The man looked at Cumley and walked away briskly towards the Waterloo Road but Cumley said he was not surprised at this because it was a cold morning. He continued his beat, patrolling the lit-tle streets and foggy riverside wharves behind the houses. At length he came back into Stamford Street again.

Something was going on at Number 118 and it was not a

jolly party. The time was now about half-past two and a large four-wheeled cab, not a hansom, was driving up at the door. Someone in the street began calling him, summoning him to the house. Then Cumley saw another uniformed constable from 'L' Division, William Eversfield, carrying a girl from the house to the vehicle. Or rather, Eversfield was doing his best to carry her as she shuddered, twisted and filled the street with her screams.

Eversfield put the younger girl, Emma Shrivell, into the cab, telling Cumley that there were two girls in this state and that the second one was still in the house. He had arranged for them both to be taken to hospital. Cumley went indoors and saw the second victim, Alice Marsh, twenty-one years old. She was grotesquely placed, on hands and knees and wearing only a nightshirt, pressing her stomach with all her strength on a chair seat in the hallway. When he lifted her to carry her to the cab, she began screaming as the pressure of the chair seat on her stomach was removed. Charlotte Vogt, the land-lady of 118 Stamford Street had found her like this. Mrs Vogt had gone to bed at about eleven o'clock and was woken just after two o'clock by cries of pain from Alice Marsh lying over the hall chair, while Emma Shrivell was writhing on the bed-room floor screaming 'Alice!' with all her strength. Charlotte Vogt called her husband and sent him for a cab to take the girls to hospital, also telling him to get the police. When the cab arrived, Constable Eversfield was with it.

The ghastly carnival of torment which the killer had staged for Ellen Donworth was now repeated. Eversfield rode in the cab with the two girls and Cumley outside with the driver. By the time they reached the hospital, Alice Marsh was dead. She had died without saying anything between her cries. Emma Shrivell lived until eight in the morning. There was no doubt that she was going to die and the medical dilemma was that every effort to keep her alive also prolonged an atrocious agony. She made an incomplete statement, which would only have been formally admissible if it could be shown that she made it knowing death was imminent. But Emma Shrivell was only eighteen and clung to the hope of life.

Inadmissible or not, her evidence was that she and Alice had a client who called himself 'Fred', a stoutly built man with dark hair and a bald dome. He wore glasses and was five feet eight or five feet nine inches tall. He wore a black overcoat and a tall silk hat. He had gone back to the house with the pair of them and, after eating tinned salmon and drinking bottled beer, he had given each of them three long thin capsules to enliven them for the three-sided pleasures that were to follow. The man had left and soon afterwards the girls' agonies began.

George Cumley asked the dying Emma Shrivell if the man was the same person he had seen her letting out of the street door just before two o'clock. He was. Then there was little more to be done as the girl passed beyond coherent replies or thought. The spasms of pain grew less frequent as she lost consciousness and died.

Dr Cuthbert Wyman at first thought that the two girls might have died of ptomaine poisoning from the tinned salmon. The salmon tin was retrieved and examined but without yielding any sign of contamination. Dr Thomas Stevenson, Lecturer in Medical Jurisprudence at Guy's Hospital, carried out a post-mortem on both girls for the Home Office. In each case, he found a fatal dose of strychnine, combined with morphia to prolong the ordeal.

Despite the notoriety of the 'Lambeth Poisonings', the investigation of the double murder was again left to Inspector Harvey at Kennington Lane. Scotland Yard contented itself with the blackmail inquiry and, of course, it was still only the Yard that knew of any suggestion of Matilda Clover having been poisoned. But George Harvey was to make progress by hard work, good fortune and without assistance from the far side of Westminster Bridge.

No one walked the pavements of the city further in April 1892 than Sergeant Alfred Ward, Inspector Harvey's facto-tum. With three street-girls dead and their killer ready to inflict a summer of havoc on others, Ward was sent 'to all parts of London to make inquiries of prostitutes'. After a good deal of useless travelling and inquiring, Ward was told by a

Lambeth girl that if he really wanted the truth about girls being poisoned in Lambeth, he should have a word with Lucy Rose.

Who was Lucy Rose? She was a servant girl now living some way off in Merrow Street, at the far end of the Walworth Road. Back in the autumn, she had been servant in a house where a young prostitute was taken ill with the 'horrors' in the top floor rooms. The young woman had died in agony after a night on the drink. Before she died, Lucy Rose heard her say that a man had given her some pills.

Sergeant Ward set off down Walworth Road and found Lucy Rose still working in Merrow Street. She confirmed the story but said that the young woman had actually died of DTs. 'During her agony she screamed as if in great pain.' Lucy Rose recalled. 'There were moments when she appeared to have relief, and then the fit came on again. When the fits were on her, she was all of a twitch.' The pain was such that the young woman had spent her last hours doubled up grotesquely on the bed, while her companions looked on in disbelief.

But what about the pills? Well, Lucy Rose had not taken much notice of that, seeing that the doctors all said the girl died of DTs. 'She told me she had been poisoned by pills given her by the gentleman.' Did Lucy Rose happen to hear who this gentleman was? Well, she had not been told his name nor anything else about him. To Ward it must have seemed as if a tenuous lifeline of investigation had snapped. Then Lucy Rose said that, though she did not know his name, she herself had met the gentleman, when she let the couple into the house.

'There was the light of a small paraffin lamp in the hall. The gentleman was tall and broad and had a heavy moustache. He had no other hair or whiskers on his face except the moustache. I should say he was about forty. He was wearing a large coat with a cape to it and a high silk hat.' After the couple had finished, Lucy Rose heard the girl say, 'Good night, dear', as she let him out. At about three o'clock in the morning the screams began. Lucy Rose went quickly up to the top floor and found the occupant pressing herself face down across the foot of the bed, 'her head fixed between the bedstead and the wall.' It was then she swore she had been poisoned. Next morning she was dead.

The drama had taken place at 27 Lambeth Road. The name of the dead girl was Matilda Clover.

Inspector Harvey sent for a copy of Matilda Clover's death certificate. Dr Robert Graham had signed it and given the primary cause of death as 'delirium tremens' and the secondary cause as 'syncope' or failure of the heart's action. He gave these as the causes of death 'to the best of my belief'. It was not an unreasonable belief. He had been treating Matilda Clover for alcoholism by prescribing bromide of potassium and various sedatives. On the night of her final illness, he had more cases than he could handle, including a baby to deliver. Because he was out on his rounds when Mrs Phillips came to summon him to 27 Lambeth Road, his assistant Francis Coppin went in his place.

Francis Coppin was not inexperienced, having been a doctor's assistant in the area for fourteen years and the son of a doctor. Matilda Clover became ill at 3 am and he saw her four hours later. She gave every appearance of having epileptic fits or convulsions brought on by excessive drinking. She had been drinking, there was no doubt of that. Her landlady and the servant girl, Lucy Rose, saw her go out again after her visitor had left. She came back, as Mrs Phillips described it, 'rolling drunk' on the proceeds of the money she had just earned. It all fitted so well. Francis Coppin knew that Dr Graham had been treating her for alcoholism. So the doctor's assistant gave her carbonate of soda to stop her vomiting but realized that she was in 'a dying condition'. She was a strongly-built young woman, the daughter of a worker in the leather trade at a tannery in nearby Southwark, but it had long seemed likely that she would kill herself by the amount she drank, sooner or later. This seemed to be the moment. Matilda Clover herself thought she was dying and asked to see her two-year-old son, who was her only child.

Under the circumstances, Francis Coppin had no reason

whatever to think of strychnine or poison of any sort. He had never come across such a case, though he was aware of the symptoms of tetanic convulsions. As any other assistant might have done, he went back to Dr Graham with news of the young woman's death and gave his opinion that it was caused by 'delirium tremens'.

Such was the story of 20 October 1891, now told to the police for the first time. Across the river, in Scotland Yard, Chief Inspector Tunbridge sat on his high counting-house stool in the Criminal Investigation Department and read with some surprise that Inspector Harvey of 'L' Division had applied to the Home Secretary for an order to exhume the body of Matilda Clover who had died on 20 October and been buried in Lambeth Cemetery seven days later. However Lambeth Cemetery was not in Lambeth. As a matter of hygiene, inner-city burial grounds had been closed thirty years earlier and each area of London had its own sculptured necropolis on the fringe of the city. Lambeth Cemetery lay between Tooting and Wimbledon. On 6 May Dr Thomas Stevenson, the Home Office pathologist, set off with police officers, a vanload from Mr Mouatt, undertaker of Waterloo Road, and grave diggers to unearth Matilda Clover.

At the grimmest moment of the case, there was another glimmer of farce. Matilda Clover had been laid somewhere in a common grave with a good few other people and no memorial. She might not be easy to find, at least not without digging up a selection of the other 'dear departed' as well. There was some doubt as to where exactly she was. It was bound to be hit or miss. A minor embarrassment was that certain citizens of Lambeth had evidently been placing flowers on the graves of strangers for years under the impression that their own loved ones were buried there. The diggers brought up one coffin after another, none of them containing Matilda Clover. After fourteen people had been exhumed from the Tooting clay, the search was over. The coffin was of the cheapest kind but it bore a plate screwed to it with the legend, 'M Clover, 27 Years'.

CHAPTER ONE

Dr Stevenson commandeered his prize. He removed the brain, stomach, part of the intestines, the liver and fluid from the chest. What remained of poor Matilda Clover was then buried again. In his laboratory Stevenson tasted the suspect substance and found the characteristic bitterness of strychnine. He mixed it with sulphuric acid and manganese dioxide, producing the most delicate violet colour which proved the presence of strychnine again. By the time he had finished, there was little doubt that Matilda Clover had ingested a dose of strychnine that was amply fatal.

A murderer was the one person certain to have known that Matilda Clover died of strychnine poisoning. And there would have been no Scotland Yard investigation but for the lunatic letters alleging the crime. But the author or authors of the letters, for they were in varying scripts, were surely not all murderers and murderesses. It was impossible to link any of them with the luckless Mr Slater who was now defending his character and his liberty in Clerkenwell. The poisoning case was far from over but Lambeth had scored one triumph at least. Scotland Yard and its blackmail theories took second place to the police work of its poor relations south of the river.

But Chief Inspector Tunbridge's evidence was increasing as well. During the inquest on Alice Marsh and Emma Shrivell, Dr Wyatt the coroner had received a note, asking him to pass on an enclosed letter to the foreman of the jury.

Dear Sir,

I beg to inform you that one of my operators has positive proof that Walter Harper, a medical student of St Thomas's Hospital, and a son of Dr Harper of Bear Street, Barnstaple, is responsible for the deaths of Alice Marsh and of Emma Shrivell, he having poisoned those girls with strychnine. That proof you can have on paying my bill for services to George Clarke, detective, 20, Cockspur Street, Charing Cross, to whom I will give the proof on his paying my bill.

Yours respectfully,
WM H MURRAY

There was, indeed, a private detective with an office in Cockspur Street, though his name was Henry Clarke, who received a similar message. But Tunbridge next heard from Dr Harper of Barnstaple. He had also received a letter from Mr Murray about his son.

> I am writing to inform you that one of my operators has indisputable evidence that your son, W J Harper, a medical student at St Thomas's Hospital, poisoned two girls named Alice Marsh and Emma Shrivell on the 12th inst., and that I am willing to give you the said evidence (so that you can suppress it) for the sum of £1500 sterling. The evidence in my hands is strong enough to convict and hang your son, but I shall give it to you for £1500 sterling, or sell it to the police for the same amount.

Dr Harper was told to insert a personal advertisement in the *Daily Chronicle*, 'W H M – Will pay you for your services. – Dr H.' Then, in an extraordinary twist of reasoning, Dr Harper was told that he could have a copy of the evidence on approval, 'before you pay me a penny', to see whether or not it was worth the amount. The blackmail letter was signed politely, 'Yours respectfully, W H MURRAY.' Dr Harper heard no more, until Chief Inspector Tunbridge arrived in Barnstaple, in consequence of the letter from 'Murray' to the coroner's jury.

With each new revelation it seemed more certain that the letters, like the murders, were the work of a mind that belonged in an asylum for the criminally insane.

IV

Scotland Yard decided to take control over the investigation of the four murder cases – Donworth, Clover, Marsh and Shrivell – from the less prestigious hands of 'L' Division. This happened on 26 May. With Inspector Harvey and his men out of the way, Tunbridge considered the possibility that the blackmailer of the Harper family might be telling the truth.

After all, there was no point to the blackmail otherwise. Could Walter Harper, who had just qualified as a doctor, be the man? True, the suspect 'Fred' had seemed older but perhaps Fred was nothing to do with it, after all.

Walter Harper was not difficult to find. He had lodged at 103 Lambeth Palace Road, just behind St Thomas's Hospital and the other buildings which looked across the Thames to the Houses of Parliament. At the moment he was in the process of moving from there to Braunton in Devon, where he proposed to set up in practice a few miles from his father. Through the web of Scotland Yard's Special Branch, Tunbridge moved upon the house in Lambeth Palace Road. It was kept by Mrs Sleaper and her daughter, Emily. Being so close to the hospital, its rooms were occupied by medical students and young doctors.

The Special Branch files showed that there was a sleeper of another kind, very close by in Westminster Bridge Road. His name was John Haynes and he had been recruited by Major Le Caron to combat Sinn Fein in its dynamite attacks on London railway stations and public buildings. Haynes was officially, though not publicly, classified as 'in the Home Office Department as a secret agent to make inquiries about a certain class of suspected persons'. The great success of the dynamiters had been to blow up part of Scotland Yard itself in 1884. Haynes' superior, Le Caron, was a legend in intelligence work who had enlisted in the United States army and penetrated the secret Clan-na-Gael organization before returning to London. John Haynes had also just spent some time in the United States as an 'engineer'. Now he was living quietly and 'unemployed' in rooms above William Armstead's photographic studio at 129 Westminster Bridge Road.

Among his contacts, who had no idea of his past, John Haynes listed one of the lodgers in the same house as young Dr Harper. This was Dr Neill, an American postgraduate student who had arrived in England several weeks earlier. He had also come over to marry his fiancée, Miss Laura Sabbatini of Berkhamsted. Chief Inspector Tunbridge now had an unwitting informant in the house where Walter Harper lodged. John Haynes, of course, kept clear of Scotland Yard. His link with Tunbridge was Sergeant Patrick M'Intyre, a full-time Special Branch officer working out of the Yard. He was, in the modern sense, John Haynes' controller.

On 1 May, six days after the first allegations against Walter Harper, M'Intyre was introduced to Dr Neill, as a friend of Haynes, by William Armstead the photographer. The acquaintanceship ripened. Sometimes with Haynes and sometimes without him, M'Intyre and Neill would meet for a drink or two in The Pheasant, a pub in Lambeth Palace Road. Yet it was Neill and Haynes who saw most of one another until 14 May, Neill talking about his other work in England as representative of the Harvey Drug Company, whose samples he displayed.

The reports that came back to Tunbridge were of a man who had 'a soft voice, though strong American accent; dressed with taste and care, and was well-informed and travelled as men go.' He was described as being powerfully built with a heavy and protruding under-jaw. He drank gin, smoked a pipe and cigars, and chewed gum. There was a suggestion that he suffered from nervous compulsions. He was observed, apparently by John Haynes, at 'Gatti's' Restaurant in the Strand, otherwise known as the Adelaide Gallery Restaurant.

> He was of an exceedingly restless temper, always pacing about, even when drinking at a bar; and when sitting, was always moving his legs like a dog dreaming, or fiddling with something on the table, and moving his head and rolling his eyes to watch every one who moved, the people who came and went, the waiters who attended on him. He appeared to hate being alone, for though he never seemed to enter with anybody, when my table was full he never went and sat by himself, but always managed to go and sit at an occupied table.

On 14 May William Armstead told Haynes that he thought the building in Westminster Bridge Road was being watched and that someone was following Haynes and Neill. John Haynes repeated this to Neill, who said that he thought so as well. He believed that he was the cause of it, because he lived at 103 Lambeth Palace Road, where there was a young man called Harper in whom the police might have an interest.

John Haynes let his friend talk. Dr Neill confessed to a dreadful suspicion that Harper had killed five girls. They were Ellen Donworth, Matilda Clover, Lou Harvey, Alice Marsh and Emma Shrivell. He knew the names because Harper confided the first three to him and asked if Neill could get him some poison to kill the other two. Dr Neill had been so alarmed that, though he was wary of finding himself sued for defamation, he had managed to discover the address of the intended victims and had written a letter to Marsh and Shrivell. He had warned them to have nothing to do with Harper and on no account to take any medicine prescribed by him.

It seemed a complete answer, except for one thing. Who was Lou Harvey? Tunbridge sent his officers to the Registrar-General at Somerset House. The register of deaths for the period showed no one called Lou, or Louisa, Harvey. Could Dr Neill add anything? He could only say that Harper had told him Lou Harvey 'dropped down dead at a music hall'. But there was no record of that death under any name. Lou Harvey promised to be a far more difficult case than Matilda Clover.

John Haynes invited Dr Neill to have dinner at the Café de Paris on Ludgate Hill and to tell him the whole story. Neill agreed and made no objection whatever when Haynes took out pencil and paper to keep notes of the conversation. Neill explained that Harper's father gave the young man more money than was good for him. Some time ago, Harper had picked up a girl at Mutton's Bar in Brighton, had an affair with her and got her pregnant. He arranged an abortion. Alice Marsh and Emma Shrivell heard about this and tried to blackmail him. Hence, Harper wanted to get rid of them – or so he had said. There was a certain plausibility in this, since

Marsh and Shrivell had come from Brighton to London just before that. It was then, according to Dr Neill, that Harper tried to get poison from him and that he wrote to warn the two girls.

Neill's relationship with Patrick M'Intyre grew less easy, as if he suspected he was being made use of in some way without being told what it was. Neill complained that a 'rip' had followed him a few nights earlier in the Westminster Bridge Road. When he turned and confronted her, she said 'she was sent after him by the police for the purpose of ascertaining who and what he was.' A little while before that, he had been stopped and questioned by a detective called Murray in Lambeth Palace Road. Murray wanted to know about Harper and his dealings with young women. Why was Neill being harassed when all he had done was to help? M'Intyre had no idea but he arranged to meet Neill five days later, on 24 May, at noon. Perhaps he would have an explanation then.

When Neill failed to appear on 24 May, M'Intyre went round to Lambeth Palace Road and found him ill in bed. M'Intyre said that he was sure there was no detective called Murray at Scotland Yard. In that case, it seemed that Neill was either 'W H Murray' or the victim of some further attempt at blackmail by the man who called himself 'Murray'. Would Dr Neill please jot down the matters complained of? M'Intyre handed him a sheet of paper. At the same time, Dr Neill showed his bona fides by handing M'Intyre the warning letter that he had written to Alice Marsh and Emma Shrivell.

It was curious that Dr Neill should have his own letter, though he insisted he had asked for its return to prevent any charge of defamation by Walter Harper. After all, Harper was going to visit the girls at their lodging and might easily have found the letter there. It was addressed to them at 118 Stamford Street and it had certainly been through the post. As Dr Neill had said, the letter warned them against Harper as the self-proclaimed murderer of Ellen Donworth, Matilda Clover and Lou Harvey. Perhaps it was more likely that young Harper had merely been boasting or joking about such murders but Dr Neill decided to take no chances.

M'Intyre put the letter down. He asked Dr Neill to compile a schedule of his movements since his arrival in England. Neill promised to have it ready for him next day. Back at Scotland Yard, the handwriting on the other sheet of paper was compared with that on the other notes. It appeared different. But Dr Neill's notepaper bore a watermark, 'Fairfield – Superfine Quality'. Brands of notepaper were widely used and might prove nothing. But 'Superfine' was not Victorian English. M'Intyre checked and confirmed that this was an American make, not available in England.

The following morning M'Intyre went round to 103 Lambeth Palace Road. Dr Neill was still in bed. Emily Sleaper, the daughter of the house, was writing out the schedule M'Intyre had asked him to draw up. M'Intyre now said that the night of the Stamford Street murders was a most important date. Neill agreed. 'So soon as I get out of bed, and I am able to look up some dates, I will be able to fix my whereabouts at that particular time, but I think I was at Berkhamsted.'

M'Intyre promised to come back the next day. Dr Neill certainly seemed in no state to leave before then. This was very nearly a misjudgement, since he was up and about on the following morning. Indeed, M'Intyre met him walking in Lambeth Palace Road.

'I am going away today at three o'clock,' Neill said casually, 'Will I be arrested if I do?'

'I can't tell you,' M'Intyre said, puzzled as to what motivated the question, 'If you walk across with me to Scotland Yard, I will make inquiries.'

The walk lasted only a few minutes. Halfway across Westminster Bridge, Neill stopped and said, 'I will not go any further with you. I am suspicious of you and I believe you are playing me double. You sent a "rip" after me to meet me outside the *British Medical Journal* office.'

M'Intyre said that this was impossible, since he had no idea that Dr Neill was going to the office. But Neill was clearly irritated, as well as suspicious. Before they parted, he informed M'Intyre that he was going to consult a solicitor as to what remedy he might seek for the annoyance caused him by the police in having him followed and otherwise harassing him. Then, in the next breath, he asked M'Intyre if he could recommend a good firm of solicitors. M'Intyre said coolly that it would be improper for him to do so.

Despite what he had said, Neill made no attempt to go away on 26 May. Yet his behaviour now became more erratic, as those who observed him reported.

> *From the time he knew he was watched and guessed he was suspected, Neill became a changed man. Every trait in his character became exaggerated. He became more nervous and excitable. He turned round and stood to see if men were following him; he made every excuse to turn down empty streets and to enter houses; he would suddenly turn round and walk back under pretence of having passed a tobacconist's, so as to see if he were followed, and would get into a cab quickly if he only saw a man crossing the street or saw any one turn and look after him. He had the air of a hunted man, and it would seem as if he was haunted in the night . . . for he kept a candle alight in his room all through the night.*

Scotland Yard had also heard of the blackmailing letter received by Dr Harper at Barnstaple. By now, his son was nearby at Braunton. On 1 June Chief Inspector Tunbridge went by express train from Waterloo to Barnstaple in Devon. He had been wired the contents of the blackmail letter, now he wanted to see the original. In Barnstaple Tunbridge looked at the letter and knew that he had solved the blackmail mystery. The letter was written on notepaper with a familiar watermark. 'Fairfield – Superfine Quality'. The message was in a neat regular script with old-fashioned capitals. It needed no expert to see the similarity to the handwriting of Dr Neill.

Chief Inspector Tunbridge knew he had his blackmailer. Had he also caught the murderer of the five Lambeth girls? That was far from certain.

On 2 June Tunbridge was back in London. Next day he

applied for a warrant for the arrest of Thomas Neill on charges of blackmail. It was 5.25 pm when Tunbridge and his officers arrived in Lambeth Palace Road and arrested him while he was out walking in his tall silk hat. He remained confident, almost truculent.

'You have got the wrong man. Fire away!'

Tunbridge showed him the envelope containing the letter to Dr Harper. 'That is not my writing,' Neill said firmly.

He was taken to Bow Street police station, where he said to Tunbridge, 'Can I send to Messrs. Waters & Bryan, my solicitors?'
Tunbridge said he would get him a telegram form so that he could wire them. 'I write nothing,' Dr Neill said, 'You do it for me.' Tunbridge went to send the wire.

On the morning of 4 June at Bow Street Police Court, Dr Neill was charged with attempting to extort money from Dr Harper of Barnstaple. He was committed to Holloway Prison to await trial on charges of blackmail. Was he also the murderer? If he wrote all the letters, which he could not have done alone, he must have known that Matilda Clover died of poison, not of DTs. Could anyone but the murderer have known that? Inspector Harvey in Lambeth had bad news for his colleagues at the Yard. Lucy Rose had heard the dying Matilda Clover say something about a gentleman giving her pills which had poisoned her. Lucy Rose was a good girl but not one to miss telling a good story. In next to no time, it seemed, half the girls in Lambeth knew it. So it was possible that Dr Neill could have heard much the same and, as Tunbridge knew, a good defence counsel would make the most of that.

Under Tunbridge's instructions, 'L' Division began to search for any other girls who might have encountered Dr Neill in the previous October. Two were found, who seemed exceptionally promising and who had known Matilda Clover. They lived in Hercules Road, just off the Lambeth Road, in adjacent apartments on the second floor of Orient Buildings. Their names were Elizabeth Masters and Elizabeth May.

Elizabeth Masters was soliciting north of the river, in

Ludgate Circus, when she was picked up by a man on Tuesday 6 October 1891. They went into the King Lud public house and then back to Orient Buildings for sex. Afterwards the customer took her to Gatti's Music Hall, nearby in Westminster Bridge Road. While they were there, they met another girl from Orient Buildings, Elizabeth May. The three of them had a drink in the bar of the music hall, then the man took Elizabeth Masters in to see the show. Afterwards they met Elizabeth May in the bar again and had another drink. By this time, Elizabeth Masters wanted to get back to her pitch in Ludgate Circus. The man hired a cab and all three of them went to the King Lud public house for another drink. The man told Elizabeth Masters that he would come and see her again. He promised to write and make an appointment.

Three days later, on Friday, Elizabeth Masters received a letter, which she subsequently threw away. Her client promised to come to Orient Buildings between three and five that afternoon. The girl sat in the window waiting, with Elizabeth May to keep her company. Presently they saw Matilda Clover, whom they knew only by sight. She was walking past Orient Buildings towards the Lambeth Road, immediately under their window, carrying a basket, wearing a hat and a white apron with shoulder straps. A man was following her, dressed in dark clothes with a tall silk hat. Matilda Clover turned and smiled encouragement at him.

Elizabeth Masters felt sure the man was her customer and that he was being poached by Matilda Clover. She and Elizabeth May put on their hats and set off in pursuit. By the time they got down to the street, Matilda Clover and her follower had vanished round the corner. The two girls hurried to the doorway of the public house which stood on the corner of Hercules Road and Lambeth Road. They saw the other two on the far pavement, near the Masons' Arms public house. Matilda Clover stopped at 27 Lambeth Road, which they gathered was where she lived. She stopped with her hand on the door knob, turning and looking at the man who had been following her. Then he came up to her and they both went inside. Elizabeth Masters waited, presumably to give one or both a piece of her mind. Half an hour passed without the man reappearing. Elizabeth Masters gave up and went home.

She never saw the man again, though Elizabeth May spotted him on one occasion. As for Matilda Clover, they heard she had died of the 'horrors', which was no surprise.

Chief Inspector Tunbridge listened to their story and arranged an identity parade in a corridor of Bow Street Police Station on 17 June. Eight months had passed since the girls claimed to have seen the man but that could not be helped. Dr Neill stood in the corridor in a line of sixteen to twenty men with their hats on. Elizabeth Masters admitted that she expected one of them to be the man she had seen with Matilda Clover. To Tunbridge's chagrin, she walked past Neill without identifying him. She did not recognize any of these men as being the one who was with Matilda Clover or the one who had picked her up in Ludgate Circus and spent the whole evening with her. It would not sound good in court.

Elizabeth May went in. She walked down the line of men, paused and pointed to Neill. It was later objected that Neill had not been allowed to shave for several days and that this growth of stubble marked him out from the rest. Or was it that he refused to shave, hoping that a beard would disguise him? At all events, Elizabeth Masters was brought back to look at the men with their hats removed. She went down the line and this time picked out Dr Neill.

For Tunbridge, this was encouraging but less than conclusive. The most important point was not whether Dr Neill was the man with them on 6 October at Ludgate Circus and Gatti's Music Hall. Was he the man with his hat on, whom they had seen following Matilda Clover three days later? Elizabeth Masters had failed to pick him out. Elizabeth May had picked him out but how well had she seen him from the window of Orient Buildings? The window was three floors up and it was shut. The girls could only have seen the man's face at an angle and in the brief period during which he was walking towards them. Thereafter, they saw him only from the back and at some distance. However, Tunbridge had done his best.

It still seemed unsafe to charge Dr Neill with murder on the present evidence. Of course he had strychnine among his other preparations because, like so many poisons, it was used routinely in prescriptions. There was too little evidence as yet to connect him irrefutably with the murder of Ellen Donworth. Even in the cases of Alice Marsh and Emma Shrivell, though he had warned them against young Dr Harper, the case otherwise depended almost entirely on Constable Cumley's identification of a man seen briefly by the light of a street lamp.

In the following week, an inquest on Matilda Clover opened at Vestry Hall, Tooting, on 22 June. It was later adjourned and lasted until 13 July. For the first time, the blackmailing letters which referred to her death were fully reported in the press. It seemed best to wait until the inquest was over before deciding what murder, if any, to charge Dr Neill with. For Tunbridge, it was a most unsatisfactory situation.

Now that Dr Neill was under arrest, Patrick M'Intyre was assigned to the search for the fifth girl, Lou Harvey, alive or – more probably – dead. He got nowhere. There was no death certificate for anyone of that name. None of the other girls knew of her. No one had heard of any girl who had 'dropped down dead in a music hall'. Another line of inquiry seemed to have run into the sand. The investigation of Dr Neill's crimes was one with so many promising starts and so few satisfactory conclusions.

But Tunbridge had finally solved the riddle of the gang of psychopaths who wrote the blackmail letters. As Walter de Grey Birch continued to assure him, they were written by a number of people, some of whom were women. The solution to this came when Tunbridge began to question Emily Sleaper, who with her mother kept house at 103 Lambeth Palace Road, and Laura Sabbatini of Berkhamsted, the genteel young person to whom Dr Neill was engaged. With Miss Sabbatini he sang hymns in the local church and to her he swore he could not sleep at night without a Bible in his room. Both these young women now admitted that they had copied out certain letters for Dr Neill. But surely they had not done

anything wrong? The doctor had explained that the Metropolitan Police had retained him as an adviser in the Lambeth
mystery because of his reputation as a toxicologist. It was
necessary for him to have copies of certain correspondence
which the authorities and others had received concerning the
case. He was far too busy to make copies for himself. He
would be immensely grateful to these two young women if
they would do it on his behalf, so that he might then return the
originals of the letters to Scotland Yard.

It was as simple as that. The letters which his victims
received were the innocent work of Laura Sabbatini, Emily
Sleaper and one or two others. Indeed, Dr Neill's mistake was
in writing any of the letters himself or using paper with an
American watermark. In his attempted blackmail of Dr
Broadbent and Dr Harper, however, he had had to move fast.

Dr Neill could be convicted of blackmail quite easily but this
prospect was soured for Inspector Tunbridge by the opinions
reaching him from the Treasury Solicitor's Department.
Under English law a man can only be tried for one crime of
murder at a time. The evidence against Dr Neill was not
strong enough in the case of Ellen Donworth, nor even in the
case of Alice Marsh and Emma Shrivell. Matilda Clover
was the best hope but she was far from certain. If Dr Neill
was tried for the murder of Matilda Clover, there was no
guarantee that a judge would permit any of the other cases to
be referred to in front of the jury.

If the murder of Matilda Clover was taken on its own, the
case against Dr Neill rested on the fact that he knew in
November that she had been poisoned and that Elizabeth
Masters and Elizabeth May swore they had seen him with
Matilda Clover on 9 October. Yet Elizabeth Masters had failed
to pick him out as the silk-hatted man she had seen with
Clover and it was doubtful how good a view Elizabeth May
could have had on that occasion. So far as knowledge of the
poisoning went, Lucy Rose and half of Lambeth seemed to
have heard about it. Why not Dr Neill as well? A prosecution
offering this evidence alone would have a considerable
struggle in persuading a jury to hang a man.

The true difficulty for Chief Inspector Tunbridge was that the decisive evidence against the killer could only come from the victims themselves. But they were all dead. So the completion of his case required a voice from the grave. It came right on cue at the end of June.

V

The voice spoke in a letter which had been addressed to the Bow Street magistrate, Sir John Bridge. Tunbridge glanced at it and saw the words, 'I had not troubled to read the case particular till Friday night, when I happened to read it in the *Star*. So I got the *Telegraph* next morning, saw my name mentioned. So I was almost sure. He being under the impression that I took the capsules, and either dropped dead in the street, or music hall.'

Tunbridge's expectations grew cooler as he looked at the signature. Mrs Harris, 87 Upper North Street, Brighton. The case had nothing to do with any 'Mrs Harris'. But then he looked closer and saw that young Mrs Louisa Harris had a pimp who was called Charles Harvey. She was known professionally as Louisa Harvey or Lou Harvey. And she was still alive. The only man who thought she was dead was surely the man who thought he had killed her, believed that he had succeeded and then talked of her death in a letter to Alice Marsh and Emma Shrivell. The man who wrote that letter, by his own admission, was Dr Thomas Neill, the soft-spoken American postgraduate.

If the story in the letter were true, it was a torpedo amidships, so far as Dr Neill's defence against murder was concerned. Lou Harvey claimed that he had picked her up outside the St James's Hall in Regent Street, just after midnight, about 20 October the previous autumn. They went to a hotel in Berwick Street and spent the night together. 'He had Gold-rimmed Glasses and very Peculiar eyes . . . He spoke with a foreign Twang. He asked me if I had ever been in America.'

When they parted in the morning, the man arranged to meet her again that evening, at 7.30 opposite Charing Cross

Underground Station. He also noticed several spots on her forehead and promised to give her some pills to get rid of them. They met that evening and went to the Northumberland public house nearby, and had a glass of wine. While they were there a woman came in selling roses and the man bought some for Lou Harvey. Then they went out on to the Embankment and walked by the river. The girl had asked him if he had brought the pills and he said that he had. They had been made up by a chemist in the Westminster Bridge Road. As they strolled in the darkness by the Thames, the man took from his waistcoat pocket two long thin capsules wrapped in tissue paper and gave them to Lou Harvey.

'He gave them to me and said I was to take them; he said I was to put them in my mouth then and there, one by one, and not bite them, but swallow them.'

Lou Harvey had been quite keen to take the pills when they first met that evening. Now she sensed that there was something not right. The capsule was an American rather than an English way of taking medicine at this time. That made them seem odd. Yet, 'not liking the look of the thing' she sensed something even odder in the man himself.

'He put them in my right hand. I pretended to take them, putting my hand to my mouth and pretending to swallow them, but I passed them to my left hand. He asked me to show him my right hand. I showed it to him. It was empty. Then he asked me to show him my left hand, in which I had the pills. I threw the pills away behind me and showed him my left hand.'

The man then said that he had an appointment at St Thomas's Hospital but that he would meet her outside the Oxford Music Hall at eleven. Lou Harvey waited until half-past eleven but the man did not return. About three weeks later, he picked her up in Piccadilly Circus, without apparently recognizing her, and they went for a drink at the Regent Bar in Air Street. He arranged to meet her later that night.

'Don't you remember me?' she asked.

'No.'

'Not that night when you promised to meet me outside the Oxford?'

'What's your name?' he asked.

'Louisa Harvey.'

When she said this, the man 'walked sharp away'. Having read Lou Harvey's letter, Inspector Tunbridge was sharp as well in his effort to catch the next train to Brighton. The result was well worth while. Not only was Lou Harvey unshakeable in her story about the capsules, she had a witness who had seen the man give the capsules to her. While she kept her rendezvous with her client that night on the long riverside promenade of the Embankment, her pimp Charles Harvey waited in the shadows, watching and listening.

Lou Harvey was soon on her way to London as the star witness at the Matilda Clover inquest. Dr Neill was present, guarded by prison officers, but he was not on trial. Therefore, there was nothing to prevent Lou Harvey telling her story, even though it related to a different crime of attempted murder. When at last the coroner's jury delivered their verdict it was devastating to his case. It took them only twenty minutes to find 'that Matilda Clover died of the effect of strychnine poisoning, and that the poison was administered by Thomas Neill with intent to destroy life'.

Yet even with Dr Neill under arrest, someone was working on his behalf. If it was his own work, he must have planned it with extraordinary foresight and the luck of the devil. Halfway through the inquest, the coroner received a letter through the post which caused something of a sensation when read out in court.

Dear Sir,

The man you have in your power, Dr Neill, is as innocent as you are. Knowing him by sight, I disguised myself like him, and made the acquaintance of the girls that have been poisoned. I gave them the pills to cure them of all their earthly miseries, and they died. Miss L Harris has got more sense than I thought she had, but I shall have her yet. Mr P Harvey might also follow Lou Harvey out of this world of care and woe. Lady Russell is quite right about the letter,

*and so am I. Lord Russell had a hand in the poisoning of
Clover. Nellie Donworth must have stayed out all night, or
else she would not have been complaining of pains and cold
when Annie Clements saw her. If I were you, I would
release Dr T Neill, or you might get into trouble. His innocence will be declared sooner or later, and when he is free
he might sue you for damages - Yours respectfully, JUAN
POLLEN, alias JACK THE RIPPER. Beware all! I warn but
once!*

If this was not somehow the work of Dr Neill, perhaps the
much maligned Mr Slater was having his last laugh at the
expense of an overworked police force.

Despite the worst that Juan Pollen could threaten, the trial of
Thomas Neill opened at the Central Criminal Court on 17
October 1892. Meanwhile Inspector Frederick Jarvis of
Scotland Yard had been sent to Canada and the United States
to see what might be known about him there. What Jarvis
discovered related not to Thomas Neill but to Thomas Neill
Cream, whom many people had thought was serving a life
sentence in Joliet State Penitentiary for the murder of Daniel
Stott.

What had happened? Neill Cream, as he was now called,
had gone to Joliet in 1881. Six years later, his father had died
at Dansville, New York, on 12 May 1887. In consequence of his
father's death, the authorities agreed to commute Neill
Cream's sentence to life imprisonment, which was in effect
seventeen years. With the allowance for good behaviour, this
brought his imprisonment to an end on 31 July 1891. The purpose of his release was to enable him to administer the family
estate, of which his father had left him the useful sum of
$16,000. And so, on 1 August 1891, the poisoner of Daniel
Stott was a free man. He first made his way to Canada, where
the executors of his father's will provided him with money so
that he could take a voyage to England for his health. His
relatives privately thought that he was going insane. On 1
October he landed from the *Teutonic* at Liverpool. Four days

later he booked into a London hotel, Anderton's Hotel in Fleet Street. Two days after that he moved to 103 Lambeth Palace Road. Six days later, on 13 October 1891, Ellen Donworth died.

The web of circumstances tightened about him as the trial began. Now there were other reports of his conduct. He had suffered from headaches and insomnia, which required medication. In all that was said about strychnine as a killer, the more common use of it as *nux vomica*, 'the vomit nut', was overlooked. In small homoeopathic doses, strychnine was used as a valuable medicine in treating disorders of the nervous and digestive systems, not more that one-sixteenth of a grain at a time. Neill Cream's nervous system was badly in need of it. More and worse was heard of him in the reports of his conduct from one of his acquaintances, reprinted in the *St James's Gazette* for 24 October 1892.

> *Women were his preoccupation, and his talk of them far from agreeable. He carried pornographic photographs, which he was too ready to display. He was in the habit of taking pills which, he said, were compounded of strychnine, morphia, and cocaine, and of which the effect, he declared, was aphrodisiac. In short, he was a degenerate of filthy desires and practices.*

After the deaths of Ellen Donworth and Matilda Clover, he had sailed for Canada on 7 January, 1892. From Quebec he had travelled to Saratoga Springs and New York, embarking for Liverpool again on 23 March. It now transpired that the circular issued to the guests of the Metropole Hotel was printed in Montreal in March and that Neill Cream had had the parcel forwarded from Montreal to Liverpool by a shipping agent, Douglas Battersby. His visit to North America had, of course, coincided with a lull in the Lambeth murders and lunatic letters.

As murderers of his time go, Thomas Neill Cream was a much-travelled man. There was one advantage for him in this. His accent was always described as 'slight' by those who heard him, but they heard him differently. In Chicago, he sounded quite distinctively a Scotsman. In London, there was no doubt among the girls that he had an American 'twang', as they called it. The authorities on either side of the Atlantic thought of him, in this respect, as two different people.

John Wilson M'Culloch of Ottawa, a traveller for Robert Jardine & Co., now came forward to testify that he had made Neill Cream's acquaintance while staying at Blanchard's Hotel, Quebec, during the first week of March 1892. M'Culloch had had a bilious attack and 'Dr Cream', as he called himself, had given him a pill to cure it. The doctor had then gone on to display his other pills and potions, saying proudly of a bottle of white crystals, 'That is poison.' M'Culloch asked him what he used it for.

'I give that to the women to get them out of the family way.' Then he produced a box of capsules, 'I give it to them in these.'

M'Culloch was left in no doubt that the doctor was an abortionist. As so often with Neill Cream, horror was enlivened by madhouse humor. He produced a false beard and whiskers and explained that he wore them, like a character in a stage farce, 'To prevent identification while operating'. He went on to tell M'Culloch of London and the fun that could be had there, especially with the women in the area around Waterloo Road, Westminster Bridge Road and Victoria Road. He described how he had had intercourse with three women in a single night between the hours of 10pm and 3am. He also entertained M'Culloch with his collection of 'improper and indecent photographs'.

The trial opened before Mr Justice Henry Hawkins with the Attorney-General, Sir Charles Russell, leading for the Crown and Gerald Geoghegan for the defence. Much of the evidence which Russell presented was beyond dispute. Yet so long as the murder of Matilda Clover was the only one to be discussed, Geoghegan held his own. As the law stood, the defendant was still not permitted to give evidence and so Neill Cream remained a spectator and object of curiosity in the Old

Bailey dock while his life or death was decided upon.

Neill Cream's defence was shattered by the evidence of Lou Harvey, who identified him as the man who had given her the pills, and the ruling of the trial judge that certain points of evidence relating to the other three murders could be introduced by the Crown. Sir Henry Hawkins disagreed with the view that these points must only be admitted to corroborate evidence already given. Such a point could be introduced as 'an independent piece of evidence'.

This remained a contentious argument but, in the case of Neill Cream, it doomed the defence and the defendant. The jury now knew, if they did not know it before, that he was accused of four murders by the same method. Geoghegan battled on and made an impressive closing speech for the defence on the penultimate day of the trial, Thursday 20 October – the anniversary of Matilda Clover's death. Neill Cream was sure that he had won. When he was taken back to Holloway Prison that evening, he sang and danced in his cell.

Next morning, leaving Holloway for the final day of the trial, he was so sure of his victory that, as the *Daily Telegraph* reported, he treated the prison governor to 'a violent outburst of foul language'. In the event, it took the jury only ten minutes to find him guilty of murder. Neill Cream, who had been boasting that he would 'give it to Hawkins' when the trial was over, stood silent in the dock as the judge put on his black cap and passed sentence of death. Only as he was led away did those close by hear the condemned man say, 'They shall never hang me.'

This was taken as a promise to commit suicide and in the death cell at Newgate gaol a special watch was kept. Yet Neill Cream left the court and ate his tea and dinner as normal, and 'conversed with the warders in his usual free style'. At 10pm he went to bed and slept well, appearing calm and composed the next day. The press spoke of his 'reckless indifference' to his fate and reported that 'His demeanour is that of a man who does not realize his awful position.' What did he hope for? Neill Cream kept them guessing to the last.

He was allowed the customary 'three clear Sundays' and

the execution date was set for Tuesday 15 November. As time passed, his composure began to fragment. Those who heard of this were gratified by his suffering or his remorse, though the withdrawal of the drugs he had been accustomed to take had a good deal to do with it. On the last night, he spent an hour pacing up and down the cell, as if to tire himself out. He lay down but did not sleep, except when he dozed for a few minutes, moaning and then waking again. By six o'clock he was up, haggard and worn, cheeks bloodless, eyes incessantly moving, hands and feet twitching. He ate no breakfast and at eight o'clock was pinioned and led across the prison yard to the execution shed on the far side. Billington, the hangman, had allowed a drop of five feet.

As Neill Cream stood on the trap with a white hood over his head and the noose round his neck, he began to gabble out a final message to the world, more bizarre than any of his letters. To the witnesses staring at the spectacle of his execution, he swore that he was a man they had sought for years, the greatest criminal of all. What he had done in Lambeth was only the last stage of an illustrious career. With Billington's hand on the lever, Neill Cream shouted,

'I am Jack – '

His final word was lost in the crash of the wooden trap-door as its two halves fell back. The bound figure dropped through, brought up short by the rope with the head just visible, at the level of the witnesses' feet. Before lunchtime, he was buried in the prison yard and an inquest at the Old Bailey had returned a verdict of death by judicial hanging.

The explanation of Neill Cream's murderous conduct eluded most of those who knew him. Perhaps the most likely truth was that he had contracted tertiary syphilis, in which case his slaughter of Lambeth prostitutes was a homicidal vengeance and the madness of his other behaviour a symptom of the disease. There seemed little doubt that his nervous system was diseased and his relatives in Canada thought him mad.

His claim to be Jack the Ripper was another matter. Those who witnessed his execution were already tense from their unenviable duty. When it was over, they were able to feel relief in the knowledge that he could not have been Jack the Ripper. The Ripper murders occurred in Whitechapel in the autumn of 1888. Dr Thomas Neill Cream was safely incarcerated in Joliet, four thousand miles away, from October 1881 until July 1891. That was the end of the matter.

Or, rather, that was almost the end of the matter. On 12 March 1985, *The Times* reported two discoveries by Donald Bell, a Canadian journalist. First a comparison between anonymous letters written by Jack the Ripper and undisguised letters written by Neill Cream suggest that both were written by the same person. If true, this would still leave the objection that Cream was in Joliet in 1888. But was he? Mr Bell discovered that in nineteenth-century America, prisoners with money could sometimes pay to have substitutes in gaol while they themselves went about their business. That would scarcely apply in the case of a murderer. Unless, of course, the man's father had died the year before and a decision was taken to free him two years later anyway.

An unlikely corroboration of this possibility came from the great English defence lawyer in murder trials, Sir Edward Marshall Hall. While Neill Cream was on trial at the Old Bailey, Marshall Hall went into court and watched him. Indeed, as he told his friend and biographer, Edward Marjoribanks, he recognized him as a client he had once defended. It was some years earlier when the man he now saw as Neill Cream was charged with several cases of bigamy. His defence was that he could not have done it because he was in prison in Sydney, Australia at the time. A cable to Australia confirmed this. Marshall Hall was convinced the man was guilty and concluded that he had a 'double' whose name and description would give him such an alibi.

Marshall Hall had not the least doubt that the man tried for the murder of Matilda Clover was the man he had defended in the bigamy case. Marshall Hall was also a close associate of Neill Cream's counsel Gerald Geoghegan, with whom he had appeared in an appeal by the murderer Frederick Deeming in May 1892. But Marshall Hall was born in 1858 and called to the bar in 1883, two years after Neill Cream began his life sentence in Joliet.

Either Marshall Hall was uncharacteristically mistaken in identifying his former client or else Neill Cream had been at liberty for several years, perhaps from the time of his father's death in 1887. That would not make him Jack the Ripper, despite their shared medical knowledge. Yet it would put him in London in ample time to be a candidate for the Ripper murders, which stopped as abruptly as the Lambeth drama stopped on Neill Cream's return to Canada and the United States in January 1892. But whatever the truth of Neill Cream's claim, it was lost forever when Billington pulled the lever of the gallows trap in Newgate on a November morning a century ago.

TWO

The Deep Blue Sea:
The Disappearance of Judge
Chillingworth (1955–61)

I

Murder and abduction have an extra dimension in Florida, whose Atlantic Ocean makes a convenient unmarked grave or an easy route for the transport of victims. From time to time murderers or abductors are caught but they seem to be the unlucky ones. One more vessel among so many hundreds of cruising yachts and ketches would scarcely attract notice, let alone suspicion. On 13 November 1961, for example, the oil-tanker *Gulflion* was north of Nassau bound for Puerto Rico. Early that morning the crew spotted a man in a dinghy waving for assistance, far beyond any sight of land. Julian Harvey explained that he was skipper and sole survivor of the Florida yacht *Bluebelle* from Fort Lauderdale. His boat had caught fire and sunk the night before. The victims were his wife Mary, and his passengers the Duperraults and the three Duperrault children. He alone had been on deck but was unable to reach them through the flames.

So much for the tragedy. Four days later, about noon on 17 November, the Greek freighter *Captain Theo* was en route to Florida from Europe. Far from land, the crew were astonished to see a blond eleven-year-old girl sitting on a balsa-wood raft with shark fins circling her. She was Terri-Jo Duperrault, weak and dehydrated, a few hours from uncon-sciousness and death. Five nights before, she had woken on the *Bluebelle* to the sound of screams and found her brother and mother lying in their blood. Julian Harvey had kept her below in the cabin, though the boat was already taking in water. As the water covered the cabin floor, the girl saw Harvey swim for the dinghy. Then she went on deck and took to the little raft before the *Bluebelle* sank. Harvey must have felt sure that Terri-Jo Duperrault had drowned.

Harvey, who had been questioned in Nassau and at Miami, heard of Terri-Jo's survival. Soon afterwards, he was found wide-eyed and dead on the floor of his motel room, his wrists, throat and legs slashed by a razor. Two months earlier, he had taken out a double indemnity policy on his wife for $20,000. Accidental death would pay $40,000 and at last he would have been clear of his unmanageable debts. It was a chance in a thousand that had caught him.

But still the chances are better when a man works alone, like Harvey. There are no consciences but his own. In 1982 Raymond Thompson had a score to settle with James Savoy, who had fitted a safe for Thompson, then returned to dig it out with a jack-hammer and empty it of its contents. Thompson, as a self-respecting Florida entrepreneur, decided to administer justice personally. His assistants found James Savoy drinking at the Cricket Club in Palm Beach on the night of 9 March 1982. When Savoy left the club, they rammed his car, seized him, and took him bound and gagged to Raymond Thompson. Two days later, several miles off the Florida coast, Savoy's head was held out over the stern of one of Thompson's yachts (in order not to get blood or brains on the deck) and Thompson shot him through the back of the head. Savoy had already been loaded with chains. His murderers had only to tip him over the stern of the yacht and watch the body sink.

Thompson should have got away with it, as he had got away with two other 'burials at sea' or 'walking the plank'. But one of his two companions was at last moved by conscience, or reward, or a feeling that he had better turn state's evidence before someone else did. Bobby Davis went to the FBI in Chicago two years later and told the whole story. Of the three men, only Thompson was sentenced to death and his personal fortune of $4,400,000 confiscated.

More sinister than murder in the criminal culture of Florida are those disappearances which may or may not end in the victim's death. In July 1989 a woman at Port St Joe saw a white van pull out of a parking space. Left behind on the ground was a polaroid snapshot of a girl in a pair of brief shorts and a sleeveless singlet. She was lying on a bed with her wrists tied behind her and a gag taped across her mouth. To police, this was no ordinary piece of titillation for the bondage market. Inquiries were made on the basis of the photograph. It was widely circulated and shown in a televised appeal. A more or less positive identification was made of the girl as Tara Calico, aged nineteen from New Mexico, who had gone missing without explanation on a bicycle trip nine months before. Thirty years earlier, in pre-Castro Cuba, the closely-organized vice rackets offered an easy destination for such teenagers, only ninety miles from Key West. Since the advent of Castro's regime in 1959, sexually motivated abductions at home or to Latin America ended elsewhere.

That they sometimes ended in death was revealed in the Gore-Waterfield case of 1983–4 in Indian River County, southern Florida. The revelations began when a man with a gun was seen chasing a naked girl, sixteen-year-old Lynn Elliott, who had escaped from his captivity. Unable to recapture the girl single-handed, he shot her dead. The reason for this need to silence her screams soon became clear when it was discovered that she was not the only adolescent being held for what could only be called white slavery. A second naked girl, fourteen years old, was found in the house with her hands handcuffed behind her. The subsequent trial revealed the price for abducted girls as $1000 a time.

Seventeen-year-old Ying Hua-Ling and her Taiwanese mother had died under the attentions of her abductors and were buried in 55-gallon steel drums. Another victim; Judith Daley was weighted and dumped in a canal after her ordeal. The body of fourteen-year-old Barbara Ann Byer was buried in a citrus grove in March 1983 and that of her companion, fourteen-year-old Angela Lavallee was 'fed to the alligators'.

Such was the underworld which had grown up alongside the 1920s real estate dream of 'Home, Sweet Florida'. Yet no case could rival the classic disappearance of two of the state's most prominent citizens in the affluence of 1950s Palm Beach.

II

If there was one place where the Florida dream remained true in the years after World War II, it was surely Palm Beach. Sub-tropical home of the Kennedys, winter resort of the Duke and Duchess of Windsor, the select community was divided by the waters of Lake Worth from the sprawling mainland vulgarity of West Palm Beach. Facing the ocean, mansions set back in green gardens looked as if they had been built for Spanish colonial governors. Their white stucco and their Roman tiles, arcaded verandas and square corner towers were the winter homes of dynasties from Boston and Fifth Avenue. The sands of Palm Beach's most expensive waterside were accessible only from the sea, the private paths barred by steel gates and locks. The town of 2,500 inhabitants was dominated by the Breakers Hotel, a 1930s venue for Wall Street on holiday, and by the expensive canopied shops of Worth Avenue. Broad sidewalks, avenues of royal palms, flowerbeds and shrubberies suggested money and self-confidence. Before the 1920s boom began, a central strip of land in Palm Beach had been priced at $240,000. Five years later it was valued at $4,000,000. Whatever else had happened in Florida, Palm Beach had held its value.

Even in the 1950s and '60s, Palm Beach remained an enclave in which the more prim and traditional standards of the old order had survived. No one – and nowhere – demonstrated this better than Judge Eugene Curtis Chillingworth and his circuit court, though the court itself now sat in the rowdy metropolitan bustle of West Palm Beach. Fifty-eight years old in 1955, Chillingworth had presided over law and order in his judicial district of Florida for thirty-four years, thirty-two of them as a circuit judge, from the time when his home had been in a small and uncluttered resort on the Atlantic sands. Apart from the enforcement of law, he was also a commander in the Naval Reserve. The press described

57

him as 'a member of a wealthy pioneer family, who reputedly has a fortune of about $750,000 which represents both in-heritance and business profits.'

With his thin pedantic face, rimless spectacles and austere manner, it appeared that he belonged to another age and perhaps to another century. Yet every morning in summer he travelled from a beach house at Manalapan to the busy and worldly circuit court of West Palm Beach, across the placid waters of the lake. He was without question a righteous judge. His application of the law was exact and his morals were firm. For more than thirty years he had been the type of law-giver whom Palm Beach wanted. Whether the same could be said of West Palm Beach was less certain. The *Washington Post* spoke approvingly of him as 'one of Florida's outstanding circuit judges' and as one with a 'reputation for dealing sternly with law violators'.

In his private life, Judge Chillingworth was a happily married man with three grown-up daughters. Much of that life was lived at West Palm Beach. However, for the humid summer months he had the beach house on the low sandy cliffs and dunes at Manalapan, a settlement of thirty people ten miles south of Palm Beach itself. Naturally the house faced the Atlantic rollers across what was virtually a private beach with a wooden stairway down to the sands. It was isolated, not to say exclusive.

Anyone who knew Judge Chillingworth understood that punctuality was a virtue with him, even a fetish. There was, therefore, surprise when he failed to appear in court at West Palm Beach at 9.30 on the morning of 15 June 1955. Surprise turned to concern when he was absent all morning and there was no reply from the beach house at Manalapan, either from the judge or from his wife Marjorie.

As it happened, two workmen were due at the house that morning. They found no one in, though the door to one side, leading to the bedrooms, was unlocked. Uncertain of what to do, they walked down the stairway to the beach. On the wooden steps were spots of red paint or blood. At the foot of the steps, the soft sand was marked by footprints going in both directions between the house and the tide line. There were signs of a struggle in the sand. One of the workmen phoned the judge's office but there was no news of him. In a little while, the men were joined by Sheriff Lawrence and his team. There was no doubt that the spots on the wooden steps were blood stains. In the porch the sheriff's men found broken glass. A floodlight in the porch, directed towards the beach, had been smashed. Someone had bled a good deal. Curtis Chillingworth's blood group was 'A' and the blood on the steps was identified as 'B'. What Marjorie Chillingworth's group might be, no one could say.

Before the end of the morning, a full-scale investigation was in progress. Leroy Collins, Governor of Florida, sent police officers from Palm Beach, Lake Worth, Boyton Beach and Lantana to join the Manalapan search party. A major figure in the judiciary had gone missing, probably snatched by criminals. As the ground parties searched the area, Coast Guard and Air Force planes droned overhead. Governor Collins also called in the FBI. It was established that the Chillingworths had last been seen at 10pm the previous evening, when they left a dinner party at the home of James M Owens, Palm Beach County Tax Assessor.

The first report from the sheriff and the search parties was not reassuring. 'Investigators found the house open, with the ventilator fans running and both of the family cars in the garage. The beds had been slept in but not made and there was no sign breakfast had been prepared.' Kidnap at midnight or in the small hours of the morning seemed the most likely explanation.

By the following day the press was running headlines such as JUDGE AND WIFE VANISH: BLOOD TRAIL IS FOUND. The Chillingworths were 'feared kidnapped and possibly slain'. The County Solicitor, T Harold Williams, had suggested that it was a case of kidnap 'by someone who was paid to do it'. W H 'Buddy' Casque, special investigator for the State Attorney-General's Office added that he thought there was no question of ransom. The kidnap had been carried out 'to throw a scare into the judge'. Whatever the motive, the judge's brother, Walter Chillingworth appointed a minister of the First Methodist Church to act as intermediary. The minister's phone rang a few times but when he picked it up there was no one on the line.

One curious factor was that two days after the discovery of the abandoned beach house, the headlines announced, POLICE TAB 3 AS SUSPECTS IN KIDNAPPING OF JUDGE, WIFE. Yet Buddy Casque refused to say anything about who the three people might be. And that was just about all. The investigators wondered whether Curtis Chillingworth might have done business with men who were more ruthless than he thought. The FBI examined 'his business deals, including several large real estate transactions, in search of information that might shed some light on his disappearance'. They found nothing. Weeks, months, and years passed without an explanation or a solution of the mystery. After two years Judge Chillingworth and his wife were considered dead for legal purposes. There was no further clue and, of course, no trace of the two bodies. Only at one moment did it appear as if the murderer had been found. He was by then a prisoner at Raiford, Florida's State Penitentiary, and he confessed to having killed the Chillingworths. Unfortunately, he was also schizophrenic and paranoid or, as Phil O'Connell, the State Attorney of West Palm Beach put it bluntly, 'Nuts'.

Judge Chillingworth was mourned as one who belonged to a world of old-fashioned values. They were none the worse for that but it was easy to see how he might have made enemies in the more brash and easy-going state that Florida had become. His own family was long-established in Florida and in the law. Chillingworth regarded with unconcealed distaste the way in which outsiders had made graft and the rackets part of municipal life.

The two most lucrative rackets in Florida by the 1950s were moonshine whisky or 'shine' and variations on the numbers game. Moonshine whisky was distilled secretly throughout the state, rather as a cottage industry. It evaded almost all the efforts of the tax-gatherers, and was shipped to the clubs of

Miami and the principal centres of consumption. The numbers racket in Florida generally took the form of 'Bolita' or 'Cuba'. It operated from the back rooms of shops in cities like West Palm Beach, the counters in the front of the premises wired to send an alarm to the back room if there was any sign of trouble. Bolita was played by the punters backing any number from one to a hundred, the stake unlimited, and the winner decided by the number on a plastic ball drawn from a bag. Not surprisingly, the operators found ways of ensuring that the heavily-backed numbers were not the ones drawn from the bag. An easy trick was to put the plastic ball with the least backing into a freezer. The stooge who drew the 'winner' could pick it by feeling its chill. After paying their expenses, the organizers took about twenty per cent of the stake. 'Cuba' was based on the Cuban national lottery, in the days when Fidel Castro was still a guerilla leader in the hills. The Florida racketeers ran their game with the same set of numbers and the same rules, except that the choice of winner was carefully regulated.

There was nothing particularly original in Florida's vices but like all rackets they needed protection. This meant advance warning of raids and a tip-off to any form of surveillance. Above all, in West Palm Beach, the operators and their runners needed protection against the austere morality of Curtis Eugene Chillingworth.

Chillingworth, though senior circuit judge, was by no means the only law-giver in the city. There was, for example. Judge Joseph Alexander 'Buck' Peel. A local lad who had made good as a State Prosecutor at twenty-six, Joe Peel was thirty-one in 1955, not even born when Curtis Chillingworth first took his place on the bench. After only six years of legal practice, Peel had already been elected twice as municipal judge. He had the offices of his law practice on the eighth floor of the Harvey Building in West Palm Beach, above those of the State Attorney, Philip D O'Connell. He drove an air-conditioned Cadillac and was a man who smiled or made friends easily. He was voted Man of the Year by the West Palm Beach Junior Chamber of Commerce. It was no secret that a

Municipal Judgeship in West Palm Beach was only the first step in a political career which he saw as leading to the Governor's Mansion in Tallahassee. A good many people liked Joe Peel more than they trusted him. He had the personable looks of a young Broderick Crawford playing the part of political office in a movie. He tried to please those who came to him, making easy promises which never seemed likely to be kept.

There were stories about Joe Peel, in his silk shirts and smart linen suits, which might have damaged a lesser man. It was said that he liked to photograph naked girls next to the framed diplomas in his office and that he would then have the film printed by the city's police laboratory. He was on first-name terms with all the officials of law enforcement. But the voters re-elected him in 1954. There are worse things than taking photographs of girls with no clothes on. Joe Peel appeared a refreshing contrast to Curtis Chillingworth, one of a new generation more suited to Florida in the second half of the twentieth century, as Judge Chillingworth seemed to linger in the nineteenth. It was true that there had been mud slung in the 1954 election and that some of it had come Peel's way. North of West Palm Beach was what was known as 'coloured town', the black quarter. It was alleged that a man whom Peel had represented in court, a Republican worker Floyd Holzapfel, had encouraged racketeers and their customers in the area to vote for Peel on the grounds that they would be less subject to interference from him as a judge. It was one among many election smears.

But that was not quite all. In the spring of 1955, Curtis Chillingworth turned his attention to the glad-handing Municipal Judge of West Palm Beach. He believed that Joe Peel had forfeited the right to sit as a judge and even to remain in practice at the bar.

Ostensibly it was nothing to do with protection or the rackets but a matter of the improper way in which Joe Peel conducted his legal practice. For he was allowed to continue in practice while also sitting as a judge who was junior to Chillingworth.

The first sign of trouble had come in 1953 when Peel improperly represented both sides in a divorce action. The complaint ended when Judge Chillingworth reprimanded him privately. But a second breach of legal etiquette might well have meant that Peel would have been disbarred. His career as a Municipal Judge would be over and his ambitions for the governorship of Florida would be a bad joke.

However, there was worse trouble in the spring of 1955. Joe Peel had told one of his clients that her divorce had gone through. She remarried, had a baby, attempted to adopt a second child and was told during routine investigation by the adoption authorities that her first marriage was still valid. She was an innocent bigamist, thanks to Peel. Charges were brought against Joe Peel to be heard before Judge Chillingworth. The senior judge was, after all, a naval commander and, so far as the administration of the law in his district was concerned, he still ran a tight ship. From more than one source, Peel heard that Chillingworth had promised 'personally to take care' of the culprit. He was going to have Peel disbarred.

This was even worse than it seemed. Peel's air-conditioned Cadillac and silk shirts were not the fruit of his law practice alone. As a youthful Municipal Judge, he was also 'protection' in West Palm Beach. Whether or not Chillingworth now knew it – and Peel feared he did – the Municipal Judge had used his office to exploit graft and corruption as a growth industry. Beyond the royal palms and expensive shops of Worth Avenue, the high-rise landscape of West Palm Beach across the lake took on a contour of judicial dishonesty. Yet without his powers as Municipal Judge, Joe Peel would no longer be able to sell protection.

How did this protection work? One of his clients described Peel's system for professional racketeers. It was so unsubtle that in a gangster movie it would have been comic relief. In the judge's office, Joe Peel explained to racketeer Bobby Lincoln that for $500 a month he would 'always be notified' as soon as a search warrant was applied for. 'I would always be notified and he would telephone me. I was to give him the

$500 a month every first Monday and it worked out fine. So whenever there was a raid we were notified. If there were any slip-ups, the fines were paid out of the take, the $500. If a fine ran too high, he could cut it.' Joe Peel could also make a legal error in the search warrant or other document, providing an easy means of appeal for the racketeer.

If the reek of corruption had not reached Judge Chillingworth's fastidious nostrils he was almost the only figure of authority to escape it. Joe Peel not only guaranteed protection but joined in the rackets. A time came when shadowy figures rode in the elevator to the eighth floor of the Harvey Building with brown paper bags of money from the Bolita games. There, in the office of the Municipal Judge, and above that of the State Attorney, the take was counted and stashed away.

State Attorney Phil O'Connell had begun to suspect the worst. Harold Gray, the young lawyer who was Peel's junior associate, told the judge that if one of these visitors 'came into the office again, I would walk out. I did not want a hoodlum and a bum hanging around.'

Time might have seemed to be almost up for Joseph 'Buck' Peel, whose immediate danger came from Curtis Chillingworth. 'When you mention his name, chills run up and down my back,' Peel told P O Wilber, a retired policeman and friend. When Peel himself was told by another West Palm Beach attorney 'that squinty-eyed old bastard is going to take care of you', he had no need to ask who the squinty-eyed old bastard might be. Chillingworth gave him until 15 June to answer the charges relating to the client who thought she was divorced.

Joe Peel was a racketeer but, ironically, he could only succeed as one by remaining a lawyer and a Municipal Judge. Without that, what protection could he offer? He must not be disbarred but Curtis Chillingworth was already promising privately that Peel would never practise law in Florida again after he had done with him. The comment reached Judge Peel. After that there was no further doubt that Judge Chillingworth would have to go.

III

Joe Peel needed a partner in murder from whom he would have nothing to fear, who would do the job while the Municipal Judge established an alibi. His choice fell on the man who hung around his office with the Bolita takings and to whom Harold Gray objected as 'a hoodlum and a bum', the political supporter who had helped the judge with the 'coloured town' vote, 'Lucky' Floyd Holzapfel.

Holzapfel had met Peel in 1953, when the judge acted for him in a small civil suit. Holzapfel had a criminal record and an interesting career. He claimed to have fought in the 101st Airborne Division during World War II but the record suggested that he failed to complete a flying course and then waited out the war far behind the front line in India. Born in 1924, he was twenty-one when the war ended and he returned to Oklahoma City as a fingerprint clerk in the local police department. The job lasted only a few months. He tried and failed as a gas-station owner, a fight promoter and an illegal bookmaker, which brought him sixty days in a Los Angeles jail.

Back in Oklahoma City on 31 December 1946, he turned to armed robbery. In the course of two nights, 'Lucky' Holzapfel and his friends with a .22 target pistol and a 1941 two-ton four-door Buick sedan held up the pay-boxes of three of the city's movie houses, the Will Rogers Theater, the May Theater and the Tower Theater. They were then caught by the police and Holzapfel went to prison for seventeen months. He was and remained a personable young man who made friends easily. To that extent he seemed like an underprivileged version of Joe Peel. On release from prison, he enrolled in the Oklahoma City University Law School and got a free pardon from the state governor so that he might later be called to the bar. He was never called.

In 1949 he gave it all up and went south to Florida. He met his third wife in Miami and drove trucks for a living. Three years later, the family moved up the coast to West Palm Beach. Floyd Holzapfel combined his work greasing cars with treasurership of a Young Republican Club as Dwight D Eisenhower began his campaign for the presidency.

In the next couple of years he became an odd-job man, married a fourth time, campaigned for Joe Peel's re-election as Municipal Judge and got a private investigator's licence. By 1954, he was working with and for Joe Peel. So was Bobby Lincoln, who owned pool-rooms and taxis in the black district of 'coloured town'. Most of Lincoln's money, however, came from the rackets. When the three men and their enterprises were threatened by the 'squinty-eyed old bastard' on the circuit bench, who else should Joe Peel turn to but those who had most to lose?

'Judge Chillingworth is going to ruin me,' Peel told Holzapfel, 'The fact is, he is personally going to take care of me when the case comes up. We'll have to get rid of the judge.'

Peel and Holzapfel took Bobby Lincoln for a ride on 5 June, ten days before the date set for the fateful court hearing. Peel said, 'Bobby, the man is trying to ruin us and I have got to kill him.' There was one logical plan, it was the only one and it seemed to Holzapfel the perfect solution. 'Joe said we could make this disappearance of the judge perfect. If we took him out in the ocean, no one would find the body, no one would be arrested.'

It was impossible that Peel himself could take part. He would be one of the first suspects and must have an alibi. But he described the beach house at Manalapan, took them past it, pointed out Judge Chillingworth whom they had never seen. 'What about servants?' Bobby Lincoln asked. Joe Peel reassured him that there were no live-in servants. 'What about Mrs Chillingworth?' Peel explained that there were nights when Mrs Chillingworth went to visit her daughters and stayed until next day. The abduction and murder would take place when the judge was alone. They would need a boat and would land on the beach by the house. Then it was simply a matter of knocking, confronting the judge with a gun, taking him out to sea, weighting the body, and dropping him over-board. No one could prove a thing.

Whatever misgivings Holzapfel and Lincoln felt, Joe Peel had logic on his side. Chillingworth could destroy them all, put them away for years. At first Holzapfel resisted, as he later claimed, 'Joe Peel told me I was his only friend in the world, his best friend, if I killed Chillingworth I would be his friend for life. "That's the only solution," he said. I told him he was crazy.' But Joe Peel, though he might be malevolent, was not crazy. As he insisted, someone was going to go down, either Chillingworth or the three racketeers. At length, Holzapfel saw reason.

The three men agreed that Chillingworth should be taken out to sea and drowned. No gunshots, no noise. They bought canvas gloves to avoid leaving fingerprints, rolls of adhesive tape, clothes-line, army belts and lead sinker-weights. Also in the boat that night was a shotgun and Joe Peel's snub-nosed .38 special. They paid $450 for the boat, $200 in one-dollar bills from a paper bag in which the proceeds of the Cuba lottery racket were carried. The date chosen for the murder was 14 June, the night before Peel's case was to come up at the circuit court in West Palm Beach.

The more the plot against Curtis Chillingworth developed, the more it resembled the moralistic melodrama of a 1950s B-movie or *film noir* as it was later and more pretentiously called. On the evening of 14 June 1955, Joe Peel was at home with ample witnesses to prove it, watching a quiz-show. 'The $64,000 Question', on television. A policeman won $16,000 that night. Holzapfel drove to 1124 10th Street, Riviera Beach, twelve miles north of Manalapan and picked up Bobby Lincoln from his house. They went to the nearby dock, got into the boat, started the engine, then followed the coast southwards. Holzapfel had brought a bottle of 'Old Grand Dad' whisky. He gave Lincoln a drink and told him, apparently for the first time, that this was not a reconnaissance but the night on which they were going to do 'a little job' for Joe Peel.

They went south until they were level with the lights of Lake Worth Casino, then pulled in towards the shore. The plan was to beach the little boat at Manalapan. Lincoln would keep the engine running, while Holzapfel went to the Chillingworth house in a 'captain's suit', with a story of his boat being stuck in the sand. He would ask to use the phone to call the coast-guard. Then he would come back with Judge Chillingworth at gun-point.

They brought the boat in just below the house. Holzapfel got out and went to the steps, saying to Lincoln, 'I'll call you when I need you.' It was after midnight as he went up the steps to the door and knocked. The door was opened by a man in faded pink pyjamas. Holzapfel asked him, 'Are you Judge Chillingworth?' 'I am.' Holzapfel drew his pistol from under his shirt and told the judge to stand still. 'Is there any-one else in the house?' The judge called out and a woman dressed in a nightgown walked into the living-room. It was Mrs Chillingworth. The plan was already going wrong. Though Joe Peel had assured them that Judge Chillingworth would be alone, he added, 'If there are any other people, they are to go too.' Holzapfel whistled for Bobby Lincoln, who stumbled up the steps. 'Knock that light out,' Holzapfel said. Lincoln broke the porch-light with his gun-butt. He rushed into the room with the .38 special drawn.

Holzapfel held a gun on the couple while Lincoln tied their hands behind their backs and taped their mouths. Then Holzapfel searched the house for witnesses. There were none. But finding the judge's wallet, Holzapfel emptied it of all but a few dollars. He left these because he did not want it to look like robbery. It seemed the taped gags were less than efficient. By whatever means, while Holzapfel was not around, Judge Chillingworth managed to say to Bobby Lincoln, 'Boy, you take care of us in this and you will never have to work any more.'

The couple were marched down to the beach, Lincoln escorting the judge and Holzapfel with Mrs Chillingworth. As they went down, Mrs Chillingworth managed to free her mouth from the tape and began to scream. Holzapfel claimed he was 'petrified'. The beach house was secluded but not beyond earshot of its neighbours or the road. He hit the screaming woman with his gun and blood dripped on to the steps. Indeed, she fell from the steps and Holzapfel had to carry her. Presently the two victims were in the boat. The boat put out to sea, beyond the southbound steam track.

The details of the crime were not working out but there could be no going back on the main plan. The two killers strapped the military cartridge belts round the waists of the judge and his wife. 'Honey, remember I love you,' Curtis Chillingworth said. 'I love you too,' said his wife. By then Holzapfel had weighted Mrs Chillingworth's cartridge belt. He rolled the bound and weighted woman over the side of the boat and she sank at once. But Curtis Chillingworth, his belt unweighted and his feet still free, struggled over the side of the boat and threw himself into the water. He was afloat and kicking his feet to propel himself clear.

Lincoln, in a panic, began to shoot at the fugitive. Holzapfel stopped him, for fear that gunshots would attract attention. He got the boat going again and went after the judge, first trying to beat him over the head with the stock of the shot-gun, then grabbing him, bringing him alongside and roping an anchor to him. The weight of the anchor was twenty to thirty pounds and it ended the struggle. 'I saw the pink pyjamas in the reflection of the light as he went down,' Holzapfel said.

The two men took the boat back to Riviera Beach Dock and phoned Joe Peel with a prearranged message. 'The motor's fixed.'

Peel was delighted, though shaken when he heard that Marjorie Chillingworth had been there and had died as well. 'Oh, my God,' Joe Peel said, 'I didn't know. Oh, my God . . . . Honest to God, I didn't know she'd be there.'

Bungled in its details, ghastly in the drama of two innocent deaths, the killers' plan still held. At the least, it might be thought that the Chillingworths had drowned accidentally in a midnight swim. However, as a matter of police routine, the waters off Manalapan were dragged but nothing was discovered. Even at the worst, as it must have seemed to Joe Peel, there would be suspicion without proof. For the moment, the rackets were safe. None of the three conspirators in the murders would dare to give away the secret. The shadow of the electric chair in Raiford penitentiary fell equally upon them all. Both Holzapfel and Bobby Lincoln stood in that shadow for love of Joe Peel, who paid them nothing for the killing.

One irony was that when Joe Peel's case came on he was not disbarred. The charges were heard by another judge and, to that extent, Curtis Chillingworth had been murdered for nothing. Yet the dead judge indirectly got his way. Shaken by the double murder and fearing a new investigation into the rackets which was soon to begin, genial Joe Peel resigned the following year as Municipal Judge and soon gave up the practice of law. The vision of the Governor's Mansion at Tallahassee, which had cost the Chillingworths their lives, was a mirage after all.

Peel's other financial interests were to thrive and he remained in partnership with Floyd Holzapfel. But there was unfinished business of a more serious kind. In August 1956, more than a year after the murders, Edna Trepp was working as secretary to Andrew O'Connell, brother of the State Attorney, Phil O'Connell. Andrew O'Connell's offices were near Peel's on the eighth floor of the Harvey Building. Edna Trepp often had lunch with Peel's secretary. She went to the offices one day and found Joe Peel's secretary almost ready to go to lunch, except for washing her hands. Waiting alone in the outer office, Mrs Trepp heard Joe Peel talking to another attorney, Frank Maynard. She alleged Peel said, 'We got Judge Chillingworth, now we got to get Phil O'Connell. He is the only one left in our way.' Edna Trepp coughed. Joe Peel came out, patted her on the shoulder and said with some relief, 'Oh, it's you.'

Long before this, the State Attorney had received anonymous phone calls in the weeks after the disappearance of the Chillingworths. The calls all said more or less the same thing. 'You're next.' Peel had even said to a friend, P O Wilber, the former policeman, 'It was either that son-of-a-bitch or me.' That was true, whether or not he was the man who killed the Chillingworths. Despite these uncorroborated and ambiguous remarks, the mystery of the Chillingworths' disappearance continued with $160,000 as a reward for its solution.

Phil O'Connell, State Attorney, had his suspicions about Peel's complicity in the Chillingworths' disappearance, as he had had suspicions of Peel's involvement in the rackets. He had been uneasy since the time when what Harold Gray called hoodlums and bums began infesting the Harvey Building carrying bags to Peel's office. Those bags were known as a kind generally used to transport the proceeds of Bolita and the Cuba Lottery swindle. In the Chillingworth case, O'Connell had as yet no certain proof, only Peel's alibi for the night of 14 June. Instead, it was Peel and Holzapfel who drove out to look at O'Connell's house in West Palm Beach to measure the lie of the land in case the State Attorney should have to go the same way as the senior circuit judge.

As it happened, the man who most nearly followed the Chillingworths was Harold Gray, Peel's associate in the law practice, who was entirely innocent of any part in the crimes or the rackets. Without telling Gray, Joe Peel had taken out a $100,000 life policy on him with an insurance agent, James W Yenzer. At this time, a year after the murders of the Chillingworths, Holzapfel was working as a bartender in the Chi-Chi club on Broadway, West Palm Beach, an establishment part-owned by Joe Peel. In fact it seemed that Holzapfel was trying to buy the club. One evening Peel brought Harold Gray there for a drink.

As they entered the club, Harold Gray went forward and was suddenly set upon by an unknown assailant who began to beat him savagely over the head. Gray yelled for Peel to help him and Peel shouted at Holzapfel, who was the unknown assailant, to stop the attack. Was it that Peel was too scrupulous or that the plan was never for Gray to be attacked in this manner? Either way, it seemed that this plan was to end in confusion as that of the Chillingworths' abduction had nearly done. It was alleged, when Joe Peel, Holzapfel and the insurance agent Yenzer were indicted, that Gray's head was to have been held under in a tub of canal water at the Chi-Chi Club until he drowned. His body was then to be dumped in the canal to make it look like accidental drowning. But surprisingly Holzapfel was acquitted, when he pleaded that Gray provoked the attack by comments on the assailant's wife. Charges against Joe Peel and Yenzer were then dropped.

Joe Peel left West Palm Beach, where grand jury hearings were soon to link his name with Holzapfel and Bobby Lincoln in the rackets. He went to Eau Gallie and became the Insured Capital Corporation. Floyd Holzapfel was one of his partners. But Holzapfel and the insurance salesman James Yenzer found themselves working together as house detectives at Miami Beach and at the Deauville Hotel. Holzapfel and Bobby Lincoln were also working together in the moonshine racket, shipping illegal whisky from Jacksonville to the thirsty stretches of Miami Beach. And then, for no apparent reason, in September 1958, the law closed in on the moonshiners. Seventy-six were arrested and gaoled. Holzapfel escaped but Bobby Lincoln went down. How had it happened?

IV

Holzapfel thought he knew the answer. A young man named Lew Gene Harvey, a small cog in the moonshine mechanism, had turned informer. It was now three and a half years since the Chillingworths' disappearance and the forces of law seemed no closer to the truth than they would ever be. Surely it was safe to repeat the disappearing act with someone like Lew Harvey whom the world would never miss? Holzapfel offered to dispose of Harvey on behalf of the moonshiners for $50,000. No one could be safe with an informer around. On 2 November 1958, Holzapfel and Lincoln, who was still on bail awaiting trial, decided they would act, with or without payment. The next night, on the pretext of doing business with him, Holzapfel and Lincoln drove Harvey inland from West Palm Beach. They stopped in the swampland of the everglades by a drainage canal. Then they pulled a gun on their victim. They bound and gagged him. Harvey was made to kneel and was shot by Holzapfel through the back of the head. A block of concrete was bound to his body and he was dumped in the canal.

But Lew Harvey was yet to cause his killers considerable embarrassment. Four days later, his body rose to the surface of the canal, bringing with it the concrete block, and was found by a startled fisherman. The block, which had been heavy enough to keep the body submerged at first, was too light as Harvey's corpse began to swell and decompose.

There was worse to come. Lew Harvey might have seemed an unsuspecting beginner but he was nothing of the kind. When his two companions suggested going for a ride to discuss a little business, he agreed, but privately made a note of their car number. He left that note with his wife. As the police began to investigate what seemed plainly a gangland killing, Mrs Harvey came forward with the note. The West Palm Beach police checked the number and identified the car as belonging to Floyd Holzapfel.

But the law bided its time, rightly believing that the body of Lew Gene Harvey would lead to far more dramatic discoveries. Certainly the connection from Holzapfel now seemed likely to lead back to Joe Peel. By staying their hand, the police of West Palm Beach had time to bring in the crime detection resources of the Florida Sheriffs Bureau at the state capital of Tallahassee. This time, they saw a chance to smash the rackets both at the top and state-wide.

The man chosen to work on the Harvey case was Special Agent Henry J Lovern, working directly under the bureau's deputy chief, Ross Anderson, a former news reporter. Lovern himself was everything a B-movie sleuth might be. A former college football star, he was slow, methodical and got results. Nor was he a novice. His first job had been in military intelligence. In this case, what he needed was a way into the criminal conspiracy and someone to open that way. Bobby Lincoln was in gaol. Joe Peel and Floyd Holzapfel seemed beyond reach. Lew Harvey was dead.

There was one man who knew the target criminals and,

though not part of the underworld, might mingle unsuspected with its members. If he failed to remain unsuspected, he might end in the canal tied to another concrete block. His name was Jim Yenzer, now a hotel detective at Miami Beach with Floyd Holzapfel, lately the insurance agent of West Palm Beach, who had sold Joe Peel a policy on Harold Gray's life. In January 1959, the Sheriffs Bureau was persuaded to take on Jim Yenzer as an undercover man in the case. Henry Lovern talked to Yenzer in March 1959, probing him about the Lew Harvey murder. Yenzer, however, began talking about the disappearance of the Chillingworths, almost four years earlier. Working with Holzapfel at the Miami hotel, Yenzer picked up a good deal of his companion's careless talk. One night, with no idea that he was talking to an undercover agent, 'Lucky' Holzapfel had told Yenzer that Judge Peel had hired someone to kill Judge Chillingworth.

Yenzer was now given the job of flushing out Joe Peel. It was not difficult to establish contact, since he knew Peel already from the sale of the policy on Harold Gray's life. In April 1959, he recalled, 'I told Peel that I knew of his participation in the Chillingworth murders. I told him that Floyd Holzapfel had told me. Joe said that Floyd should be careful who he talks to.' It was scarcely a confession but Yenzer had moved closer than anyone to the truth. He warned Peel of what Holzapfel would do 'if he ever starts talking'. Peel said helplessly, 'I know, I know.'

By now surveillance on Peel and on Holzapfel, more likely of the two to be a weak link, had been stepped up. Conversations were secretly recorded and more than eight hours of tapes compiled. So far it was to no purpose. To arrest Peel and Holzapfel on the present evidence still risked the collapse of a prosecution.

The next development was Floyd Holzapfel's plan to hijack a $60,000 shipment of arms, intended for the rebel movement in Cuba, and sell them to other Latin American revolutionaries. Holzapfel invited Yenzer to join him in the enterprise. On instructions from Henry Lovern, Yenzer agreed. The arms were commandeered but when the two men were driving a truck load of them by night, they were intercepted by the police near Miami. In the confusion, Yenzer ran for his life and Holzapfel was caught. To Holzapfel it seemed a matter of luck that he had been caught while his companion got away. As it happened, even Holzapfel escaped punishment. Though tried and sentenced to fifteen years imprisonment, he appealed at once and was released on bail.

There was to be a re-trial. However, Floyd Holzapfel had a good idea of how it would end and he decided not to await the result. In December 1959, he travelled to Washington DC and caught a plane to Rio de Janeiro. In Rio, he would be safe from justice, even if he remained poor. It was not justice that was his greatest concern but Joe Peel and the money that might be due from the Insured Capital Corporation. By this time Peel himself was in a panic at the way that his former partner was hinting to anyone who would listen that the former judge was the killer of Curtis and Marjorie Chillingworth.

Faced with the flight of Holzapfel, Peel did two things. He sent money to Rio with promises of more to follow. Holzapfel would surely hesitate to expose such a benefactor to Phil O'Connell or the Sheriffs Bureau. And then Peel offered Jim Yenzer payment plus expenses to go to Rio and wipe out 'Lucky' Holzapfel.

Joe Peel still had no inkling of Jim Yenzer's concealed loyalty. Presumably, Peel felt that a man who had sold life insurance on the unsuspecting Harold Gray might be open to a different kind of offer on Holzapfel's life. Jim Yenzer recalled how it came about. 'I told Joe that when and if he decided to hit Floyd to let me know definitely. Later he asked if I would kill for him. I said yes. He said how much would I charge. I said: "Normally, five to ten thousand." He said he might go to two thousand.'

Yenzer's reference to his 'normal' charges set him up as an experienced hit-man in Peel's opinion. The odd thing was that Joe Peel, who had made so much money and had so much to lose, would only go to $2000 dollars to get rid of the man who might cost him his own life. In the event, Yenzer persuaded

Peel to offer more. As time went by, the sum reached $5300, provided Yenzer also employed an assistant.

Seldom was there a conspiracy in which so many people were double-crossing one another. Jim Yenzer took advantage of this to stir up the participants a little more. He telephoned Holzapfel in Rio to tell him that the Insured Capital Corporation was making big profits and that 'Lucky' Floyd was losing most of his share to Peel. He telephoned Holzapfel again, a little later, and informed him that Joe Peel was being seen around a lot with Mrs Holzapfel in various parts of the country. He told Peel that the West Palm Beach State Attorney was now offering $100,000 for the discovery of the bones of the Chillingworths. However, instead of looking anxious, Peel grinned and said that anyone who wanted to find them should look off the shore of Manalapan, about a hundred yards beyond the southbound steamer track. But still there was no substantial confession and, of course, Peel's alibi for the evening on which the two victims had disappeared remained unbreakable.

After nine months of living on a subsistence in Rio, Holzapfel had had enough. He decided to return to Florida secretly and under an assumed name. Joe Peel would have to finance him or risk being given away. After all, his buddy Jim Yenzer had assured him that he was owed a small fortune from his partnership in the Insured Capital Corporation. Peel could not afford to hold out on him now. Perhaps he might simply collect the money and then disappear again. In September 1960, Holzapfel flew from Rio to Mexico and then to Houston, Texas. The authorities had guessed he was coming back to Florida and they watched for him in vain at Miami International Airport. Safely and unobserved, he reached Florida overland, booking into a motel in Melbourne on the Florida east coast. Yenzer found him and then went to Peel, warning him that Holzapfel was back and ready to spill everything about the Chillingworth murders.

Yenzer met Peel in a room at the Melbourne Holiday Inn, just south of Eau Gallie, and again warned him of what Holzapfel would do. He urged Peel to make a decision about the contract on Holzapfel's life. And then Yenzer raised another problem.

'After I kill Floyd, the other persons in the Chillingworth thing will come looking for me. What can I do to protect myself?'

Joe Peel reassured him: 'Don't worry. The other person is in the penitentiary.'

That evening, Henry Lovern knew for the first time that only two men apart from Peel had been involved in the Chillingworth murders. The 'other person' must be Bobby Lincoln, associate of Holzapfel and Peel, now in the penitentiary as a moonshiner.

Yenzer's improbable masquerade as a hit-man for the rackets was almost over, though not before Joe Peel had handed him the first instalment of $500 as down payment for the murder of Holzapfel in Florida, Brazil or wherever else he might be. It seemed that Jim Yenzer could do little more for the Sheriffs Bureau unless there was another witness to his conversations with Peel. And Joe Peel was increasingly careful that there should not be.

Even now the most unhappy man was Phil O'Connell, State Attorney for West Palm Beach. A tough but fair-minded prosecutor, who had been a well-known amateur boxer in his youth, O'Connell had been one of the first to suspect Peel's connection with the rackets. After the disappearance of the Chillingworths, the grand jury hearings in the city had linked Peel more or less publicly with Holzapfel and Lincoln, in the business of protection offered to illegal gambling and moonshine. No further progress had yet been made in the grand jury hearings. O'Connell had come close but never quite close enough. In the Chillingworth case, the Sheriffs Bureau had provided him with ammunition but in court, as O'Connell knew, it was still too little.

Too much of Peel's 'confessional' evidence would sound flimsy, even if it could be corroborated. When he told Yenzer that the bones of the Chillingworths were somewhere off Manalapan beyond the steamer track, he was only saying what half of Palm Beach might have said. When he admitted to P O Wilber that 'it was either that son-of-a-bitch or me', he was stating a publicly-known truth. Even if his remarks could be proved, which they seldom could be by corroboration, they were at least ambiguous.

The State Attorney faced one or two other difficulties. As the threat of grand jury revelations increased, Peel had moved north to Eau Gallie, on the east coast of Florida not far from Cape Canaveral. It seemed that he could have had no part in the murder of Lew Gene Harvey, despite Holzapfel's known connection with it. The Harvey case was still the best lead but Phil O'Connell had no wish to find that he was trying Holzapfel and Lincoln while Peel went free. The case with the best proof was therefore of no use in bringing Peel to justice. And, whatever case was tried, O'Connell faced Joe Peel's easy glamour and assured style as a courtroom performer. Unlike most defendants, he would be in his natural element. Despite the former judge's breaches of legal rules and etiquette, he played to the jury and the gallery as a debonair matinée idol as well as an advocate. Like a matinée idol, he drew the crowds. The public gallery was always full, its occupants mainly female, for Peel's performances. The State Attorney drew no crowds at all. On the witness-stand, Joe Peel would be a match for Phil O'Connell.

Phil O'Connell knew that his case against Joe Peel would have to be watertight. After five years, it was still far from that. His one hope was Jim Yenzer. Peel had offered Yenzer money to kill Holzapfel, whom the former judge now described as a raving maniac. Even so, O'Connell only had Yenzer's word for this. In September 1960, according to Yenzer, he had met Peel in a motel at Cocoa Beach, south of Eau Gallie. Peel was nervous and suspicious. He searched behind the curtains of the room and examined the bases of the lamps. There were no hidden microphones. All the same, he insisted that they should hold their conversation in the open air. Once again, if the case came to court, Yenzer's story would have no corroboration.

By 30 September, however, 'Lucky' Floyd Holzapfel was

back in Florida. He was a hundred miles or more north of Palm Beach on the Atlantic coast and a few miles south of Joe Peel in Eau Gallie, staying at the Haven Aire Motel, Melbourne, under an assumed name. Yenzer took Peel to the nearby Holiday Inn, Peel being accompanied by a former plumber, Donald Miles, who was now another partner in the Insured Capital Corporation. The three men met in Room 217, which had been skilfully bugged. In the adjoining room, 219, sat Henry Lovern and his technical assistant, ready to record every word.

It should have been the end of Joe Peel. Unfortunately, the recording was almost incomprehensible, the words obliterated by the air conditioner and other background noises. Henry Lovern never heard Yenzer telling Peel that Floyd Holzapfel was half a mile away and Peel telling Yenzer to go down there and kill him.

Yenzer agreed. It was arranged that Peel and his partner should leave at once with their families for Daytona Beach, far to the north on Florida's Atlantic coast, and establish alibis for the time of Holzapfel's death. 'I intend to get Floyd out of the way,' Joe Peel said, 'because he has enough on me to put me in the electric chair.' He asked Yenzer if he had recruited an assistant yet and Yenzer said that 'a man from Jacksonville' was going to help him. There was only one possible hitch. John Peel, Joe Peel's brother, might have gone to have a drink with Holzapfel. What was to be done if he was there when Yenzer arrived? 'Then Jim will have to take him too,' Joe Peel said, philosophically passing sentence of death on his brother. 'I love you,' he told Yenzer as he left, 'I hope everything goes all right.' With that, Peel and Miles set off for Daytona Beach. They would listen for a radio report of Holzapfel's death or disappearance. When he heard it, Peel would phone a message to Yenzer, 'Go and collect the package.' The package would contain payment for the murder.

All this was lost to Henry Lovern and his tapes. However, as soon as Peel and Miles had left, he rang the next room and told Yenzer to turn off the air conditioner. Then Yenzer was to phone Floyd Holzapfel and get him to the wired room at the Holiday Inn by any means necessary. It was not difficult. Yenzer had only to hint to his former partner that Joe Peel, far from making him a present of the profits owing to him from the Insured Capital Corporation, was going to send him the same way as Judge Chillingworth.

Floyd Holzapfel arrived and the tapes in the next room began to run again. Holzapfel, as a failed racketeer and hitman, was at his lowest ebb. 'I walked in cautiously,' he said of his arrival at Room 127 of the Melbourne Holiday Inn, 'because I thought Mr Peel had set me up to be killed.' Alone and depressed in his own motel room, he had reached a point where he was even signing the wrong false name for his meals. Now his old buddy Jim Yenzer poured him a glass of whisky and took a lemon soda for himself. Holzapfel relaxed a little in the company of the partner with whom he had worked as a house detective at the Deauville Hotel in Miami Beach and who had been his partner again in the failed arms hijack. Jim Yenzer poured him another whisky and they began to talk.

Presently another informant and candidate for reward money, P O Wilber, entered the room. Holzapfel relaxed a little more. Wilber was the man who had stood bail for him over the arms hijack and who showed no animosity when Floyd Holzapfel skipped. For the first time in almost a year it seemed that he was among friends. Holzapfel began to unburden himself of troubled thoughts. 'I didn't know there was a policeman within a hundred miles of me,' he said later, 'We talked about companies Joe and I had set up. I had definitely been swindled by Mr Peel. We discussed past activities of ourselves and Mr Peel. We had a plan. Yenzer was going to call Peel and tell him I was dead. Then have Peel come over to the hotel, get him talking and I was going to walk out of the bathroom. During this part of the conversation, we found out how we had been damn fools.' Yenzer refilled his friend's glass.

When the conversation came back to Joe Peel again, Holzapfel said, 'I was completely disgusted with his underhand tricks, cheating, robbing, and killing people.'

CHAPTER TWO

Jim Yenzer filled Holzapfel's glass from time to time and the conversation continued. Indeed, it continued for three days and nights of dedicated drinking. At the end of that time, Jim Yenzer may have held the world record for non-stop consumption of lemon soda. There were also three empty bottles of Scotch and two of vodka, on Holzapfel's account. In an outpouring of self-pity, he told his companions of his 'wasted life'. At last he talked in a rather confused manner about the Chillingworth murders, how he had told the judge it was a stick-up and how he had dropped Marjorie Chillingworth to her death in the sea with a final derisive salute of 'ladies first'. He and Peel and Lincoln deserved all they got, he said. 'People who have done what I have done – and what Joe Peel has done and what Bobby Lincoln has done – should be stamped out like cockroaches because they aren't fit to be with decent people.'

There could only be one conclusion to his self-accusation. On 3 October 1960, when the drinking and the self-pity had reached a fourth day, Ross Anderson of the Florida Sheriffs Bureau, with Henry Lovern and two deputies, entered Room 127 of the Holiday Inn. Though they had drawn their guns, 'Lucky' Floyd Holzapfel was no longer in a state to realize fully what was happening, let alone resist. He managed to lift his hands and say, 'I'm not armed.'

Betrayal, justice, or snare, whatever the term used, the work was now almost complete. Holzapfel was taken to Titusville gaol, the nearest to Melbourne. That night, coming to his senses and knowing what his prospects were, he slashed his left wrist and lay on the floor of his cell, trying to pump his hand to increase the loss of blood. But they found him after half an hour and patched him up in hospital.

Ross Anderson and Henry Lovern had their tapes. The recordings were still a disappointment. Where there was so much drink – Scotch or lemon soda – there was also a good deal of urination. Every time the lavatory was used in the motel suite, the extractor fan came on automatically and blotted out everything else on the recording for the next ten minutes. The Sheriffs Bureau had a lot of tape by this time.

According to the *New York Times*, they had recorded seventy-two hours of conversations between the conspirators and the undercover men, however imperfectly. But whether tapes that were recorded in such a manner and were so incomplete would be admitted as evidence in court was another matter.

At Daytona Beach, Joe Peel listened to the news on 3 October and heard an unwelcome report.

> *Floyd A Holzapfel, a Florida criminal, was arrested today. Police claim that the five-year-old mystery of Circuit Judge and Mrs C E Chillingworth is now cleared up.*

Joe Peel and his partner, Miles left Daytona Beach in a hurry for Georgia, where Peel said that he was going to get hold of poison and commit suicide. Miles thought the poison was actually intended for Holzapfel. But then Peel changed his mind and said that Miles, with his skill as a plumber, should construct a bomb. Peel would book an airline ticket and smuggle the bomb on to the plane, blowing up the plane, himself and everyone on board. That way it would not look like suicide and his wife Imogene would collect his life insurance.

Joe Peel was no longer at his best in a crisis. He now returned to the very place where he was most likely to be caught, Room 127 of the Melbourne Holiday Inn. What did he expect to find there? In the event, men from the Sheriffs Bureau were waiting for him with Phil O'Connell, State Attorney of West Palm Beach. Joe Peel looked at them with all the surprise of an innocent man. His conscience was clear and he had nothing to answer for.

V

On the following day, Joe Peel and David Miles were charged with conspiracy to murder Floyd Holzapfel. Bail was set at $25,000 but Peel, who denied the charge, raised this easily. Not so the luckless plumber, Donald Miles. As soon as Peel was released, he left Miles in gaol and vanished. Phil

O'Connell knew that the best chance of keeping track of him was to release Miles as well. Where else would the poor dupe go but to his master? In this O'Connell was right. So Miles was released and he followed Peel to a hotel room in Chattanooga, Tennessee, which he reached the following week. Again the law officers broke in upon the two men but this time Joe Peel was arrested and charged with the murders of the Chillingworths.

It was unfortunate for the State Attorney that the Chillingworth case was almost impossible to prove without granting immunity to one or other of the conspirators. Joe Peel, Floyd Holzapfel and Bobby Lincoln were clearly implicated but only two of them could be brought to trial. The evidence of what Peel had said to Jim Yenzer or P O Wilber was at best fragmentary. Reports of Joe Peel's 'It was either that son-of-a-bitch or me' comments were sensational but not enough on their own to convince a jury. And, of course, Yenzer and Wilber would have to admit in court that they were hoping for a prime share of the $160,000 reward money. As for the evidence of the tapes, it was not enough for a conviction. In any case, because they were so patchy it was possible that a judge would refuse to admit them in evidence.

As it happened, each of the three accused was hungry for immunity as the price of turning state's evidence against the other two. They all faced first degree murder charges and the spectre of the solid oak-framed electric-chair in Raiford penitentiary. Though Peel was accessory before the fact this was still a capital charge if the crime was a first-degree murder. When he made a bid for immunity in exchange for giving prosecution evidence, Phil O'Connell turned him down flat. The one candidate whose immunity offered the least affront to justice was fifty-year-old Bobby Lincoln, boss of the 'coloured town' rackets.

Even here there was a problem. Phil O'Connell was uneasy at the effect of a black man giving state's evidence against two whites. In 1961, how would an all-white Florida jury react? The only effect would be, however little, to increase sympathy for the two white men. But there was no other way. Lincoln was still serving his moonshine sentence and when the offer of immunity was made to him, he took it at once. In exchange, he agreed to be the star witness against Holzapfel and Joe Peel when the Chillingworth case came to trial. It was Floyd Holzapfel who now found himself isolated. Bobby Lincoln's evidence would condemn him. But there was no longer anything that he could offer the prosecution. After all this time, no one needed 'Lucky' Floyd Holzapfel. The best that he could do was to plead guilty to a charge of first-degree murder and hope that he might draw a life sentence rather than the electric chair. He might not be the state's witness but if he helped to put Joe Peel in the chair, the state might look more kindly on him.

As for Joe Peel, his courtroom performance would be impressive but it could scarcely disguise the fact that he was virtually his only material witness. If the jury accepted the stories of Floyd Holzapfel and Bobby Lincoln, the 2,000 volts that might send the former Municipal Judge to eternity would be almost humming in the courtroom air. Since Peel could only be tried for one murder at a time, O'Connell decided to begin with that of Judge Chillingworth. Yet the world was also going to know that Joe Peel stood charged with the murder of Marjorie Chillingworth, the attempted murder of Floyd Holzapfel and more than a hundred and fifty counts of fraud relating to the activities of the Insured Capital Corporation. Joe Peel was not charged with offences as a racketeer but his West Palm Beach protection system was soon to be described vividly and publicly by Bobby Lincoln on the witness-stand. The trial was set for March 1961. By November 1960, Peel sat in Cell 305 of West Palm Beach gaol, to which he had sent other men in his capacity as a judge.

Edward Johnson was a trusty in West Palm Beach gaol and one of his jobs was carrying meals to the cells. Though his evidence was not corroborated, he alleged that one day in November 1960, when he took food to Joe Peel's cell, the ex-judge talked to him about the forthcoming trial. He showed Johnson a packet of cigarettes. The top had been peeled back a little and the ends of several cigarettes could be seen inside.

When these were shaken out, the rest of the packet contained a white powder, which was apparently potassium cyanide. 'He told me,' Johnson said, 'that if he got Floyd Holzapfel, he would beat the Chillingworth rap.' And then Peel said, 'If you put that in the food or milk, you will be well taken care of.' Joe Peel himself denied the entire story, pointing out that he was being held in a maximum security cell without being allowed cigarettes or cigarette packets.

Edward Johnson said that he took the packet from Joe Peel and hid it behind the pipes of the washroom. Several times, Peel asked him about it and told him exactly what to do. But Edward Johnson went to the State Attorney instead.

Peel won a tactical victory in getting the trial transferred from West Palm Beach. He was no longer 'Man of the Year' in the Junior Chamber of Commerce. The new venue was to be Fort Pierce, about fifty miles north on the Florida east coast. As the *New York Times* reported, 'The trial has shifted to this tomato-growing and cattle town, north of Palm Beach, on the defense's contention that Mr Peel would not receive a fair trial in the home town of the Chillingworths.'

So in a courthouse, which unlike his Cadillac had never had air-conditioning, Joseph Alexander Peel Jr was arraigned. The press reported that 'Mr Peel was pale from long weeks in a jail cell but was nattily suited today.' His attorney, Carlton Welch, tried to invalidate much of the prosecution evidence by arguing that his client should not be tried for his life on 'the testimony of hoodlums.' He lost that point. Then he tried to cross-examine Floyd Holzapfel over his part in the Harvey killing. The state knew Holzapfel had committed the crime and yet it had taken no action to prosecute him for it.

'I want to ask Holzapfel if he has ever been arraigned or entered a plea in the Harvey case. I propose to show that he has not been asked to plead, that he has a hope of leniency.' But the judge ruled against him on this point too.

So the participants in the drama told their stories again, encouraged much of the time by Phil O'Connell as State Attorney, who now saw his chance of ridding the world of Joe

Peel. Yet the best defence was Peel himself. He was a plausible, tricky, fluent and quick-thinking witness. He denied all connection with the murder of Judge Chillingworth and presented himself to the small-town jury in the St Louie courthouse of Fort Pierce as a victim of big city politics. As for Holzapfel and his story of Peel's involvement in the murder, it was Holzapfel who was the true gangster and who had even threatened Peel's baby daughter.

'Floyd asked me to go into an eight per cent loan business. I said no. He persisted. His friends offered to come in on a building business in Orlando at eight per cent. I said okay. Floyd was dangerous. One day he phoned and all he said was that he had a friend who had a little girl and the little girl was killed because her father talked too much. He made a special point of telling me the story.'

Under cross-examination, Joe Peel held his own against Phil O'Connell. When Peel was first arrested O'Connell demanded, 'Did you state that you would tell about the Chillingworth case if you were granted immunity for any participation you may have had in it?'

Joe Peel smiled his silk-shirted smile.

'Mr O'Connell,' he said patiently, 'if I had tried to talk to you about immunity in the Chillingworth case, you would have arrested me that night.'

But O'Connell had not arrested Peel in that case for another week or more and had meantime let him out on bail over the attempted murder of Holzapfel. Though O'Connell spoke the truth and Joe Peel did not, the well-groomed West Palm Beach lawyer now made the State Attorney sound like a deliberate and rather inept liar.

On the evidence, however, there could only be one verdict and the Fort Pierce jury brought it in. They found Joseph Alexander Peel guilty as accessory before the fact in the murder of Judge Curtis Eugene Chillingworth. But then, to the visible consternation of the State Attorney, they recommended mercy by a majority vote. The spectre of Raiford's electric chair receded and vanished. Joe Peel had given the performance of his life in the sweltering and old-fashioned St

Louie courthouse and it had paid off. Despite a second-degree murder conviction and a life sentence, he looked and spoke that day like a man who had beaten the rap.

He had also been indicted for the murder of Marjorie Chillingworth but when that trial came on it was something of an anti-climax. Joe Peel withdrew his plea of 'not guilty' and entered one of 'no defence'. He was again convicted of second-degree murder, since his part in the two killings was the same, and drew a second life sentence. In theory, he might be released after seven years – or never.

Bobby Lincoln, having been given immunity, was released from prison in the following year when his moonshine sentence had been served. Floyd Holzapfel had pleaded guilty to first-degree murder in the Chillingworth case and came up for sentence in West Palm Beach on 3 May 1961. Judge Russell O Morrow showed some sympathy with the man whose nickname, by a grotesque irony, had always been 'Lucky'. He told the self-confessed killer, 'You have done an excellent job in helping the state and in laying an example before all people, young and old, that crime does not pay.' Holzapfel alone faced the electric chair, though he had been of more use to the prosecution case than Bobby Lincoln and less the prime mover of the killings than Joe Peel.

And yet, Judge Morrow insisted, Holzapfel had perpetrated crimes which were, 'gruesome, vicious, cold-blooded, premeditated, designed, the like of which the history of Florida had never seen.' As the law stood, there was only one sentence that the judge was permitted to pass and he did so. The court decreed that Floyd A Holzapfel 'be taken by the Sheriff of Palm Beach County and by him delivered to the State Prison of the State of Florida, and there by the process of electrocution be put to death.'

In the game of winners and losers, Floyd Holzapfel was a natural loser. Joe Peel, by whatever freak of fortune, had been a survivor. How, then, could Peel have imagined that he would be brought to justice not by the bodies of the Chillingworths but by the body of a man who had nothing to do with the Chillingworths and of whose very existence Joe Peel was unaware?

At the end of 1958 and even in 1960, five years after the deaths of their victims, the three men had every reason to think that they had escaped justice. And yet, at the end of 1958, it was another freak of fortune which had brought to the surface of an everglade drainage canal the weighted corpse of a small-time crook, Lew Gene Harvey. The odds against the body ever surfacing greatly favoured the killers. Unlike the Chillingworths, Harvey would be little missed and scarcely looked for. Yet he had left a car number with his wife, which led to Floyd Holzapfel, to Rio, and to a hotel room in Melbourne, Florida, where Joe Peel was trying to arrange a murder contract.

By means he could never have envisaged, Joseph Alexander Peel, a State Prosecutor in West Palm Beach at twenty-six, a judge the next year, a man who controlled the very system by which he had been caught, had been trapped as surely as if he had gone on the witness-stand like Floyd Holzapfel and confessed everything. It was the final irony of the case that he was not brought to justice by the bones of the Chillingworths but by the unexpected discovery of the corpse of this complete stranger. If the state truly wanted to acknowledge the man who convicted the former municipal judge of contract murder, it should have paid the $160,000 reward money into the estate of a small-time racketeer and informer, Lew Gene Harvey, whose body floated when by all the laws of probability and gangland science it should have sunk.

THREE

Serenade in Scarlet:
Melvin David Rees Jr
(1957-61)

I

When Curtis Chillingworth and his wife went missing on 15 June 1955, they only made page three of the next morning's *Washington Post*. The banner headline on the paper's front page described a bizarre and apparently motiveless double murder that was far closer to home. The previous morning, hours before the Chillingworth disappearance was reported, fourteen-year-old Ann Ryan and her sixteen-year-old friend, Nancy Shomette, left home shortly before eight o'clock. They lived just outside Washington DC, at Lewisville, Maryland. Their route lay across North-Western Park.

Later that morning, twelve-year-old Barbara Huff was exercising her dog in the park. She was near the trees of the picnic site with its 'fireplace' on which visitors could cook their barbecues. The dog ran off and began to investigate something under a loose pile of small branches. Underneath lay what looked like a life-sized doll. It was the body of Ann Ryan, the younger of the two friends. The police of Prince George County sealed off the area, erected plastic screens and began a search for further clues. Thirty-two feet away they found the body of Nancy Shomette, also covered loosely by twigs and branches.

The first thing the investigators noticed was that the heavy structure of the barbecue fireplace had been moved. Had the killer been going to attempt a cremation of the girls, at least sufficient to make the bodies hard to identify? Or were they

89

to be placed, alive or dead, on the structure for some other ritual? There was no answer to that.

Police Chief George Panagoulis held a press conference later that day. The two girls had been shot. There was no evidence that they had been raped. So far, there was no specific lead but the police were attempting to trace and interrogate anyone who had been in the park that morning. In answer to further questions, he revealed that this was no ordinary shooting. The bodies had been dragged to the places in which they had been found and the girls had first been shot some distance away. The evidence indicated that they had been crossing open ground when the gunman opened fire on them. Ann Ryan dropped at once while Nancy Shomette ran for the trees. But the killer caught up with her, either dropping her or making her lie down. He then used the girl's body as if for target practice. He shot her in the stomach first and then in the breasts - more than once in each area. After he had reloaded and put a total of ten shots into her, the sixteen-year-old-girl was still alive. He had dragged her to the place where she was found, put the muzzle of the gun to her head and given her the *coup de grâce*. The bullet that had finally killed her was found on the earth under her head. It had come from a .22 Marlin rifle, a calibre which had enabled the man to put so many bullets into the girl, causing smaller wounds, before she was killed.

Superlatives of horror greeted the news of the killings and relegated the Chillingworths to page three in the Virginia and Maryland press. Though there was no rape, this particular double murder had overtones of sexual violence. No one needed to read Sigmund Freud before guessing which organ of the killer's body the gun symbolized. That it was not a sex crime in the more obvious sense was a cause of foreboding. It was the work of a mind more deranged than that behind most sexually motivated crimes, a display of sado-sexual ambition at its worst.

Events moved quickly overnight. By the day after the killings, the police of Prince George County had a youth in 'protective custody'. Eighteen-year-old Norman Hager of

Lewisville knew the two dead girls and had been in the park that morning. Because the two seemed to have gone missing, he had actually driven with some friends to the park to see if they were there. When he came home, a little later, the police were already on the scene. 'Sonny' Hager was questioned for twenty-four hours. He protested his innocence and offered to take a lie-detector test. On the third day of the inquiry, 17 June, the Hager family's attorney successfully applied for a writ of *habeas corpus* and secured the young man's release. Though the Hager parents agreed that the police should search their home, Norman Hager was entirely innocent and had nothing to fear. 'Sonny' Hager had been doing his friends a good turn when he went with them to the park to look for the girls. He was now out of the case.

Half the entire police resources of Prince George County were diverted to the investigation. The only remaining clue to the 'Sharp Shooting Killer', as the press now dubbed him, was his use of the .22 Marlin rifle, Model 88-DL. As the month of June 1955 passed, Police Chief Panagoulis cast his net wider and with a suggestion of increasing frustration. A friend of Nancy Shomette's in New Jersey was interviewed as a new 'key witness'. It came to nothing. Engineers from Fort Meade blasted a hole in the wall of the park lake to drain it. An army mine-detector squad then searched the lake bed and found nothing that gave a clue to the murder mystery. Planes and helicopters carried out a low-level aerial scan of roof-tops and tree-tops. Plans were made to search the sewers. Six hundred more people were questioned. One hundred and fifty purchasers of Marlin rifles were checked. Captain Richard Felber, Chief of Washington's Metropolitan Homicide Bureau, visited the scene and loaned a number of his officers to Prince George County. A modest reward of $200 was offered for information leading to the killer's conviction.

The inquiry was still almost where it had been on the first day. However, a woman came forward to say that she had heard shots from the park as she did her washing-up at about 8.00 to 8.15am on the morning of 15 June. Other witnesses also thought they heard shots, suggesting that the girls were killed very soon after leaving home. Had the killer been watching for them? The police further revealed that they had read two diaries and that they had found slips of paper on the barbecue fireplace which were intended to burn but had not caught fire. Whatever was written on the slips of paper, it seemed to do no good to the investigation.

And that was very nearly the end of the case for Police Chief Panagoulis and his men. When, on 25 June the *Washington Post* announced, 'Wanderer is "Definite" Suspect in Dual Slaying', the entire story had a ring of desperation. But at least the inquiry was on the front page again. The suspect was an unshaven armed wanderer with a .22 rifle. The gun looked new and he had been seen near the park. 'A bandolier-decked Pancho Villa-style character was seen wandering in the woods before and shortly after the crime.' He was described as a white man, five feet ten inches tall, thirty years old and weighing about a hundred and sixty pounds. 'He had a dark full head of hair, bushy in front, and needed a shave when last seen. He has a weathered complexion, like he spent most of his time in the open. He was wearing a blue shirt and dark khaki pants with a web belt. On one side of his belt was a sheathed dagger, on the other side an Army canteen.'

By 28 June, police searches had failed to find any sign of this wanderer. Maryland police now made a new appeal to the nation, at least as far north as Connecticut. They needed to find a college man who 'acts peculiar' and had not been seen for the past five weeks. This appeal sounded even more desperate than the last. Like the bearded wanderer, the 'peculiar' college man failed to appear again. Next day, 29 June, the gloom at Police Headquarters in Prince George County was reflected in the press. 'Police officials continue to feel that the thousands of hours of unending legwork they've invested in the past two weeks will be rewarded with a break in the case, but at day's end it seemed the killer's trail was cold.'

Waiting for a break now became the official policy. By 30 June, the police had received seventy-five 'Pancho Villa' calls. These did nothing to forward the inquiry. At that point, so far as the press was concerned, the case became yesterday's news. On 1 July it disappeared from the banner headlines and even from the third page.

Almost a year passed without further developments. It was June again, in 1956. On the first day of the month, eighteen-year-old Mary Elizabeth Fellers and sixteen-year-old Shelby Jean Venable were given a lift by a young man with a scar on his face. The vehicle in which they hitched a lift was a blue Ford and it picked them up on Route 1 at Beltsville, Maryland. Mary Elizabeth Fellers lived in Beltsville and Shelby Jean Venable's home was nearby in North Laurel. Those few witnesses who saw the girls get into the car never doubted that they had hitched a lift with someone they probably knew. In any case, with two girls together there was safety in numbers.

A week passed and nothing more was heard of them. The disappearance was inexplicable and sinister. Even if they had decided on a shorts-and-shirt hitch-hiking escapade of some kind, surely the police search would have found them. After nine days, Shelby Jean Venable was found, floating in the Potomac near Brunswick, Maryland. She was nude, having been raped and then strangled. The state of her body also indicated that she had been in the hands of a man who was a pathological sadist. The leisurely and casual torment of the victim was uneasily reminiscent of the way another sixteen-year-old, Nancy Shomette, had been used for target practice the year before.

Five more days passed. Then the body of Mary Elizabeth Fellers was found in the Catoctin Creek, in Loudon County, near Wheatland, Virginia. She was also nude, had been raped and strangled and showed signs of sadistic maltreatment.

The police of both states, with the assistance of Washington's Metropolitan Homicide Bureau, launched murder inquiries. But they neither found the young man with a scar nor his blue Ford. It was not their fault if the witnesses were vague. Blue was a popular colour and Ford cars filled the roads like summer flies. As for the autopsies, the bodies of the two girls were nothing but mute testimony of a sadistic imagination.

The murders were technically different from the killings in North-Western Park the year before. The second pair of girls had been strangled, not shot. In the light of what was later discovered, it seems the killer may actually have hanged them. Moreover, these two had been raped and the first two had not. The bodies of the second pair had been found far apart but it seemed likely that they had been tied up, raped, tormented and then murdered either in one another's presence or at least very nearly so. The network of roads in the tide-water country would not make it difficult to dump them miles apart. In such respects the killings differed from the North-Western Park murders. What linked them was the almost lascivious cruelty of the murderer. Such a sardonic taking of life was less common in the 1950s than it was to become. That aspect was the worst part of the crime.

Once again, after a few months the police had got nowhere. By making the girls strip before he tied them up, even by removing any remaining clothes after death, the wanted man had deprived the police of a whole set of clues which such garments might offer. The bodies had been in water for between five and fifteen days, a little less if the killer had kept the girls as his captives for a day or two. Whatever the period, the immersion made the time or date of death difficult to establish. The place of death was impossible to determine. It could have been anywhere within a hundred square miles. Having no scene of the crime to search, the police lost another set of clues.

A year passed and it was June 1957 - another June, the month in which the two previous double killings had taken place. Very little was known about the killer but there was no need to be superstitious in order to wonder if some kind of periodic planning or simply the compulsion of a deranged mind might be at work. What would June 1957 bring?

The month was very nearly over and there had been no repetition of the type of sadistic murder which had occurred in the two previous years. On Monday 26 June, at about 1.30pm, Master Sergeant Roy D Hudson drove out of Fort

Meade towards Laurel, Maryland, where he lived at a motel with his wife and two young children. Shelby Jean Venable had lived nearby, at North Laurel, but Master Sergeant Hudson was well able to take care of himself and was certainly no one's idea of a murder victim. On this particular afternoon, he gave a lift to a civilian worker at the base, an attractive married woman who lived with her husband and children in Baltimore. Margaret Harold, thirty-four years old, had been on her way to Glen Burnie to catch the Baltimore bus. Sergeant Hudson offered to take her to the bus stop.

They drove out of the base, each having changed into off-duty clothes, and put their other clothes on the back seat of the car. Margaret Harold was wearing a pink blouse and a pair of black pants. Because she had been given a lift, she was going to be early for her bus. Sergeant Hudson was in no hurry, however, and they stopped for a drink at an inn on the main road. Then, with time still to spare, Sergeant Hudson turned off on to a dead-end forest track or dirt road. He turned off at the junction of Maryland interstate highways 424 and 450, some ten miles west of Annapolis. There was a derelict farm building on the corner with a green car parked near it. He and Margaret Harold could sit and talk for ten minutes, away from the busy main road, before they went on to the bus stop. The way things had been in Maryland, it was better and safer for the young woman to be in his company than standing on her own until the bus came.

But when the two friends turned off the main road and disappeared along the dirt track of the old logging route, they left the warm summer world and entered a land of nightmare.

For almost three hours there was no sign to the rest of the world that anything was wrong. Then, at about 4.30, a farmer working on his land saw a man running towards him shouting for help. The farmer was Mr F L Burden and the man who wanted help was Sergeant Hudson. If Roy Hudson ran as though a devil of hell was at his heels, he had good reason for it. A few minutes later, Mr Burden was phoning the state police with a story he only half-believed, about a man running for his life and a young woman dead in a car.

What had happened? Roy Hudson and Margaret Harold had been sitting in the car, talking. A man approached them, walking alone towards the highway intersection. He was wearing a faded and dirty workshirt with khaki denim pants. Sergeant Hudson described the man as about five feet eleven inches tall, unshaven with a pale skin. He had black hair combed straight back and bushy eyebrows. Sergeant Hudson got out of the car and the man began to shout at him. Some of his words were indistinct but the general message was that he was annoyed to find the couple sitting there. 'What do you think this is?' he yelled, 'A national park?' He claimed that he was a caretaker of the woodland. Hudson protested that he and Margaret Harold were just sitting there and talking, which they were entitled to do. The man said he guessed it was all right, so long as they were just talking.

He came right up and asked Hudson for a cigarette. The sergeant went back to the car for a packet of cigarettes, gave one to the man and took one for himself. Then he lit the cigarettes. 'I walked this far,' the man said, 'how about giving me a ride back to my shack?' Hudson thought this might be the broken-down farmhouse at the main road junction, where the green car was parked. He ignored the request and got back into his driving seat. Again the man asked for a lift. Hudson said there was no room, he and Margaret having piled their working clothes on the back seat. By now he wanted to get rid of the unkempt scrounger.

Instead of accepting this explanation, the man opened the door and got into the back of the car. Sergeant Hudson, losing his temper rapidly, turned in his seat. The man showed him what he had in his hand. 'He had a blue-steel, snub-nosed revolver and was cocking it.' As he settled himself in the back, the stranger said, 'Both of you put your arms over the seat.' Hudson obeyed. Margaret Harold simply put her hands behind her. 'I need money,' the man said, 'Have you got any?'

Hudson saw that the man had some electric cord in his hands. He guessed what was about to happen. He would be tied up and Margaret Harold with her wrists pinioned would be taken into the trees. Next day the police would be looking for her body. To forestall this, Hudson quickly said that he had money but that he wouldn't be able to get his wallet out if his hands were tied. For some minutes he argued and pleaded with the man, telling him to put the gun away. But the unkempt stranger sat in the back of the car with his gun pointing at the couple. Then he reached forward and began to fondle Margaret Harold. Repelled and frightened by this, she twisted and struggled to evade him. The man became annoyed as she continued to resist him. As if there were nothing else for it, he raised the gun and shot her through the back of the head. She was killed outright.

As Margaret Harold slumped forward with blood pouring from the exit wound in her face, Sergeant Hudson brought his hands forward, opened the driver's door, rolled out of the car and scrambled behind a bush. Even as he rolled out of the car, the stranger fired but missed. There were two more shots as Hudson reached the bush. Two further bullets remained before the man would have to reload but Hudson took a chance. He got up and ran, expecting a bullet in his back at any moment. But despite the accuracy given to hand-guns on the screen by Hollywood, to hit someone at more than six feet or so was not always easy. A man running was an even worse target. With two shots left in the gun, the pursuer held his fire in hope of coming up close behind Hudson but the sergeant was fitter and a lot more frightened. 'I heard him coming after me,' he said, 'but I lost him.'

While Hudson was gasping out his story to the startled farmer, a truck driver was unloading gravel several miles away. A light green saloon car, moving at speed, swerved into a ditch as it took the main road junction too fast. The trucker came across and helped the driver, a young man with bushy eyebrows, to get his car back on the road again. The young man thanked him and drove off. That was the last anyone saw of him.

The hunt for Margaret Harold's killer seemed even more short-lived than those for the murderer or murderers of Nancy Shomette, Ann Ryan, Mary Elizabeth Fellers and Shelby Jean Venable. Several suspects were detained, only to be released when Sergeant Hudson did not identify them as the killer. The *Washington Post* printed a superfluous warning to its readers of a 'thug' on the loose. The month of June 1955, 1956 and 1957 had brought headlines to the front page, reporting the murders of girls or young women, five of them so far. Would the killer reappear again in June 1958?

There was a further macabre curiosity revealed by the investigation into Margaret Harold's death. Near the scene of the murder was a semi-derelict cinder-block cottage. It was scarcely fit for shelter, let alone habitation. Yet someone had been living there. The police search revealed a curious mural or montage in the basement room. An entire wall of the basement room was covered by cuttings from detective story monthlies and from magazines. The cuttings were of sexual offences with photographs of the victims. They were interspersed with what were euphemistically called 'pin-ups'. Some of these anticipated the type of cult fetishist 'comics', in which the young women were no more erotic, to most eyes, than trussed chickens. The setting was suggestively depicted but the actual moment of criminal violence left to the reader's imagination, thus warding off a censorship which still operated in America in the late 1950s.

The police and the FBI had little doubt that this was the hide-out of Margaret Harold's killer. Yet there was something potentially more sinister than the montage of explicit sexual violence on the basement wall. In the centre of this strange mural was a photograph of a girl who was fully dressed and who in no way reflected the dramas and suggestiveness of the rest of the exhibits. The propriety of the photograph made it the most incongruous item of the entire display.

This was the only photograph which had not been cut from a newspaper or magazine but was actually a print from a negative. By this time the FBI had been called in and the photographic paper was examined. It bore a serial number which showed that it had belonged to the University of Maryland. From that, it was possible to trace the girl in the picture. She had been a student there. To say that she was shocked by the discovery of her photograph in such circumstances would be an understatement. Yet she had no idea who had taken it or even that it had been done. As a student, she had naturally been out with quite a few boyfriends but none that could be connected with the case or who resembled the suspect. Perhaps he had watched from a distance, unable to win her friendship as others had, and perhaps he made his own photographic record of her. The worst of it was that she held pride of place in the murderer's display. Was she shown at its centre because he intended her as his next victim?

Yet the Margaret Harold inquiry was running into oblivion even more rapidly than the others. On 28 June, the police released details of the 'Cottage Hide-Out of Bushy-Haired Killer'. They had no further doubt that Margaret Harold's murderer had been using or living in the half-ruined building. They revealed the murals of 'pin-up girls' and 'detective story magazines detailing sex crimes'. The conclusion was that 'Everything points to our theory that the man we seek is mentally disturbed, probably with strong sex manifestations.'

As a statement of the obvious the last comment was masterly. Like the previous year's inquiry and the one before that, the Margaret Harold investigation died with the passing of the month of June. Four months later, another shock from as far away as Los Angeles reached the East Coast as a distant tremor. Yet it was enough to wake apprehensions. The Los Angeles police had arrested a thirty-year-old television repairman after a patrolman arrived on the scene of a fight between the man, Harvey M Glatman, and the passenger in his car, Lorraine Vigil, who was twenty-six. It occurred on a desert road at night and Lorraine Vigil had been shot in the thigh by her companion's gun during the struggle.

Glatman's Los Angeles apartment was searched. He was a photographer rather than a collator of such cuttings as had been found in the basement of the cinder-bloc cottage. Among his prints were a number showing young women lying on the ground in the desert, bound and gagged. Others were shown tied into chairs. They were generally gagged and most looked very apprehensive. Glatman's line of patter was to boast of being the cover designer for a New York magazine which specialized in crime stories of the kind that involved the heroine being tied up and then rescued. Glatman had hired professional models to pose for some of these. Among the photographs were three which were recognized as showing professional models. Shirley Ann Bridgeman was twenty-four and lived in Sun Valley. Ruth Rita Mercado was the same age and lived in Los Angeles. Judy Ann Dull was nineteen and lived in West Hollywood. All of them had been missing for some time. The evidence of Glatman's photographs and his confession established that he had abducted them, held them at gunpoint for several days, ill-treated them and then strangled them. Two desert graves were found in a remote area near Escondido in San Diego County. A body already found the year before near Indio, in Riverside County, was now assumed to be that of Judy Ann Dull.

Glatman went to the electric chair in August 1959, saying philosophically, 'I knew it would end like this.' So far as the people of Maryland and Virginia were concerned, he did not match the description of the killer of Margaret Harold and four others, though he had East Coast connections. The true cause for alarm was that a terrible sexual rage seemed to be breaking out in 1950s America, now in Maryland or Virginia, then in California. The deduction was that the series of killings in Maryland and Virginia was something the people might have to live with. It was just a matter of time before the killer of Margaret Harold and the four schoolgirls – or one of his competitors – struck again.

II

Unlike the month of June in the previous years, June 1958 passed with no further killings. Indeed the 'Wanderer' or 'The Bushy Haired Killer' was not heard of again in the whole of 1958. Then on 14 January 1959, the front page of the *Washington Post* had another banner headline, the most sensational of them all. 'VIRGINIA FAMILY VANISHES' Carroll Vernon Jackson, a twenty-nine-year-old salesman, had set out on the afternoon of Sunday, 11 January from Apple Grove,

Virginia, to visit friends in the state capital, Richmond. With him was his twenty-seven-year-old wife Mildred, known as Millie, and their two little girls, five-year-old Susan Anne, and Janet Carroll, just eighteen months. On their way home, they called on members of their families and left Millie Jackson's parents at about 9.40pm, some fifteen miles from Apple Grove. They had not been seen since.

Next morning, Millie's aunt was surprised to see the Jacksons' Chevrolet saloon parked on the main highway, Route 609, on their way home. There was no sign of the four occupants. What possible reason could they have for leaving the car on a lonely stretch of road late at night? A phone call established that the family had never reached their home. The state police were alerted. In a little while, unease turned to alarm.

'Skid marks indicated the car had been forced to the shoulder, and the car's interior indicated that it had been deserted in haste. The keys were still in the ignition which had been turned off, and police ascertained the car was still in good working order.' There was ample fuel in the tank and the car started as soon as the ignition key was turned. After all, Mr Jackson was a salesman and needed his car in good order. Millie Jackson's purse was still on the dashboard with money inside it. The children's toys were on the back seat.

A team of three hundred people carried out a fruitless foot-by-foot search of the surrounding countryside. Local people thought the disappearance of the family was 'one of the strangest things that ever happened round here'. The police thought the crime was probably a kidnapping. No one yet mentioned murder, though the *Washington Post* headline on 15 January, four days after the disappearance, proclaimed, 'Fears Rise for Family of 4'.

Fears rose most sharply of all in Washington's FBI headquarters. Inevitably many incidents were recorded there which were not revealed to the public. The mystery of the missing family had no necessary connection in the public mind, as yet, with the five previous murders. But the truth was that the Jacksons' car was not the first to be forced off the road, not even the first to be forced off the road on the night of 11 January. On 24 August the previous year, Mrs June Tuozzo, an attractive dark-haired woman of thirty-three, had been driving at night with her husband. They were on a lonely stretch of road near Laurel, Maryland. Another car forced them aside and blocked their way. A man pulled a gun on the couple. He forced Mr Tuozzo to get into the boot of the car and locked him in. Then the man drove the car for about twenty minutes to a wooded area. Mr Tuozzo used his feet and fists in an attempt to force the boot open. But the abductor told Mrs Tuozzo to warn her husband that she would be beaten or killed unless he stopped.

In the wooded area, June Tuozzo was made to get out of the car and the man carried out a sexual assault on her. As she was dressing again, his aggression seemed to vanish and he became almost considerate. 'He told her to put her clothes on. He was going to let her go,' the press later reported. Her assailant said, 'I'll be all right as soon as I get a cup of coffee . . . I'm glad this wasn't any worse than it is. You get yourself a cup of coffee too . . . You're a good woman. You're quiet. You don't make much noise. I'm glad it wasn't any worse than it was.' Her description of the man matched the one given by Sergeant Hudson of Margaret Harold's murderer.

Nor was that all. Keith Waldrop and his wife had also been driving by night. A light-coloured 1952–54 Ford bore down on them from the rear with its headlights glaring. Its driver forced them towards the ditch and they came to a halt. The other driver then opened his car door but he had not forced them over quite enough. There was just enough room to get round him on the right. Mrs Waldrop took one look at the stranger, guessed what was in store for her, and said to her husband, 'Go!' Their car shot forward through the gap between the other car and the ditch. In a few seconds they were clear and safe.

This incident had happened fifteen miles from where the Jackson family had apparently vanished on the night of 11 January. Indeed, it had happened at about 9pm that same evening, about forty minutes before the Jacksons disappeared.

January and February passed without any further clue or explanation in the Jackson mystery, except for a single letter. It was an anonymous letter to the police written on 29 January and posted in Washington DC. It was signed with a line-drawing of the sun and it assured the police that the Jacksons were alive and well.

On 4 March, at about 3.20pm, two men who worked for the American Viscose Company were trucking decomposed saw-dust as garden compost, about two miles west of Fredericks-burg. It was some forty miles from the place where the Jacksons had disappeared. They were loading their truck from a pile of sawdust when the wheels sank into ground which was waterlogged from winter rain. James Beach and John Scott decided to put some dead tree-branches under the wheels of the vehicle to get it moving again. As they gathered the dead branches from the ground, they saw a man's foot. They had found Carroll Jackson. He was lying on his back in a blue business suit, his hands tied behind him, and a gash in the nape of his neck. He had been brutally beaten, then shot. Underneath him was the Jacksons' eighteen-month-old daughter, Janet Carroll. The baby had suffocated under her father's body.

The horror of the discovery was equalled only by the fears of what had happened to Millie Jackson and her five-year-old daughter Susan Anne. Perhaps it was best to hope that Millie Jackson was being held to serve her captor's sexual needs and that perhaps Susan Anne had been taken so that threats against her daughter would make the young woman obedi-ent. To hope that this might be so seemed preposterous in other circumstances. Yet the alternative was that Millie Jackson and her daughter were both dead, having been beaten and sexually abused beforehand.

But even the hope that the two might be alive under these circumstances was short-lived. About seventy miles north of Fredericksburg, across the state border in Maryland, two boys were out shooting rabbits in Anne Arundel County on 22 March. Beside the lane, where the earth had been disturbed, they noticed some reddish-brown hair poking through the soil. Thinking it might be a rats' nest, they fired into the soil with their air-rifles. Then they decided to dig for the nest. The russet hair belonged to a five-year-old girl who was lying face-down in a shallow grave.

There was little doubt of what else the police of Anne Arundel County would find. The news broke in the press the next day. 'Slain Virginia Mother, Child Found in Woods.' Millie Jackson lay under the body of the child, killed by pistol-whipping to the face and head. Susan Anne had been killed by a blow to the back of the skull. All this had apparently happened close to the burial spot, a hundred miles from the place where the Jacksons had disappeared. One of Millie Jackson's stockings was found round her neck, used as a halter to lead her by rather than to strangle her. The other stocking was found nearby.

Millie Jackson and her daughter had been buried close to the place where Margaret Harold had been shot. In the basement of the nearby cinder-block cottage with its montage of words and pictures on one wall, a button from Mrs Jackson's dress was found on the floor. Whatever had been done to her was carried out in this sanctuary of a deformed mind.

Once again, searches and questions produced nothing more than the police already knew about the appearance and manner of the suspect. Though a 'Supersquad' of detectives from Virginia, Maryland, Washington DC and the FBI was operating on the case, it was making little progress. 'I believe if we get the Jacksons' killer we will have the murderer of Margaret Harold,' announced Chief Wade of the Anne Arundel County Police. But anyone in the state could have told him that. Morale was not improved when, on 26 March, the hunters seemed to have nothing better to offer than an appeal to the killer to give himself up.

'Top Washington officials called yesterday on the shadowy killer of the Carroll V Jackson family to surrender himself before his twisted mind ordains the death of other innocent victims – or he himself is killed in the pursuit of his mad fancies. They promise prompt medical attention for the killer in voicing the conviction that the man they are hunting is a sex pervert who kills almost casually, unable to resist the tragic mental quirk that drives him.' A conference of Virginia, Maryland and Federal investigators was held and agreement was reached that the wanted man was a pervert. Once again, any newspaper reader could have told the delegates that before the conference began.

And still the 'shadowy figure' remained a shadowy figure. Despite all the descriptions and the corroboration of them, there was no clue as to who the man might be. 'Supersquad' got nowhere.

Another year passed and three more months after that. It was June 1960, five years after the pair of schoolgirls had been shot in North-Western Park. There had been no more murders and, indeed, most people were not sure whether there was any more investigation. Had the whole thing just been closed down?

One of the people who wondered about this was Glenn L Moser. He was thirty years old, a sewing-machine salesman and cab-driver who had once studied criminology at the University of Maryland. One day, as he was passing the FBI office in Norfolk, Virginia, he went in and asked if anything had happened about his letter. What letter? It was one he had written to them well over a year before. But no one had taken any notice of it and he assumed that perhaps they had found it to be unimportant. He just thought he would ask what had happened to it. But what had Mr Moser's letter said? 'I wrote to the authorities in Maryland and Virginia about Dave,' he explained. Who was Dave? 'Melvin David Rees Jr,' he added, 'But I suppose they thought I was just another crank with an axe to grind.' That seems to have been exactly what they thought, both in Maryland and Virginia.

Who was Melvin David Rees Jr? He had been a student at the University of Maryland with Glen Moser and had shared Moser's home for a few weeks. All this had been several years before. After that, Melvin Rees worked by day in a Washington music school. After dark, he played in the band at

Harrigan's, a night club in the south-west of the city. While at the University of Maryland, Rees had read economics but it was evident that his real talent was musical. Apart from the Washington school and the night club he was a 'pick-up musician available for emergency fill-in engagements and proficient on the saxophone, clarinet and piano.'

Glen Moser and Melvin Rees had grown up together in the spacious Hyattsville suburb of north Washington. But by the time they got to the University of Maryland, Rees was a benzidrene addict. Moser alleged that Rees had been wild-eyed with benzidrene on the night after Margaret Harold's death. He had certainly been close to the scene of that murder as well as to the abduction of the Jackson family. Moser had been so uneasy that he had asked Rees outright whether the killings were his handiwork. Rees would never give him a straight answer. All this might have been conjecture. But then Moser described Rees to his FBI interviewers as being thirty-one years old with dark bushy hair and a thin pale face.

The FBI knew that the odds were still in favour of the Virginia and Maryland authorities in their assumption that Moser was a crank with an axe to grind. At the very least, however, Rees would be worth a look. They went to the address which Moser had given them, 3908 Madison Street in Hyattsville. It was where the Rees parents lived. They were still living there and so were Melvin Rees' wife and child. Rees was trying to get a divorce but he was long gone from Hyattsville. No one knew where he was.

So far as the FBI were concerned, this could well become a fruitless nationwide hunt for a man who had no connection with the murders. However, Melvin Rees had left some of his possessions in his parents' house and those, too, would be worth a look. FBI Agent Gene S Weiner was searching a room on the upper floor of the Madison Street house, and not finding very much, when he noticed an open closet with a few pieces of furniture and some cartons of books inside. The suspect was a reading man. Weiner noticed *A History of Prostitution*, Aldous Huxley's *Ape and Essence* and Sigmund Freud's *The Future of an Illusion* among the titles. There was also an accordion case. Weiner opened it and found a pistol and a diary. He opened the diary and read a page of randomly punctuated prose.

'Caught on lonely road after pulling them over levelled pistol and ordered them out into car trunk. Was open for husband and both bound.' The account went on to describe the killing of the others, leaving only the young woman and her daughter. 'Now the mother and daughter were all mine.' After he had finished with the young woman, he 'tied and gagged led her to place of execution and hung her.' Among the papers in the accordion case was a press cutting from the *Washington Post* of 14 January 1959. It was a photograph of Millie Jackson and her daughter Susan.

Nor was this the only homicidal drama described in the document. The rapes and murders of Shelby Jean Venable and Mary Elizabeth Fellers were there. So were the murders of Margaret Harold, Nancy Shomette and Ann Ryan. And so were a score of others, including crimes for which other men had long since been tried and condemned. The document could scarcely be accurate in all these cases. However, it described the unsolved murders with chilling plausibility. There were, of course, discrepancies. Millie Jackson had been led gagged and with her hands tied behind her. The nylon stocking round her neck was thought to have been used as a halter to lead her. Yet there was no evidence that she had been hanged rather than clubbed to death with a pistol. Perhaps the hanging of the young woman was a gloss of fantasy added by the killer afterwards. On its own, the document would not be enough for a murder conviction. But the route to other evidence had now been opened.

The blue snub-nosed .38 was another possible lead. Those intended victims who escaped had described the man as carrying just such a gun. It was a common type of weapon but it might yet link the suspect to the murders. When Gene Weiner made his report, the hunt for Melvin Rees began.

His car was found easily enough, a blue and grey 1954 Ford located at San Antonio, Texas. Melvin Rees was nowhere near it. Then a letter, addressed to the young man's parents, was intercepted by the FBI. It had no sender's address but it was postmarked 'West Memphis, Arkansas'.

When the FBI descended on West Memphis, its agents looked first for any connection that an itinerant musician might make in the town. At 317 Broadway, there was the West Memphis Piano Company. One of its employees was a bushy-haired piano salesman who taught music in his spare time and played in local jazz combos.

The FBI brought their most important witness to West Memphis. He was Master Sergeant Roy Hudson who had seen the murderer of Margaret Harold three years earlier. On 24 June 1960, the piano salesman left work and walked home to a garage apartment, at 525 Stonewall Street, where he lived with a tall good-looking night club dancer, Pat Whitinghouse Rees. As he reached the apartment the agents closed in. Melvin Rees was arrested and identified by Sergeant Hudson as the man who had killed Margaret Harold.

The arrest of Melvin Rees was far from being the end of the case. Master Sergeant Hudson identified him as the killer of Margaret Harold but Mr Hudson had seen the killer briefly, if memorably, three years before and there were no corroborating witnesses. No one could positively identify Rees as the bearded 'Wanderer' near North-Western Park five years earlier. No one could identify him as the young man with a scar seen giving a lift to Mary Elizabeth Fellers and Shelby Jean Venable four years previously. Even after a few months, identification might be difficult. How good would it be after three, four, or five years?

In the case of the Jackson family, eighteen months earlier, there were no witnesses to the crime. However, the Waldrops identified Rees as the man who had tried to run them off the road the same night as the abduction of the Jacksons, fifteen miles from where the disappearance of the Jackson family occurred and less than an hour before it. June Tuozzo identified him as the man who had sexually assaulted her after stopping the car which her husband was driving. Yet none of these identifications, except for Sergeant Hudson's, tied him to murder. And Sergeant Hudson was a lone witness.

There was, of course, the secret diary of rape and murder. Yet it might be suggested, as it soon was in court, that the events were mere fantasy. To fantasize responsibility for sexually motivated murders reported widely in the press might be unappealing but it was not a criminal offence. It was impossible that Rees could have committed some of the crimes he described and, in the case of Millie Jackson, he wrongly described the method of her death.

For the moment, the question was where he should be tried. The evidence was that he had committed crimes in both Virginia and Maryland. The murder of Carroll Jackson and his younger daughter, as well as that of Mary Elizabeth Fellers seemed to be a matter for Virginia, on the basis that their bodies were found in that state. The others, six in all, had been found in Maryland. Indeed, there was no doubt that Margaret Harold had been murdered in Maryland.

It mattered very much to Melvin Rees where he was tried. Virginia still had the death penalty and very little compunction about carrying it out. Though capital punishment was still the law in Maryland, no one had been executed since 1921. Moreover only one charge of murder could be tried at a time, though the court might permit evidence from the other charges to be admitted. It was decided that Melvin Rees should stand trial in Maryland for the murder of Millie Jackson. The hearing began on 25 January 1961 in the elegant high-ceilinged courtroom of the Federal Court for the District of Maryland at Baltimore.

A jury of eleven men and one woman tried the case. Rees sat at the table with his attorneys and 'rocked gently in a leather chair and kept his eyes on the Federal judge and the prospective jurors who will determine his fate.' He had no money and was represented by two court-appointed attorneys, W J O'Donnell and William J Evans. The specific charge against him was that he kidnapped Millie Jackson 'for the purpose of beating, having sexual gratification upon her body, and killing her.'

The prosecution based its forensic argument on the blue snub-nosed .38, found in the accordion case. Neither Millie

Jackson nor Susan Anne had been shot, of course, though Carroll Jackson had. This case was concerned solely with Millie Jackson who had been killed by blows to the head and face with a pistol. Forensic examination showed traces of blood on the trigger, safety level and screws of Rees' gun. Unfortunately, the traces were too small for analysis to determine the blood group. There was no bullet fired and, therefore, no ballistic evidence to identify the weapon beyond dispute in that way.

The defence naturally objected that such a common type of weapon 'could be in the hands of thousands of people.' That was certainly true. This particular gun had been improved by having bone grips screwed to the butt in place of whatever was there before. He insisted that the bone grips were on the butt when it came into his possession.

Defence counsel also warned the jury against accepting the confessional 'diary' as evidence of anything but a vivid imagination. The crimes included those for which others had been convicted and which Rees could not possibly have perpetrated. Nor were they to condemn Rees merely because he was 'a nonconformist, an irregular musician, a man who lived with a married woman, and a consumer of benzidrene.'

In his favour, Rees had been regarded as a 'very satisfactory' music teacher and he had an alibi for the night of the Jacksons' abduction. At the time that it happened, he was in his usual place on a Sunday night, playing in the band at Harrigan's night club, fifty miles away in Washington. At the trial, neither Robert Earle, the manager of Harrigans, nor bandleader Phil Trupp could remember whether or not Rees was there on that particular Sunday evening two years before.

Glenn Moser, the former friend of Melvin Rees, told his own story of the night of 11 January 1959. He and Rees had hired a cottage at Norfolk, Virginia on 2 or 3 January 1959. they took a couple of girls there, Pat Routt a night club dancer being the one who accompanied Rees. On Sunday 11 January, Rees left alone in his car for Washington to play in the band, just as it was getting dark. He had cut it fine, Glenn Moser recalled. 'I told him he'd have to hurry if he was going to make it on time.' Rees drove off in his 1954 Ford. 'I've never accused him of the crime.' Moser insisted under defence cross-examination, 'I wanted him investigated . . . I wanted to get the truth.'

When the trial of Melvin David Rees opened in Baltimore, the evidence against him might have seemed strong rather than conclusive. But that was deceptive. The prosecution spoke of a surprise witness. When that witness appeared, he added weight to one of the most disputed items of the prosecution evidence, the snub-nosed .38. It was an unusual gun because of the bone grips which had been added to its butt but there was no way in which it could be scientifically connected with the murder of Millie Jackson. However, three weeks into the trial, the judge had ruled that relevant evidence from the murder of Carroll Jackson was admissible in the present case.

The surprise came in the evidence of George A Berley who had worked with a comparison microscope in the FBI laboratory. Near the place where Carroll Jackson's body was found, the search had revealed a discarded pair of brown plastic grips from the butt of a handgun. At the time they offered no direct clue to the killer, though it was thought likely that they had come from the murder weapon. Gordon Berley had removed the bone grips from the butt of the gun found in the Rees home. He made an impression of the surface of the steel butt and, using a comparison microscope, compared its surface with the discarded plastic grips found at the murder site. The minutest markings of the screw holes and scratches and markings on the butt corresponded precisely, under considerable magnification, to those on the plastic grips. There was no doubt that they belonged to one another and that the gun owned by Rees had been at the scene of Carroll Jackson's murder. Though the bullet had not been found and there was no ballistic evidence, no two gun butts could have been so alike.

Where the evidence of murder had been strong, it now became conclusive. The Maryland jury convicted Rees on

23 February 1961. The jurors refused to recommend a death sentence, though it would not have been carried out in the state anyway. Rees was sentenced to life imprisonment. As he escaped execution in Maryland, the press reported, 'A faint trace of a smile appeared at the corners of Rees' mouth.' The smile was short-lived. As soon as Maryland had tried him, the state of Virginia applied for the extradition of Rees to stand trial for the murder of Carroll Jackson, for which he would face the electric chair if found guilty. The second trial was very much a re-run of the first, at Spotsylvania, Virginia, in September 1961. As at the first trial, the evidence of the discarded grips and the microscopic examination of the gun butt seemed conclusive. Rees was found guilty of first degree murder on 28 September and sentenced to die in the electric chair. He was executed a few months later. On the night of his death, as he walked to the room where he died alone, the executioner and audience invisible to him, he was asked by the prison warden if he had any final words. He shook his head and said nothing. Then, as an afterthought, he said, 'I'm very sorry.'

Melvin Rees was intelligent and articulate, a skilful musician if not a gifted one. Yet his five years of murder without detection had very little to do with intelligence or cunning. The police of two states and the nation's capital, as well as the FBI, had simply failed to find him. Widespread searches and inquiries were instituted without result. The desperate appeals for a bearded 'wanderer' or a college man 'acting peculiar', even for the killer to give himself up in exchange for medical treatment, presumably followed by the electric chair, suggested that the investigations were at an impasse. Such appeals generally came within a couple of weeks of the crime and advertised to the killer how far behind him his pursuers had fallen.

Perhaps he would never have murdered again, once settled in West Memphis. Or perhaps, in time, he would have begun a career of homicide in Arkansas. The only prevention of that possibility was an almost casual doubt in the mind of Glen Moser. Had Mr Moser not chosen to walk into an FBI office and inquire about his letter of the previous year, Melvin Rees would almost certainly have passed beyond danger. And even Rees could not have guessed that such persistence from a friend who hoped to clear him of private suspicion would make him very publicly an occupant of the electric chair.

FOUR

'How Can They Be So Sure?' The Christine Darby Investigation (1967–69)

I

North of Birmingham, on the trunk road to Stafford, Stoke-on-Trent and Manchester, the landscape of the Industrial Revolution retained many of its century-old characteristics in the 1960s. For almost fifteen miles north-west of Birmingham, there was little break in the drab urban landscape, through Aston, Walsall and Bloxwich. After that, the factories and terraced housing opened out into Cannock Chase, much of it planted by the Forestry Commission with rows of fir trees, growing among tall bracken, geometrically divided by forest roads, paths, and rides that doubled as fire-breaks. Close to Cannock and Walsall, it was an area for walkers, picnics and exercising the dog.

Just south of Cannock, a road ran east to the pleasant cathedral town of Lichfield, where Samuel Johnson and David Garrick had been born two centuries before. North of Cannock, another road ran east to Rugeley where the most celebrated of English poisoners, Dr William Palmer, had practised his curious arts in the 1850s. Still further north on the main road from Cannock was the county town of Stafford, about ten miles away, with its Shire Hall and Assize Courts. Such was the area in which the events of 1965–69 took place.

By the 1960s, the landscape of towns like Bloxwich and Walsall saw the first signs of renewal. The shabby lines of Victorian terraced housing, doors opening on to the street, still rose row upon row across the view. But in this workshop of England there were also brave new worlds of high-rise flats for the engineering workers of the vast Austin car works at Longbridge or the factories of Lucas components at Wolverhampton. Idle smoke-stacks were not yet a characteristic of the English Midlands and the automobile industry was still the nation's earner.

The people of the West Midlands had shown strong feelings in matters of politics and society. Throughout the country, manufacturing workers had played a part in returning a Labour government to power in October 1964, for the first time since 1951. By a substantial majority, Wolverhampton sent to parliament a Conservative MP, Enoch Powell, whose attacks on the policy of allowing coloured immigration from the British Commonwealth caused uproar elsewhere but won him his seat. In nearby Smethwick, the Labour Foreign Secretary elect, Patrick Gordon Walker, preached racial tolerance and equality. Though his party won elsewhere, he was humiliatingly defeated by an anti-immigration Tory, Peter Griffiths, in what should have been a Labour stronghold.

Most of the people who lived in the terraced streets of Walsall or Wolverhampton were kindly and generous folk, not embittered racists. Yet they struggled to make ends meet and many of them had seen little of the good things of life. It dismayed them that scarce municipal housing and declining employment, in towns where they had lived all their lives, might go to strangers who had never set foot in the country until a few months before. How little, it seemed to them, did the prosperous advocates of racial mixing understand them from the remoteness of Whitehall or the Downing Street cabinet room. Perhaps they were misled or ill-informed but the election results at Wolverhampton and Smethwick exemplified the quick and intense public emotions that characterized such industrial towns.

On 8 September 1965, it was almost a year since the election of the new Labour government. In the Birmingham suburb of Aston, where the A34 began its northward stretch to Bloxwich, Walsall and Cannock, the local children were back at school after the summer holidays. Among the pupils who went home for lunch that day were eleven-year-old Susan Reynolds and her six-year-old sister Margaret. After lunch, their mother saw them off from their home in Clifton Road. Because of the difference in their ages, the two girls went to separate schools but the first part of the route was the same for both. About six hundred yards from the Prince Albert Primary School, which Margaret Reynolds attended, they took their different directions. Margaret Reynolds was never seen alive again.

There was a delay in alerting the police because the girl's mother had no cause for concern until Margaret failed to return from school. The teachers assured her that the six-year-old had not been at school that afternoon. Aston divisional police began a search at once and did everything that could be expected of them. With the aid of civilian volunteers, they searched the area, its buildings, waste land, parks. They issued posters with Margaret Reynolds' picture, reconstructed her last known movements and her appearance at the time. They undertook a thorough search of her home and garden, for not even parents are above suspicion when a child goes missing. Ponds, lakes, canals and rivers were dragged. Residents and travellers were questioned. Weeks became months and nothing was found.

There were alleged sightings from all over the country, each prompting hope and then ending in despair for the bereaved parents. Nothing resulted from any report. Margaret's birthday came and went in October, Christmas passed as well. When the next news came, it was not about Margaret Reynolds. Another little girl, Diane Tift, vanished four months after the first. She disappeared on the afternoon of 30 December, while walking home the short distance from her grandmother's house. This had happened in Bloxwich, about ten miles north of Aston on the main A34 road out of Birmingham.

Margaret Reynolds might possibly have died in some misadventure. The disappearance of Diane Tift altered that perspective at once. In any area of this size, a number of sexual assaults on girls of their age, however deplorable, were likely to be recorded. But the case of the two missing girls pointed to something much worse.

CHAPTER FOUR

Again the police began a search of the area and a house-to-house inquiry on the local estates. But Diane Tift had vanished as surely as Margaret Reynolds. The Walsall CID collated reports of men who had attempted to entice little girls into their cars. There was one common feature in several of the incidents. The man had black or dark hair, brushed back but perhaps wavy at the front. In one case, where this was the description, the girl had been brutally attacked by the man and almost killed. He had never been caught nor plausibly identified.

Once more, all the searches and the inquiries produced nothing. Then, on 12 January 1966, almost two weeks after Diane Tift's disappearance, it was reported that a man had found a child's body on Cannock Chase, beyond the area of the search. Tony Hodgkiss had been cycling across the winter countryside on a narrow road, just west of the A34 a few miles north of Cannock. In the ditch to one side, he saw a child's clothing and then saw that it shrouded the body of a little girl, lying face-down in the undergrowth.

Mansty Gulley, as it was called, soon became the site of a mobile police station. An inquiry was launched by the combined forces of Scotland Yard and Staffordshire CID. Two Yard officers, Detective Superintendent Cyril Gold and Detective Sergeant Eric Bailey, joined the murder squad. The little girl's body was that of Diane Tift. She had been sexually assaulted and her attacker had evidently suffocated her by pulling the woollen pixie hood over her face and drawing its string tight round her neck. In the winter night that followed, plastic tenting covered the site and floodlights illuminated it. At daylight a routine search of the surrounding area was begun. Before long, a uniformed policeman noticed an object in the silt in the ditch. It was a child's skull. The bones of Margaret Reynolds lay almost at the same spot as the body of Diane Tift. It was impossible to tell, after five months, how the first little girl had died or whether there had been a sexual assault upon her. The pathologist thought she had probably been strangled.

Outrage at the fate of the two little victims united the Midlands towns of Cannock, Walsall, Bloxwich, and the

Birmingham suburbs. As the news spread, the entire country seemed moved by the killings. The Labour government would fulfil its pledge to abolish capital punishment for murder. Yet, whatever the politicians might think, opinion polls showed that the electorate was seldom less than 10–1 in favour of hanging killers and, indeed, of whipping juvenile delinquents. In the case of the two little girls, the view of the Midlands towns was that hanging was 'too good' for the beast who had defiled and killed them. But combined with a sense of outrage, local people had a preoccupation that was not felt by the country at large. In the little streets and in the tower blocks, they felt a dread of what might happen to their own children. Hatred of the killer was balanced by fear of him. An urge to vengeance was tempered by a longing to be told that he had been caught, that they and their children were safe again. If the truth were told, the assurance of safety was even more important to most than the satisfaction of revenge.

But the people were cheated both of safety and revenge. For six more months, the Staffordshire CID, under the direction of the two Scotland Yard officers, carried out house-to-house inquiries and vehicle checks, followed up statements and information and investigated known sex offenders in the area. An identikit picture was produced, based on such information as the CID could gather.

Yet again, it all came to nothing. No one was ever to stand trial for the murders of Margaret Reynolds or Diane Tift. Six months later, in June 1966, the Scotland Yard men went back to London and the inquiry was closed. There was, simply, nothing else to be done. The people of Cannock, Walsall, Bloxwich, and Aston were left with a killer still at large. Vengeance had been frustrated – the man had got away with it – and the people feared more than ever for their children.

II

Christine Darby was seven years old in 1967. She lived with her mother and grandmother in one of the Victorian terraces in the centre of Walsall. The family income depended on her mother's earnings as a supermarket assistant and the little girl was looked after much of the time by her grandmother. Like other children of her age, Christine Darby was still on holiday from school on 19 August 1967. In any case it was a Saturday and the child was left much to her own devices. Summer holidays for most people in Camden Street meant staying at home. There might be a trip to relatives or perhaps a day out by Midland Red coaches to the nearest seaside at Weston-super-Mare, more than a hundred miles away, but that was the limit of ambition.

After lunch that day, Christine went out to play in the street with her friends. She was not going more than a hundred yards or so, perhaps as far as the junction with Corporation Street. It was now more than a year since Scotland Yard had given up the inquiry into the deaths of two other girls and almost two years since Margaret Reynolds had disappeared. While it was true that no one had been brought to justice, there had been no further crime of that sort for eighteen months. Perhaps the killer had moved away, or committed suicide, or perhaps been frightened off by the murder investigation. Christine and the two little boys played in the street for an hour or so. Then a car drove past and stopped. The driver wound down the window on the passenger side and asked them the way to Caldmore Green. He called it 'Carmer Green' which was the local pronunciation. Caldmore Green was no distance at all, just beyond the end of Camden Street and round the first corner of Corporation Street. A good many cars went down there to the car wash, just beyond Caldmore Green in St Michael Street. But the driver opened the passenger door and asked Christine if she would show him the way. The Darby family, like many of its neighbours, did not own a car. It seemed that Christine, at seven years old, had seldom ridden in one. The glamour of it appealed to the child. She got in and sat in the passenger seat beside the driver and smiled at her two friends.

The other two children were bystanders. One of them, eight-year-old Nicholas Baldry, was surprised, when the car turned and drove off away from Caldmore Green. He ran to the house in Camden Street and told Christine's grandmother that the child had gone off with a man in a car. The Darby family had no telephone. However, there was one in the near-by off-licence, just round the corner, and a message was telephoned to the police and logged at 2.52pm. Few people keep track of time in such emergencies but, given a total distance of a couple of hundred yards and the obvious sense of urgency, it seems unlikely that more than a few minutes passed between the abduction and the phone call.

After the earlier abductions, the Staffordshire police had a contingency 'Stop Plan' for establishing road blocks if another child went missing. This was put into operation at once, piling up traffic in Walsall centre that afternoon as cars and car boots were searched. Nicholas Baldry had been able to tell the police that it was a light grey car and driven by a man in his thirties, thin-faced and with dark hair. But the hours passed and there was no sign of Christine Darby in any car that was stopped, nor of the man who was regarded as her abductor. When the girl was missing overnight, it seemed unlikely that she would be found alive. On Sunday morning, the Staffordshire police assumed that they were now looking for a body.

The procedures which had followed the disappearances of Margaret Reynolds and Diane Tift were implemented again. There was a renewed determination – perhaps desperation – on the part of the Staffordshire police. No one could forget the failure to catch the murderer of two girls in 1965. Yet there had at least been a sense of relief that no other child had followed them for the past eighteen months or more. Now it seemed that the same man had reappeared and that a new series of killings had begun.

By the next morning, Sunday, an extensive search was in progress. North of Cannock, to the east of the A34 on the Rugeley road, part of a child's underwear was found on the branch of a fallen tree on Cannock Chase. Christine's grandmother identified it as belonging to the girl. On Monday, not far from this spot, a forestry worker found a child's plimsoll lying in the bracken. It was identified as the type that Christine Darby had been wearing.

The search teams concentrated on the nearby Forestry Commission woodland of Brindley Heath, along the north of the side road that ran east to Rugeley. Five hundred policemen were supplemented by two hundred and fifty servicemen from the army and the Royal Air Force. The entire area was marked out with binder twine and the men moved forward in a continuous line, using sticks to probe the terrain. Over much of the ground through the forest, the bracken was waist-high. It was on Tuesday evening, more than seventy-two hours after Christine's disappearance, that a solider discovered a child's body in the area known as Plantation 110.

Christine Darby had been roughly covered by bracken. It seemed unlikely that she would have remained undiscovered for long. She was naked below the waist except for her white socks. The position of the body graphically suggested a sexual motive for the killing.

The scene at Mansty Gulley twenty months earlier was re-enacted, this time a few miles to the east of the A34. A tent was erected over the spot and floodlights were turned on. It was another six hours before enough forensic work had been done for the child's body to be removed. She was formally identified as Christine Darby and the cause of her death established as suffocation. As the first indications suggested, she had been sexually assaulted and it was assumed from bruising on her face that suffocation occurred from a hand being held over her mouth or a cushion pressed over her face to silence her cries. It was possible that she had not died where the searchers found her. Though her plimsolls were missing, the white soles of her socks were clean, which indicated that she might have been carried dead or unconscious to the place where she was found.

Detective Superintendent Cyril Gold had retired by this time. The new team from Scotland Yard consisted of Detective Superintendent Ian Forbes, a formidable and aggressive Scot who had been a Flying Squad officer, and Detective Sergeant Tom Parry. This time there was no thought of failure. From the very start and throughout a long and unproductive period of the investigation, Forbes had one message for the public and the press. 'We are going to get this man.' Or, as he instructed his officers privately, 'Bring the bastard in.' It seemed he had no option. To fail again, as the earlier inquiry had done, leaving the Midland towns at the mercy of a child-killer, was an appalling prospect. There had to be a result. Yet months passed without one. Like his predecessor, Forbes would return empty-handed to London before there was any hint that a man had been caught.

Public anxiety produced a press coverage that was nation-wide. Even on the afternoon of Christine Darby's disappear-ance, radio news bulletins had alerted their listeners and appealed for information. In a few more days, as the murder inquiry developed, there was national coverage on television, then in its first decade of general availability. From time to time, as the inquiry dragged on inconclusively, Super-intendent Bob Booth would appear as Scotland Yard's spokesman on late night television news programmes and would give the same answers to his interviewers. 'We are going to catch this man.' People hoped he was right but, as the months passed, more and more began to doubt it.

The Wolverhampton *Express and Star* broke the story in full to the Midland towns on Wednesday 23 August, reporting a 'leaf by leaf' forest search, which detectives had now begun. The paper carried the suggestion that all men in the Walsall area should be finger-printed and Ian Forbes stated what was cruelly self-evident. 'A man who kidnaps a little girl and deals with her like this is indeed dangerous.' The paper reported the growing anxiety of parents for their children's safety and the Mayor of Walsall's letter to Lilian Darby, promising her that the prayers of the people were with her. There was a map and photograph of the murder site.

But unlike the deaths of Margaret Reynolds and Diane Tift, there were witnesses to the apparent fate of Christine Darby.

First there was Nicholas Baldry, the eight-year-old who had been with Christine when she was abducted. He described how the driver of the car had asked for 'Carmer Green' which was the local pronunciation. He identified the type of the grey car from a selection shown him. He was sure that it was larger than his father's Austin A55 and thought it was either a Ford Consul or a Vauxhall 101E. He also gave a general description of a man with dark hair, probably in his thirties.

Since the alarm was telephoned to the police at 2.52pm, it seemed unlikely that Christine could have been abducted before about 2.45pm. But that was not positive. At about 2.40pm, a television engineer, David Hunt, saw a grey Austin turn out of Camden Street into Corporation Street. It was driven by a dark-haired man about thirty years old with a girl of seven or eight beside him.

A third witness offered a sighting which was less conclusive but it gave a precise time. Mrs Nancy Daniel was due to attend a wedding at 3pm at Bloxwich parish church, on the road north from Walsall to Cannock. She arrived outside the church and looked at its clock to check the time. It was 2.53pm. As her husband parked the car, she saw another car drive past going north towards Cannock. It was a dark grey car, possibly a Vauxhall, driven by a man with a girl of five or six in the passenger seat. The girl did not appear distressed and, if anything, was enjoying the experience of riding in the car. The man was thirty-five to forty years old, of medium build with dark brown hair. He was wearing a dark jacket with a white shirt.

The fourth witness was regarded as the most important. Victor Whitehouse had been walking alone on Cannock Chase that day. He had parked his blue Volkswagen car quite close to Plantation 110 where Christine's body had been found. Because he was misled by the police map into thinking that the body had been found further off, Mr Whitehouse did not come forward and was not questioned until twelve days after Christine's disappearance. On that Saturday afternoon, however, he had started walking at about 2.15pm and returned to his car after covering 'about four miles'. It was then 'about four o'clock'. Four miles was not a great distance for an experienced walker to cover in an hour and three-quarters. Other things being equal, it seemed likely that Mr Whitehouse returned to his car a little before rather than a little after 4pm. Near the place where he had parked, Mr Whitehouse passed a 'ride' as the fire-breaks were called. At a distance of 'fifteen or twenty yards' down the ride a car was parked. It was 'slate grey or bluey grey' and he identified it as either an Austin A55 or an Austin A60. A man was standing beside the driver's door. Mr Whitehouse described the man as being about forty, five feet ten inches tall with dark hair brushed back. Though the man was standing on the far side of the car, he turned full face as Mr Whitehouse passed him at a little distance. He finally identified the car as an Austin A60 and pointed to the place where he had seen it parked, about two hundred yards from where Christine Darby's body had been found.

There was a fifth witness, Mrs Jeanne Rawlings, who had driven to Cannock Chase with her husband and also parked near this area in order to exercise her dog. They had parked on a road which was hidden from Mr Whitehouse and the grey car but was only a few hundred yards away. The witness and her dog were outside the car. Mrs Rawlings heard another vehicle coming, which she afterwards recalled as a grey Austin A55, and she went to hold back her dog from the forest road. The grey car passed and, her attention divided between the vehicle and the dog, she none the less had a brief glimpse of the driver in profile. He was on his own, a dark-haired man in his thirties. Jeanne Rawlings also gave a specific time. It was 4.20pm when she and her husband parked their car and a few minutes later when the grey Austin A55 passed them.

Further evidence, though it seemed to contradict the time given by Mr Whitehouse and Mrs Rawlings, was offered by Mr James Deakin. He claimed that he had almost been knocked down, when he was crossing the A34 road just north of Cannock at 3.47pm by a grey car travelling very fast from Cannock Chase. Mr Deakin was precise as to the time he saw the car. He thought he would recognize the driver again. Like the evidence of the other witnesses, his story was of interest but the sighting was half an hour too early to tally with that of

Victor Whitehouse. Indeed, the A55 car which Mrs Rawlings saw would not have reached Cannock until almost an hour after Mr Deakin had his narrow escape.

To fit all these times together would involve the murderer abducting Christine Darby soon after 2.45pm, driving to Cannock Chase and then parking there at about 3.20pm. In no more than ten minutes or so, he would have to assault and murder the girl, carry her body at least two hundred yards and conceal it, and be on his way again. Almost immediately after passing Mr Deakin, he would have had to turn back on his tracks, heading fast for Cannock Chase in order to be seen there by Mr Whitehouse at about 4pm. Such a sequence of events seemed more suited to the convenience of the witnesses than to the facts of a murder.

III

The two immediate tasks of the inquiry were to issue an identikit picture of the suspect and to track the grey car. To track every grey Austin A55 and A60 registered in the Midlands was a daunting prospect. There were 23,000 of them. The cars were made at the Longbridge works in Birmingham, where local loyalty and a discount system made them very commonly purchased. In any case, throughout the entire country, the cars were among the most popular models on the market. Suppose the car were a Vauxhall or a Ford, which was what the only witness sure to have seen it thought? Suppose, for whatever reason, the murderer's car was registered a hundred miles away? Merely to check 23,000 cars would not suffice.

A clue might have been offered by the tyre tracks on the earth of the forest ride. Yet, though they were consistent with the Austin A55 or A60, it was impossible to say much more than that. Superintendent Ian Forbes thought the tracks had been made in daylight, since few drivers would have wanted to reverse down such a track in total darkness. This would confirm that the little girl's body had probably been placed in its makeshift grave on Saturday afternoon or evening, somewhere between about 3.30pm and 9pm.

There was nothing for it but to check 1,300,000 files for cars in the Midlands area and weed out any vehicles that might have a connection with the case. In the event, it took months. If that produced nothing, there would have to be a decision as to whether to spread the net wide or whether to give up checking cars. As it happened, the search produced nothing.

An identikit picture of the man whom Mr Whitehouse and Mrs Rawlings recalled seeing was produced, based on their instructions. It received national publicity. The *Daily Express* had found an entirely innocent man with a resemblance to the suspect. A make-up artist then refined his appearance on the witnesses' advice. On 25 October, more than two months after the murder, the paper's front page showed a photograph of this man as the 'Murderer's Double'. He was standing behind the door of a grey Austin car, as Victor Whitehouse had seen him. The identikit picture was also printed underneath. The wanted man was now called 'The A34 Murderer', after the road connecting the towns where the killings occurred. Surely this new nationwide publicity would produce some result. With the man's double, as seen by the two principal witnesses, published on the front of a national newspaper in millions of copies, someone must recognize him. They would recognize him even if he had been innocently on Cannock Chase. They would recognize him even if they had no reason to suspect him of murder. There was a multitude of calls to the police but not one of them produced a result.

'We are convinced that the man who murdered her is the man in the identikit picture,' Superintendent Ian Forbes insisted, 'and that it is a good likeness. His is a face well known to someone – probably to several people. He is being sheltered either by a relative who knows of his guilt but is prevented from coming forward by misguided loyalty or fear, or by people who recognize a resemblance in an acquaintance but cannot bring themselves to believe that the person could be a child-killer. The innocent – and many innocent men may well resemble the picture – have nothing to fear.'

No one, innocent or guilty, matched the identikit picture or that of the murderer's double, as seen by Ian Whitehouse or Jeanne Rawlings. When the investigation ended, not a single member of the public had offered a plausible identification. If the witnesses were right – if such a man existed at all – where was he? Had he no family, no acquaintances in the same street or who went to the same church, pub or football matches? Did he never go to work? Or was the identification system flawed? The earlier identikit picture was so bad that it was hard to imagine anyone looking like it. Indeed, as someone remarked privately, with a little more hair its nearest resemblance would have been to one of the senior police officers involved in the case.

In defence of the identikit, it was said that the points of resemblance would be specific details rather than the general look of the man. Those who had not seen him to begin with would not appreciate its worth. But Victor Whitehouse had seen the man at a distance of fifteen to twenty yards where it was the general impression rather than specific details that would have been most clear. Mrs Rawlings had never seen him full face, as the picture showed him, but only in profile. The question was whether the art of the identikit was too subtle for ordinary people to appreciate or whether it was mumbo-jumbo.

But with every extension of the police investigation, now based at Cannock rather than Walsall, the stakes were raised. Success would vindicate Forbes and his team. Another failure would carry the simple and devastating signal to the people of the Midlands that the police could no longer protect them or their children against this most feared and abhorrent crime. Because the inquiry had become national news, that suggestion would be widespread. As for the killer – or killers – such a man would feel that he could select his victim, assault and murder her, and still have an excellent chance of getting away with it.

This last consideration was a stark reminder that there was no alternative to raising the stakes. Accordingly, the largest house-to-house inquiry in the history of criminal investigation was announced in January 1968. Every man who lived in Walsall, aged between twenty and fifty, would be asked to account for his movements on the afternoon and evening of Saturday 19 August. This might require 35,000 interviews. If the killer happened to live twenty or thirty minutes' drive away in the densely populated areas of Birmingham, house-to-house inquiries in Walsall would be a waste of time. A similar house-to-house check in Birmingham might involve half a million interviews, an impossible task. If the killer lived there, even though he had been born in Walsall and said 'Carmer Green' for Caldmore Green, he had got away with his three murders and one brutal attack on another girl.

Such was the knife-edge on which the inquiry team walked while its publicists insisted to television viewers, 'We are going to catch this man'. CID officers set out with their questionnaire forms and began the task. In the event, they visited 40,000 homes and questioned 28,000 men. Some answers were not satisfactory and the men were seen again. They were innocent but some could not remember precisely what they did on that afternoon, four months earlier. Some had difficulty in finding alibi witnesses. Because it was a Saturday afternoon, most were not at work and many had only their families to support their stories.

The house-to-house inquiry got no further than the identikit picture. Worse still, the murder squad was plagued by cranks and misfits through letters and telephone calls, most of them anonymous. One man who telephoned was traced, arrested and fined £75 for wasting police time. Anonymous letters which named a man as the murderer were, not surprisingly, often in female handwriting. A good few faithless lovers and tiresome husbands were getting their just desserts.

In an age before computerization, the inquiry was in danger of collapsing under the weight of its own documentation. Detective Chief Inspector Pat Molloy, joining it at Cannock in January 1968, recalled that he found thirty-six four-drawer filing-cabinets, three hundred card-index drawers, as well as twenty to thirty trestle tables stacked with card-indexes and a two-tier wooden rack for 'Action' boxes. And then the house-to-house inquiry added some 40,000 documents. The index cards alone grew to 1,500,000. There were details of more than 20,000 telephone messages, almost 14,000 statements and more than 10,000 letters. There were false alarms and innocently misleading reports from a pubic made increasingly anxious and apprehensive over the crime. As always, there were downright malicious leads from those with a grudge to work off against the police. Almost beyond belief, as morale was at its lowest, there were threatening letters to the bereaved mother of Christine Darby.

Superintendent Forbes and his 'bring the bastard in' tactics led to the arrest and questioning of known offenders against children in the Walsall area. Forty-four of these men were detained when their answers to the questionnaires caused suspicion. Despite what was later said, those with a sexual interest in children were not that rare. As Chief Inspector Molloy put it, 'The Midlands were crawling with such people.'

There was no ceremony in these detentions. One man had been left in a cell for two days after questioning without any charge being brought. He protested against the violation of his rights and demanded an apology. Forbes, as reported by Chief Inspector Molloy, told him to tell the first people he met in Cannock that he had been held on suspicion of murdering Christine Darby. 'They'll fucking lynch you. Now fuck off.'

The investigation got rougher as it got nowhere, though Ian Forbes insisted that the police were closing in and that the man must be very 'worried'. The reassurance lacked conviction. But then, on Saturday afternoon 21 May 1968, nine months after the murder of Christine Darby on another Saturday afternoon, a man was arrested. Two sisters, aged five and two, had been enticed into his Morris Minor in Stag Crescent, Walsall and driven off. There were ample witnesses to the scene. Half an hour later the police 'Stop Plan' went into action and the Morris Minor was intercepted. The man and the two girls were inside it. The elder girl claimed that the man had put sticking plaster over her mouth and had then indecently assaulted her. Though there was no evidence of injury to her, sticking plaster was found in his pocket. But despite police questioning, it soon became apparent that he could not have been the killer of Christine Darby. He had no previous convictions, was tried at Stafford Assizes and put on probation for two years.

Soon there was nothing for it but to scale down the Christine Darby inquiry, though this decision was not made public. Ian Forbes and Tom Parry returned to other duties at Scotland Yard in August 1968. Forbes still insisted that 'We will catch him.' Once again, everyone hoped so but it was increasingly difficult to see how. The disquieting thought in most minds was that the man would only be caught if he killed another little girl. Was that not too high a price to pay, even for bringing him to justice?

Three months passed without any further development in the case of the 'A34 Murder' or the 'Cannock Chase Murder', as it was now variously known. At the beginning of November, a number of bonfires were being prepared to celebrate Guy Fawkes night in Walsall. One of these, on a piece of urban waste land, was organized by John Aulton and his family. At about 7.45pm on 4 November, ten-year-old Margaret Aulton was at the bonfire site while her mother was briefly absent. A green car with a white roof stopped on the garage forecourt across the street. The driver came over and asked who had built the bonfire and whether Margaret Aulton would like some fireworks for the next night's display. 'My mum won't let us have any until tomorrow,' she said. Then the child walked back with the man to the parked car. The driver opened his door and pointed to the passenger seat, saying that the fireworks were there. But though there was a news-paper on the seat, Margaret saw no fireworks. She said that the man took her by the arm and pushed her towards the car. 'He tried to push me into the car, but I ran away and sat on the wall.' As he walked round to open the passenger door for her, the girl sat on the low wall of the forecourt.

Wendy Lane, a young married woman, had been buying fish and chips for supper on the far side of the road. When she saw the man and the girl, she called Margaret across the road to her. The man got into his car, sitting with his face lowered, and then drove away.

Wendy Lane went home as Margaret Aulton was rejoined by her mother. The child was unhurt but the incident was at least very odd and, in Walsall at that time, seemed sinister. Wendy Lane thought about it and, half an hour later, telephoned the police. She was able to describe the car as being green with a white top and even to give them a registration number. It was 429 LOP. She described the man as being five feet ten inches in height, about average. He was well-built with dark hair and was wearing a suit. Like some of the earlier descriptions, this might have fitted thousands of men in the area. He was average height, average appearance, and almost average age. There was nothing in the description to distinguish him from those thousands of Midlands men. Moreover, it proved impossible that she could have seen the car which was registered as 429 LOP. It was a grey Ford Anglia and was in Yorkshire. The CID did a permutation of the letters and numbers. Most were useless but, by changing the order of two numbers, so that it read 492 LOP, they found a green and white car. It was registered in Walsall as belonging to Raymond Leslie Morris. He lived in Flat 20 of Regent House, a council block on the northern side of the town. It overlooked Walsall police headquarters.

Raymond Morris had not been connected by the police with the murder of Christine Darby. He had been interviewed, like thousands of other men, about his movements on 19 August 1967. His wife, Carol Morris, confirmed that they had been shopping together that afternoon and had then visited her parents. The police discovered that they had a statement volunteered by Morris's brother saying that Raymond Morris was a sexual deviant and naming him as a possible suspect for an A34 child-murder. He was interviewed again. Again his wife assured the police that they had been together on 19 August 1967. Morris was clearly annoyed at being visited once more and complained that he was being pestered by the police. It was later alleged that he said, 'I do not see any reason why you should want to see me again. Are you trying to catch me out?' They could not, of course, tell him of the statement his brother had made. At the time, it may have seemed to be part of a family vendetta.

The question for the Walsall police was whether Morris had attempted to abduct Margaret Aulton. For the Cannock investigation, the question was whether, if he had attempted the abduction, he might also have been the abductor and murderer of Christine Darby. Who was he? Raymond Morris was thirty-eight years old and a local man. His first marriage, at the age of twenty-two, was to a girl he had known since childhood. After thirteen years and the birth of three sons, the marriage ended in 1964 with no suggestion that Morris had been a guilty party. He then remarried. Carol Morris had been twenty-one, fourteen years younger than he. Morris had had several jobs in the past sixteen years but was currently employed as a foreman engineer at L J Taylor Precision Engineering Ltd at Oldbury, on the southern fringe of Walsall. His employers thought highly of him. He was smart, conscientious and efficient. His IQ was 120. He was a good amateur photographer and had considered going into business in partnership with a man in Perry Barr, Birmingham.

The matter of attempted abduction was for the Walsall CID to investigate. Next day they went to L J Taylor Precision Engineering to bring Morris back to Walsall police headquarters. He seemed happy to co-operate, though he was not told the nature of the inquiry until they reached the headquarters. When faced with the accusation of attempting to abduct a child, he called it 'too ridiculous for words'. He had left work the previous evening at about 7pm and would have been home by 7.45, when the bonfire incident had occurred. When he was asked to go on an identity parade, he agreed. 'It was not me, so I have nothing to fear at all about standing on any identification parade.' He had one reservation, however, which was that he would like to telephone his solicitor first. He telephoned John Benton and, having been reassured, went on the parade. Both Margaret Aulton and Wendy Lane attended it. Neither of them identified Morris as the man they had seen the previous evening.

The Walsall police had informed the Cannock murder inquiry of what had happened. However, they now had too little evidence to hold Morris and he was duly released. He would be shadowed but the evidence of failed identification and a car number that was inaccurate would not support a prosecution. Had the child run off to sit on the wall without the man taking her by the arm as she stood by the car and pushing her towards it, there might have been no case of any kind. The girl had certainly been sensible, resourceful and self-confident enough to go only a short distance to sit down on the forecourt wall. As for the witness, if Wendy Lane could not identify the man next day, how much could she prove that she had seen in the darkness from the far side of the road? For the moment there was no more to be done.

It was the murder squad's investigations which now brought Ian Forbes and Tom Parry back to Cannock from Scotland Yard. As for evidence against the new suspect, there was the letter from Morris's brother. And though the suspect had no previous convictions, there had been a complaint to the police about him in October 1966. Two girls, aged ten and eleven, were playing truant from school. They took shelter from the rain in a doorway at L J Taylor Precision Engineering. A man asked them if they would like to come home with him at lunchtime. The girls agreed. While they were in his flat, he persuaded them to undress as far as their underwear and he took photographs of them. The man was Morris and the photographs were taken in the Regent House flat while his wife was out at work as a wages clerk. No prosecution was brought because the girls could not sufficiently corroborate one another's stories.

Could Morris have been at the scene of the abduction of Christine Darby and at that of Margaret Aulton's attempted abduction? In travelling home from work, he virtually crossed Walsall from Oldbury in the south to Regent House in the north-west. It was possible to drive through the town or skirt it on what was, in effect, a ring road, a longer but faster route.

The route through the town would have taken him close to the scenes of the two incidents. However, at the time of Christine Darby's murder, Morris claimed that he generally took the route round the town to avoid the heavy traffic in Walsall centre.

His present car was a green Ford Corsair with a white top, 492 LOP. At the time of Christine Darby's murder, he had a light grey Austin A55. So had thousands of other car owners in the Midlands. Jeanne Rawlings identified the car on Cannock Chase as an A55. David Hunt briefly saw a grey A55 turn out of Camden Street at 2.40pm. Victor Whitehouse, who had perhaps the best view of the car on Cannock Chase, thought it was an A60 rather than an A55. The car which Mrs Daniel saw was apparently a Vauxhall 101E and it was dark grey.

The one witness who could be certain of the car which abducted Christine Darby, because he saw her getting into it, was eight-year-old Nicholas Baldry. He was sure that it was not an A55. His father had a grey A55 and the abductor's car was different. It was larger, apart from anything else, and he identified it as a Ford Consul or, like Mrs Daniel, as a Vauxhall 101E. Was it possible that the car on Cannock Chase, a common make and colour, was not connected with the murder? The police checked almost six hundred cars on Cannock Chase on the day of the child's disappearance. The A55 was certainly not the only car parked close to the spot where Christine Darby's body was found. Mr and Mrs Daniel were unwittingly just as close. Moreover, was the body there at 4pm? It may have been but there were certainly several more hours of daylight when it could have been taken there and when the area would have been less frequented than in mid-afternoon.

It was a matter of opinion whether this was splitting hairs or a conflict of evidence. With Superintendent Forbes and Sergeant Parry back in Cannock a decision had to be taken on whether to arrest Morris for Christine Darby's murder. A good many people might not think he looked like the identikit picture and certainly not like the man who had been worked on by the *Daily Express* make-up artist. Then there was the major difficulty posed by Carol Morris having twice given her husband an alibi. If that could be broken, then the prospects of a conviction would improve beyond measure.

Superintendent Forbes gave his orders. At last the exhortation to 'bring the bastard in' had a specific objective.

IV

On the morning of 15 November 1968, Raymond Morris had taken the lift from Flat 20 of Regent House down to the service road. As usual, he left for work at 7.30am. By now, he had been under surveillance by the murder squad for ten days and they had established his daily routine. He got into his car and drove a hundred yards before he was flagged down at a road block of police Panda cars. A uniformed officer asked him for his driving licence. He produced it and was sitting in his driver's seat when an unmarked car stopped. Chief Inspector Molloy got out, walked across and took Morris's keys from the ignition of his car, then told him that he was being detained in connection with the murder of Christine Darby. Morris was stunned but before he could respond he was dragged from his car to the unmarked vehicle and was driven north to Stafford police station.

According to police witnesses, when Morris was arrested, he said, 'Oh, God! Is it my wife?' He denied it. If he did say it and then denied it, he was unwise. The police argued that he thought his wife had withdrawn the alibi she had given him. But it was soon apparent that Morris had other secrets. He had indecently assaulted his wife's niece. He had taken indecent photographs of the child. Supposing his wife had discovered the photographs or the assault and told the police? Was he not then the kind of man who would be suspected of killing Christine Darby? That a man who took the photographs was indeed such a potential killer was soon being claimed in court by the prosecution. Morris also had a first wife who soon told stories of his sexual oddity. 'Oh, God! Is it my wife!' It was unlikely that he meant his first wife but not impossible. Though witnesses heard him ask the question, it may not have been as open and shut as the police interpretation suggested.

To establish the reputation of the man who had been taken into custody was not easy. His brother had told police that Raymond Morris was sexually odd and a suspect child-killer but offered no evidence. His first wife spoke of such aberrations as wanting her to undress and make love during the day. His mother-in-law spoke vaguely of him always looking at girls when she was out with him and her daughter. His neighbour called him a perfect gentleman and his father thought him an ideal son. His employer called him 'a really nice chap', and praised him as smart and efficient. Within his family there seemed to be a split between those who thought he was go-ahead and ambitious, working hard to save for the bungalow the couple were hoping to buy, and those who thought he was trying to get above himself. Ambition and self-improvement were not universally admired.

Morris was left in a cell at Stafford police station. Before beginning a thorough interrogation, Ian Forbes wanted the ground well prepared. A CID officer went to the firm where Carol Morris worked as a wages clerk and told her of her husband's arrest for the murder of a little girl. She was devoted to Raymond Morris and had no idea that he could be capable of such a thing. Numbed by the news which Detective Inspector Norman Williams brought, she returned with him to Regent House and allowed the police to search the flat. Several boxfuls of evidence were taken away.

Then it was time for her to be driven to Hednesford police station, just north-east of Cannock, well away from Raymond Morris at Stafford. The couple were to be kept apart. Ian Forbes and Chief Inspector Pat Molloy interrogated Carol Morris at Hednesford that afternoon. To say that she was shaken by the events of the day or in a state of shock would be an understatement. But she repeated her alibi for her husband and insisted that she had not been mistaken. Ian Forbes left the interview room and Carol Morris was in the company of Chief Inspector Pat Molloy and Sergeant Tom Parry. Chief

Inspector Molloy, in his later account, described how he told her that her husband was another Ian Brady, the Moors Murderer; that she was unlikely ever to see him again; that the police now had to decide whether or not Carol Morris was 'another Myra Hindley', Brady's partner in the torture and murder of four children. Carol Morris was so innocent that she did not even know who Myra Hindley was and Mr Molloy had to explain that she was a Moors Murderer.

Chief Inspector Molloy recalls that he 'launched into a graphic description of what Myra Hindley had done to little Lesley Anne Downey while Ian Brady was raping her and the tape machine was recording the events in all their gory and sadistic horror.' This account lasted twenty minutes for Carol Morris's benefit. 'She sobbed as I painted a lurid picture of poor Lesley Downey's death-throes, of the bestial things done to her, and of the child's pitiful cries for her mother.'

During the course of this, Sergeant Tom Parry turned pale and left the room. Carol Morris now knew in detail who Myra Hindley was, a public enemy, a reviled and despised child-killer who was unlikely ever to see the outside of the prison to which she had gone at twenty-four years old – almost the same age as Carol Morris herself.

Pat Molloy records laying his hand on her shoulder at the end of twenty minutes of this and asking, 'Well? Are you a Myra Hindley?'

The young woman who had lived a blameless life until that day was suddenly confronted by the possibility of a trial for a murder she had known nothing about and life imprisonment at the age of twenty-five. She was crying, shocked and be-wildered, by no means in a normal state of mind but now, questioned gently, she went back on her previous story. Ian Forbes returned. Instead of a difficult witness who might have to be cajoled or intimidated, he saw at once that this young woman was in a state to be won over. Chief Inspector Pat Molloy watched him sit next to Carol Morris and ask gently, 'How are you now, my dear?' In his presence and that of Chief Inspector Molloy, Carol Morris produced a new statement. Raymond Morris had come home late on 19 August 1967, between 4pm and 4.30 rather than 2pm. 'I trusted my husband implicitly and if I was mistaken, it was an honest mistake and with no intention to cover up for my husband.'

To Chief Inspector Molloy, she said nothing about a mistake but, 'He was there and he told police and I just said yes when they asked me if I agreed. I didn't think it mattered.' Not thinking it important and being mistaken were not at all the same thing.

Though she was to be a crucial witness for the Crown at her husband's trial, Carol Morris's part in the investigation ended with the destruction of her husband's alibis. She also gave evidence that on the evening of the 'Bonfire' incident, he arrived home ten minutes later than he had claimed. Because the law cannot compel a wife to give evidence against her husband, she was not obliged to be a prosecution witness. Her readiness to be one might have been attributed to police pressure. But almost certainly she was moved by some of the items found in the flat at Regent House. Not by pin-up magazines of a routine kind in the spare room and also under the bathroom carpet. But among the photographic prints and negatives in the spare room were those of Carol Morris's five-year-old niece. The child had stayed with the couple the year before and again in August 1968. These photographs, presumably taken with a timer, showed the child undressed with a man's hand indecently assaulting her. The background of the photographs was the spare room of the flat and there was no doubt that the disembodied hand and the watch on the wrist were those of Raymond Morris. Carol Morris did not see these photographs until 26 November, the day after she agreed to give evidence for the Crown. Whether she had remained unaware of their existence since the police search is another matter.

Having broken Morris's alibi and found the indecent photographs, Ian Forbes turned to the suspected killer and began his interrogation that evening. According to Morris, though Ian Forbes denied it, Forbes had already been to his cell and said, 'Well son, you are on your own now. Your wife's left you. No one wants to know you.' He also alleged that Forbes said, 'Well, we know that you've done it. We know you are sick in the head. Why don't you tell us why you've done it? You won't see the outside of this cell for thirty years.' There were no witnesses to these remarks and only Morris's word that they had been made.

Morris added that he had also asked for his solicitor when he was brought to Stafford police station that morning. He alleged that Chief Inspector Pat Molloy 'pushed me against the wall and punched me in the stomach. I put my hands over my stomach and doubled up and he punched me in my left-hand side. He punched me again and then got hold of me by the lapels of my jacket and he said, "Now do you want a fucking solicitor?"' There were, of course, no witnesses to this alleged incident in the cell. In exoneration of Chief Inspector Molloy, it was soon pointed out that if he had punched Morris like this, he would have done so in the knowledge that the suspect would soon be examined naked by a prison medical officer as a matter of routine.

The practice of tape-recording interviews was some years in the future. When Morris was questioned at 7.05pm, two versions emerged, his own and that of the police. His solicitor was not present because, in the official report, he had not asked for him. Morris, who had declined to go on the Walsall identity parade ten days earlier without first speaking to John Benton, insisted that he asked for a solicitor throughout the interview on this far more serious charge. The police version was that he did not even refer to the possibility of having a solicitor. Had a lawyer been present, the disputes over what was said would have been avoided.

The interview was not productive for Ian Forbes. Morris lapsed into silence from time to time and repeated such answers as 'Whatever I say will make no difference . . . I'm finished . . . Oh, what's the use of all this. . . . ' Whatever Forbes may or may not have said to him in his cell, Morris appeared to know that he was on his own, that his wife wanted no more to do with him. He denied ever having seen Christine Darby. When Forbes questioned him as to his movements on the afternoon of 19 August 1967, Morris repeated that he had arrived home from work at about 2pm and had later gone shopping with his wife for an hour and a half. They bought postal orders to pay the rent. Postal orders were certainly bought, though Mrs Morris later said that on this particular Saturday she bought them in the morning.

'Mr Morris,' said Forbes, 'I have interviewed your wife and she tells me that you did not arrive home that afternoon until at least 4.30.'

As it happens, independent evidence was to show that this was probably not correct, whether or not Morris was guilty of the murder. However, he now put his head in his hands, shaking his head as if in denial, and said, 'Oh, God! Oh, God! She wouldn't.' Did he mean she wouldn't betray him by telling the truth or by telling a lie?

Forbes tried to tackle him on why, according to his mother-in-law, the couple had not arrived at her house until about 5pm. Morris ignored the question. He had not claimed to have arrived there until 4.45pm anyway. There was silence again. Forbes tried to revive the interview by telling Morris that he would be put on an identification parade.

'No, no, no.' Morris said, 'I won't go on one. Nothing . . . nothing will . . . You can't make me.'

'Why not?'

'Mr Forbes, I think you are being a bit over-zealous in this case. You are trying to put a fitting end to an illustrious career.'

There was no doubt that Forbes quite legitimately hoped to do so, the question was one of motive. But Morris apologized for the remark and said, 'My whole life, my marriage, my job, my future. What does it matter now? I'm finished. There's nothing for me now. It's the end.'

As for the identity parade, he refused again.

'If you feel as confident as you are making out, you had better charge me and have done with it.'

By the end of the interview, the hostility which Morris felt towards the police was blatant. He had no criminal record and his previous brushes with the law had been the allegation of attempted abduction ten days earlier and the allegation of photographing the two girls in his flat in October 1966. But neither case had been proceeded with. Ironically, Morris might have seemed to most people the pattern of the law-abiding citizen, neat, industrious and frugal. He neither smoked nor drank but saved for the future. Yet he had flared up when the police returned to check on him after his brother's statement and now behaved like a prisoner-of-war in enemy hands.

Ian Forbes solved the problem of the identification parade as best he could. The next morning his prime witness, Victor Whitehouse, was brought to Stafford police station. Morris, who still refused to go on an identification parade, was taken to the police station yard and made to stand with his back to the wall. Victor Whitehouse and Ian Forbes walked into the yard and stood about five or six yards in front of the suspect, far closer than the range of fifteen to twenty yards on Cannock Chase.

'Have you seen this man before?'

There was a very long pause, ten to twelve seconds. It was a year and three months since Victor Whitehouse had had his relatively brief glimpse of the man near Plantation 110. Not for twelve more days had he known that there was any significance in it. Was he now uncertain or just being very careful? At last he said, 'Yes. I'd say yes.'

It was not the most positive response but it was enough. That morning, after Morris had at length contacted his solicitor, he was charged at Cannock with the murder of Christine Darby and remanded in custody by Cannock magistrates.

The news of an arrest for the murder of Christine Darby spread with dramatic rapidity in Walsall from a radio news-flash. One report alleged that more beer was drunk in the town on the night of 16 November 1968 than since V-E Day ended the war against Germany in 1945. It seems improbable. An incident was also reported to the police after a man drinking alone in the Green Rock in Walsall had said of the murder squad's identification of the killer, 'How can they be so sure

that they've got the right man after all this time?' Other customers picked up the doubter and threw him through a plate-
glass window. It was, Chief Inspector Molloy recalled, 'a
touching demonstration of faith in their police force.' The
injunction to 'bring the bastard in' was now replaced by a
public urge to 'string the bastard up' or to 'give him to us!' as
the crowds shouted outside the court buildings. Seldom had
the command of the Queen of Hearts found a plainer echo.
'Sentence first – verdict afterwards.'

V

The trial of Raymond Morris was to take place three months
later, in February 1969, at Stafford Assizes in the Shire Hall.
Before that, however, there were hearings before the
Cannock magistrates and one incident which was scarcely
reassuring to the prosecution. The committal proceedings
took place at Cannock Magistrates Court. Staffordshire Police
had brought the grey Austin A55 to Cannock and parked it in
the yard outside. Morris had sold it some time before and
there was no forensic evidence to connect the car with the
murder.

During the hearing, however, while young Nicholas Baldry
was giving evidence of Christine's abduction, the Crown
asked that the child should be taken into the yard to see the
car. Perhaps he would now recognize it as the one he had seen
in Camden Street when his friend was abducted. The defence
objected on the grounds that, while it was proper for him to
be shown several different types of car and asked if one of
them was the vehicle, it was not correct to show him Morris's
A55 alone.

The defence objection was dismissed and the court
adjourned to the yard outside. Back in the courtroom, prose-
cuting counsel asked the child.

'Was that anything like the car you saw in Camden Street?'
'No.'

This unexpected answer brought the questioning to a halt
for a moment.

'How did it differ?'

'In its shape.'

'How about the size?'

'The car the man had was a bit bigger than that.'

The answer was a reminder that Nicholas Baldry was the only witness who beyond all question had seen the abductor's car. Unless he was regarded as an unreliable child, he was the best witness. But he had one of the best reasons for saying that the car was the wrong shape and the wrong size for an A55. Like thousands of people in the Midlands, Nicholas Baldry's father had a grey A55. Quite simply, the child knew that this was not the same as his father's car.

Mr James Deakin, who had just been missed by a grey A55 north of Cannock, now repeated that it had happened at 3.47pm, which would have undermined the evidence of Mr Whitehouse and Mrs Rawlings, so far as the prosecution was concerned. He was asked whether the man now in the dock was the one he had seen briefly, a year and three months before, through a car windscreen. 'I think that is the man,' he said.

Jeanne Rawlings had seen a man briefly and in profile a year and a quarter before, as his car passed her while she was holding back her dog. Asked if she could identify the defendant as that man, she said that she would need to see Morris's right profile. When he turned his head, she said, 'That definitely is the gentleman who was driving the car.'

Carol Morris was called and, though not obliged to give evidence against her husband, she said she wished to do so. She admitted that she first said that Morris had arrived home about 2pm on that Saturday afternoon. Her evidence now was that he got home 'between 3.30 and 4.30'. They reached her parents' house about 5.30pm. There was considerable doubt on this last point when the time of arrival at her parents' house was indicated as just after the football results ended at 5.11pm.

But Carol Morris's evidence, if it was accepted, would still not ensure a conviction. If Morris was home at 3.30pm it was almost impossible that he could have driven to Cannock

Chase and back, let alone murder Christine Darby. If he returned home any time between 3.30 and 4pm, it was unlikely that he could have done it. If he returned home at 4.30pm, which was the time that Carol Morris later gave, he would have had time to commit the crime but it was impossible that Mrs Rawlings could 'definitely' have seen him on Cannock Chase at 4.20pm. It was possible that Mr Whitehouse might have seen him at 4pm but not much after that. Mr Whitehouse saw a man standing beside a car, not yet driving away. A police driver followed the routes between Morris's flat and Plantation 110. The three journey-times which he recorded were thirty-five minutes, twenty-nine minutes and twenty-one minutes. It would then have taken about two more minutes for Morris to park his car and go up in the lift to Flat 20.

His clothes were important. Mr Whitehouse thought he saw a blazer. Mrs Daniel, who saw the car she thought was a Vauxhall pass Bloxwich Church at 2.53pm, described a man in a dark jacket. Carol Morris's evidence was that her husband, as usual, wore a grey suit for work and that neither the suit nor his underclothes showed any unusual stain or mark. He was alleged to have committed assault, murder, carried a body two hundred yards and concealed it. His clothes bore no trace of this. Apart from the question of his clothes, if Morris had done all these things, he would at least have needed more time to tidy himself up.

The trial began at Stafford Assizes on 10 February 1969. Morris had a quite good defence to the murder charge, if the Crown was required to prove guilt beyond reasonable doubt. The police acknowledged that there was not a scrap of forensic evidence linking Morris to the crime. The circumstantial evidence was questionable, though Carol Morris had by now refined the time of her husband's return to 4.30pm. Evidence of identification was uncertain. The only witness who definitely saw the abductor's car was positive that it was not an Austin A55.

However, by the time committal proceedings were over,

Morris faced other charges. There was the attempted abduction of Margaret Aulton on 4 November 1968. Because Morris was accused of murder, the attempted abduction took on a more sinister possibility. Only Morris could say what his intentions were. Perhaps he meant to entice her into the car and fondle her or perhaps he would have driven her to a remote spot, sexually assaulted and killed her. The answer depended on whether he was a murderer or not.

The indecent photographs of his wife's niece were found in the search of the flat. It was easy to show that the hands in the picture were Morris's and that his watch was on one wrist. After his arrest he managed to transfer the watch to his ankle, where it was soon found. He had taken those photographs and was guilty of the assault they showed. He had no alternative but to plead guilty to two charges of assaulting the child, once in 1967 and once in 1968.

The Crown now proceeded with three charges: murder, attempted abduction, and the 1968 case of indecent assault. The threat to the defence came on the first day. Brian Gibbens QC, who led for the Crown, asked that all three charges be tried simultaneously. The defence objected. If the three charges were tried together, the jury would be told that Morris had admitted indecent assault, and that he was charged with attempted abduction. How could that not influence their decision as to whether or not he was guilty of murder?

Ironically, if Morris had murdered Margaret Aulton and his wife's niece, he could not have been tried simultaneously for the three crimes. If he had a long list of previous convictions for sexual offences, those could not have been brought forward in the prosecution case. But the prosecution argument was that, whether or not witnesses could identify Morris, he could be identified by what was later called psychological profiling. Sexual interference with little girls was so rare a perverted lust, Mr Gibbens argued, that it was found only in 'a small proportion of the population'. He cited the fact that only eighty-one men had been convicted of having sexual intercourse with girls under sixteen in the whole of 1966.

Morris also employed the unusual method of enticing girls into his car, at least he was accused of doing so on two occasions.

Was it possible to examine this theory in the light of other views? No one could reasonably believe the eighty-one cases in 1966 represented absolute truth. Forty-four known sex offenders had been arrested in the Walsall area alone for questioning in the Christine Darby case. Chief Inspector Pat Molloy's view was that 'the Midlands were crawling with such people'. He was perhaps better informed than Home Office statisticians. Twenty years later there were more precise figures. A MORI poll in May 1988 reported that one in twelve respondents had been abused as children. Before hysteria broke out in Cleveland and elsewhere in the late 1980s, figures for the county of Hereford and Worcester, not far from Walsall, ran at 150 a year. As the zealots moved in, the figures doubled. Of course it was argued that increases were due to social services imperialism – devise a problem needing more funds and staff, thereby improving career prospects. Or that it reflected a feminist urge to show what a rotten lot men were. Child abuse and wife-beating documentaries on television alternated unconvincingly. But that Morris's type was very rare is hard to sustain.

It was also argued that Christine Darby had been found with her legs apart in much the same posture as Morris had induced his wife's niece to assume. That apparently established a link. Did it? Chief Inspector Molloy's view was that the murdered girl had been found in 'the classic rape position'. What was so distinctive about that? Morris, said the Crown, tried to abduct little girls by enticing them into his car. However repellent, that must have been one of the most common ways of enticing a child or even an adult from public view.

Psychological profiling was not an art, let alone a science. Years later, the Yorkshire Ripper, Peter Sutcliffe, was interviewed nine times by the police who knew the psychological profile they were looking for. Nine times he got away because he did not fit it. The Boston Strangler was profiled as a man who hated his mother. He was, as it turned out, devoted to her. He killed elderly women because their resistance was weaker.

But Keith Mynett QC, for the defence, lost the first battle for Morris. Mr Justice Ashworth accepted the profile argument. The three charges would be heard together. It would be, as Bryan Gibbens QC for the Crown described it, 'highly prejudicial' to the accused man's interests but in the interest of justice.

Morris seemed doomed. The judge insisted that he would direct the jury not to be influenced on the murder charge by Morris being already guilty of indecent assault and charged with attempted abduction. This was curious because the whole point of the profile argument was that one crime should be very closely associated with the others. If he was the sort of person to commit one of the crimes, as he had admitted, he was the sort of person to commit the rest.

On that basis, the trial went ahead. In the defence case, Morris certainly did not help himself by his accusations against Chief Superintendent Ian Forbes and Chief Inspector Molloy. There was no proof of his allegations. Even had there been, Morris's complaints would not have proved his innocence one jot. It sounded like an attempt to smear the police. Much harder to believe, though it might still be true, was that Morris did not mention a solicitor until the second day of his detention. He had been so quick to want one when detained over the attempted abduction case ten days before.

Carol Morris timed her husband's arrival home on Saturday 19 August at 4.30pm. She also said it would take an hour from then until they reached her parents' house. After returning home, Morris washed, shaved and changed. They had had a meal, cleared away, went down in the lift and drove to Walsall centre. The traffic was bad because of the road blocks. However, they parked the car, walked to Marks and Spencer to buy cream cakes for her mother, returned to the car and drove for ten minutes to her parents' house. Without delays all this could be done in an hour.

According to Carol's father, the couple arrived at the parents' house just after the sports news ended on the television. An engineer testified that it had ended at 5.11pm on 19 August 1967. In that case, Morris had arrived back at his flat just after 4.10pm. If that was so and if Mr Whitehouse and Mrs Rawlings were accurate in the times they gave, they could not have seen him on Cannock Chase at 4pm and 4.20pm respectively. And that would put the suspect grey Austin A55 in limbo. Far the best witness still was Nicholas Baldry who picked it out as a Vauxhall 101E or a Ford Consul. If Christine Darby was abducted in a car of either make, psychological profiling counted for nothing.

At last Morris himself was escorted to the witness box. His defence was simple. Carol Morris was not telling the truth. He had arrived home at about 2pm on 19 August 1967. They had gone shopping together for about an hour and a half, buying postal orders to pay the rent among other things. Then, at about 4.45pm, they had gone to his in-laws. His own parents lived next door and they gave evidence that his car had been parked outside by 5pm.

The question of times and places, how long it took to drive from Cannock Chase to Regent House, did not concern Morris. He had been at home with his wife when Christine Darby was abducted and was probably out shopping in the centre of Walsall at the moment of her death. When his wife changed her story, and if Morris was guilty, he might have been tempted to offer some explanation for his late return home. But there were no such excuses. He stuck to his original account and said it was Carol Morris who now gave false evidence.

If so, why should she have done that? Perhaps from the fright that the police gave her by threatening to treat her as another Myra Hindley. It was absurd, of course. Carol Morris had confirmed an alibi which was false. But Myra Hindley had helped to torture a girl to death, unmoved by tears or screams. Possibly, however, something was also said to her of the photographs which Morris took of her niece and of the two assaults on the child carried out a year apart.

Yet Carol Morris's change of heart was only the first of the two forces that doomed the defence. After Morris had given his evidence, he was cross-examined. He had performed reasonably well when questioned by his own counsel but Brian Gibbens had Morris at his mercy. The most significant part of the cross-examination, quiet and lethal, dealt not with the murder of Christine Darby but with the indecent photographs of Carol Morris's niece, copies of which were now in the hands of the jurors. According to the judge's ruling, these might identify Morris as a killer.

In a more usual trial, a man may be guilty as sin but the jurors' knowledge is limited to the facts of one accusation. The man may be acquitted, only for it to be discovered that he had a criminal history of impressive dimensions. But Morris had had no alternative but to plead guilty to the charge of indecent assault. His own photographs were there to prove it – and to move the jurors to revulsion. His counsel had asked him what he now felt about the photographs and Morris replied, 'They are revolting, sir.' What did he now feel about taking them? 'I am disgusted, sir.' But there was worse to come when Brian Gibbens got up and the cross-examination turned to the same topic of the photographs.

'Will you first tell the court how it was you came to take the photographs in that bundle? That little girl was aged five. And your wife was in the house when the photographs were taken, in the kitchen?'

Morris's defence was that he had molested the little girl but that whether he had murdered Christine Darby was a matter of fact, not character. Now he tried to counter with an answer which described his wife's niece falling back on the bed and having no knickers on. He insisted that it happened in a couple of minutes and that he had never done anything like it before in his life. He explained that he intended to throw the photographs away and forgot they were still in the flat.

There was a terrible stillness as the questioning closed a last escape route for Morris, that of the fundamentally decent man who had taken such photographs in a moment of opportunity and had meant to destroy them. Did he notice the similarity of the position in which his wife's niece was photographed and in which Christine Darby had been found, the legs open and knees raised? In case he missed the point, Morris was handed a photograph of Christine Darby lying as she was found.

Brian Gibbens pointed out that the photographs of Mrs. Morris's niece had been taken on 17 August 1968, almost the first anniversary of Christine Darby's death. 'What you did to the girl in the photograph was, in some respects, the same thing that must have happened with Christine Darby.'

'I don't follow you, sir,' Morris said but by that time his last hope had gone.

Mr Justice Ashworth, in summing up, told the jurors that their decisions on the murder charge must not be influenced by Morris's guilt of indecent assault and the strong evidence of attempted abduction. They were not to say, 'Well, he did one so he must have done another.' As for the other strand of the prosecution case, Carol Morris's change of heart, the judge warned the jury to approach her evidence with very great caution. One or other of her stories must be untrue, he told them. That being so, 'Can you rely on her at all?'

The jurors retired. They were out for an hour and forty minutes. When they came back, it seemed they felt they could rely on Carol Morris after all. Raymond Morris was found guilty of murder and guilty of attempted abduction. News of the verdict reached the crowd that was waiting outside in Stafford's Shire Hall Square. A chant rose of 'Hang him! Hang him! Hang him!' In the quiet formality of the assize court, the judge looked at the man in the dock.

'I do not intend to keep you there more than one moment, nor do I intend to make any comment myself about this terrible murder. There is only one sentence, as you know, and that is life imprisonment. That is the sentence I pass on you.'

The press were ready for the verdict. Comments on the case itself were not enough. 'From an early age he had shown strange tendencies and was cruel, hard and over-sexed.' Who said so? Not his wife, nor his parents, nor those who knew him. 'He had big ideas from his early days,' the *Daily*

Telegraph insisted. But was this not the get-up-and-go which the paper elsewhere encouraged? 'He began to antagonize his family even before he left school.' That was not really what his family said. 'Morris was vain and very conscious of his good looks.' The same characteristics in another person would have been commended as taking pride in his appearance. Of his first wife, the press wrote, 'She was 11 when he met her.' Of course she was a schoolchild, so was he. There was a difference of two years in their ages, but the phantom of the grown man hanging round the school playground was conjured up once more. Claptrap of this kind was a traditional privilege of the press after a murder conviction.

Morris tried to overturn his conviction. Nine months later, in November 1969, Keith Mynett QC appeared before the appeal judges and sought leave to appeal against the verdict. His reasons were plain enough. The murder charge should have been tried separately. Evidence relating to the charges of attempted abduction and the indecent assault should not have been admitted at the murder trial. The appeal judges heard his argument and that of the Crown. They denied leave to appeal.

At one time, Morris required round-the-clock protection in Winson Green Prison, Birmingham. After his trial, he was transferred to the high security wing of Durham Gaol. His companions included Ian Brady, the Moors Murderer, and two other child-killers. Many years later, he was said to have been diagnosed as psychopathic. Under the circumstances, an innocent man might have shown symptoms suggesting that state as easily as one who is guilty.

'After so long, how can they be so sure they've got the right man?' The words of the rational sceptic who was thrown through a plate glass window for thinking such thoughts still echo in the case. But to depart from the orthodox view that Raymond Morris got what he deserved is to encounter two considerable difficulties.

The first is the tragedy of the Darby family in the loss of their child. Surely, as the mayor of the town said, the prayers of everyone in Walsall must have been with them. And yet if justice was not done, it and they and Raymond Morris were equally victims. However repellent the sexual character of Raymond Morris, if he did not murder one and perhaps three little girls, the person who did so was allowed to go free.

The second difficulty is that, in one area of his life at least, Raymond Morris was a thoroughly unpleasant individual. That was true whether or not he committed murder. He may have been a 'perfect gentleman' to his neighbours, an 'ideal' son to his parents. His employers 'could not say a word against him'. Yet he was a self-confessed molester of at least one little girl. Though the two witnesses failed to identify him as the man who tried to entice Margaret Aulton into his car, the identification of the car was strong evidence that he was guilty of attempted abduction. And if he was guilty of that and guilty of indecent assault on his wife's niece, he was regarded as having the 'hallmark' of a murderer. By assuming that to be true, the enticement of Margaret Aulton would have been the prelude to her death.

At the very least, the circumstances of enticement were different. Christine Darby, Diane Tift, and Margaret Foster had been abducted in daylight, in the early afternoon. When Morris saw Margaret Aulton, it was a dark November evening and he was due home in a few more minutes. He had already had three visits from the police over his alibi for Christine Darby's death, and he had argued with them. His wife had confirmed his alibi. If it was false, as she soon claimed, how would he explain a long absence on this November evening? And what would Carol Morris do, if another little girl died while he was unaccountably absent? If he was the cold and cunning villain that the press claimed, surely all this crossed his mind.

The time of day was important. If he had Margaret Aulton in his car, did Morris really propose driving for an hour to somewhere like Cannock Chase and back, spending further time in committing the offence? Even if he went there, it was absurd to risk driving off the main road on to a muddy forest track in total darkness. A cold and calculating mind would surely have thought of that. And ultimately, when he arrived home at about 9.30pm instead of 7.50, he must explain to his wife the state of his shoes or clothes as well as the reason for his absence.

One need not believe in Morris's innocence of an attempt to molest Margaret Aulton to suggest that murder was no part of it. Even in the place where he was parked, he might have enticed the girl into his car and fondled her or persuaded her to fondle him. A darkened garage forecourt or an ill-lit street of business premises would do. What need of murder if he could do this, then drive on, arriving home only fifteen or twenty minutes late? A less serious indecent assault made sense in such circumstances. Murder in the middle of Walsall did not. If that was so, then the use of attempted abduction as part of the profile of Morris as murderer was a poor fit.

Yet murder was at the heart of it all. The acts that could be clearly proved against Morris – taking indecent photographs, molesting the little niece with his hand and the attempt to entice Margaret Aulton into his car – did not involve murder. The two girls whom he was alleged to have invited to his flat and photographed in 1965 were not in danger of their lives. There was no 'hallmark' of murder in such conduct, however repulsive the conduct might be. Yet the crime that had murder at its heart was brought against him in court on the grounds that he must have done it because he was the sort of man who would have done it. If the facts needed support of such a kind, Keith Mynett QC was surely justified in calling them 'a pretty weak case'.

Did Raymond Morris kill Christine Darby? Setting aside the contentious issue of 'profiling' his personality, could he have done so? Twenty-five years later, the possibilities can be discussed without the risk of being thrown through a plate-glass window.

1. The Timing
If Carol Morris was right in the evidence she gave against him, it took her husband an hour to wash, shave, change, eat a meal, clear up, drive with her into town, park the car, go to

Marks and Spencer and back, and then drive with her to her parents' house.

What time did they arrive at her parents' house? Her mother put the latest time as 5.30pm, though Morris's parents claimed that they saw their son's car parked outside at 5pm. Even his mother-in-law thought, at one point, that he might have been there as early as 5pm. When Carol Morris's father said that the football results had just ended on ITV as the couple came in, an engineer pegged the time at 5.11pm.

That was the worst case that could be put against Morris on the question of arrival at his in-laws. He claimed to have arrived at 4.45pm. But if the time of 5.11pm was right, and if his wife was right in her evidence given against him, that it took an hour from the time he got home, then Morris arrived home in Walsall at about 4.10pm and it took a minute to go up to the flat by lift.

Morris himself claimed to the end that he had come home about two hours earlier. But if he was lying and his wife spoke the truth at his trial, he could only have arrived home at 4.10 by leaving Cannock Chase somewhere between 3.35pm and 3.45pm, according to the timings of the police driver. If he left Cannock Chase then, Ian Whitehouse could not have seen him there 'about four o'clock', unless that meant anywhere within about three-quarters of an hour. It was quite impossible that Jeanne Rawlings could have seen him at a few minutes after 4.20pm. He had already been home in Walsall for ten minutes by then. If she had seen Morris on Cannock Chase after 4.20, he would not have reached his in-laws until just before 6pm, half an hour after the latest time that the most hostile witness had suggested.

Of course, if Morris was on Cannock Chase and left between 3.30pm and 3.40pm, it was perfectly possible that James Deakin saw him speeding towards Cannock at 3.47pm. The witness gave that time very precisely. However, Mr Deakin's evidence again contradicted that of Victor Whitehouse and Jeanne Rawlings.

At Morris's trial, it was suggested that the times given by witnesses should be treated sympathetically. People are not always looking at their watches, Mr Justice Ashworth said. And it was a long time ago. But evidence of times was given to the police within a few days of the event, the longest delay being Victor Whitehouse's twelve days. Much was made elsewhere of Mr Whitehouse's powers of observation and memory, when it came to identifying the suspect. If those powers were what they seemed, it was reasonable to assume that when he said 'about four o'clock', he meant something very close to it. Many of the times given by witnesses were extraordinarily precise. Mrs Daniel saw a car going through Bloxwich at 2.53pm. Mr Deakin saw a car speeding towards Cannock at 3.47pm. Mrs Rawlings parked on Cannock Chase at 4.20pm and saw a car driver in profile a 'few minutes' later. The ITV football results ended at 5.11pm. Far from being vague, the times given in the case were unusually exact.

Morris stuck to his story of coming home before Christine Darby was abducted and being with his wife thereafter. The only change was when he timed his arrival home at 2pm to 2.15pm, rather than 1.45pm. He had forgotten that his employer had just come back from holiday. Morris clocked out at 1.13pm but stayed on, briefing him on the previous week. His employer confirmed that he had indeed just come back from holiday, that Morris stayed late to brief him but he could not say how long. In the end, it was Carol Morris, not her husband, who changed her story. As the trial judge put it, 'On any view she has told lies. I say that without hesitation. Either she lied originally in confirming his alibi, or she is lying now. . . . Can you rely on her at all?'

In fairness to Mrs Morris, there were pressures of which the jurors did not know. There was the police interview, 'Are you another Myra Hindley?' Twenty minutes of this changed a firm witness for her husband's innocence into a tearful and shaken witness against him. Then there were the appalling photographs of her little niece, Raymond Morris's hand sexually assaulting the child. She was not shown these until after agreeing to give evidence against him but did she not know of them? She was present when police took them from the house and, presumably, received a receipt for them.

Though not compelled to give evidence against her husband, she was thereafter willing to do so.

Yet after all that, Carol Morris's evidence contradicted Victor Whitehouse and Jeanne Rawlings who were central to the prosecution's story.

2. Identification

For twelve days after the murder, Victor Whitehouse did not know that the man he saw in passing, at forty-five to sixty feet, had any connection with the murder inquiry. He had no specific reason to fix that man's appearance in his memory. Nor, unlike other witnesses, did he give the time to the minute. He had no reason to remember that either. He did not see Morris for a year and three months. Asked if this was the man he had seen on Cannock Chase, he paused for a long time, ten to twelve seconds. To sit and count this out is to realize how long that silence in the police station yard must have been. Then he replied, 'Yes. I'd say yes.' Whether the hesitation was born of uncertainty, conscientiousness, or both, no one could say.

Mr Whitehouse and Mrs Rawlings guided the artist who produced the identikit picture of the wanted man. But if he truly looked like the picture, he was not Raymond Morris, as any comparison of Morris's photograph and the drawing would show. The drawing and the 'look-alike' of the man on Cannock Chase appeared on posters, television, and in the press, including a front-page feature in the mass-circulation paper, the *Daily Express*. In the year that followed, not a single member of the public came forward to identify Morris as either the face in the drawing or the figure in the look-alike photograph. His wife did not come forward. His parents-in-law, according to Chief Inspector Molloy were 'willing recipients to suggestions that their son-in-law was the Cannock Chase Murderer.' Yet they saw no likeness between the picture and Morris, despite their cordial dislike of him and their accusations by hindsight of the odd way he looked at girls. His first wife who thought him sexually odd did not come forward. Not even his brother made the identification, though he had actually gone to Cannock police station, as Pat

Molloy later discovered, and named Raymond Morris as a suspect for child-murder, specifically the murder of Diane Tift. The fault, surely, lay not with the brother but with the lack of resemblance between Morris and the pictures. As for those anonymous people who allegedly came forward after the trial to say what a cold and perverted character Morris had always been, not one of them reported any likeness between him and the published pictures.

It was not good enough for the police to suggest that people had misunderstood the technique of the identikit, that it relied on particular features not general appearance, which people would normally expect. The public was asked, 'Do you recognize this man?' The unanimous answer so far as Morris was concerned was 'No.' There was, of course, the further difficulty that only Victor Whitehouse had seen the man on Cannock Chase full-face, as in the drawing. Mrs Rawlings had only seen him in profile and could not identify him in court until he turned that profile. The identikit picture, whatever its virtues, described a view of him which she had never seen.

Other evidence of identification was thin. In court, Mrs Daniel the wedding-guest was disqualified because it proved she had identified Christine Darby from a newspaper photograph and not from the little girl she had seen in the passing car. As for Mr Deakin, he had seen the driver of an A55 briefly as it sped past him. Eighteen months passed before he saw Morris in court.

3. The Car
Mr Deakin, Mrs. Rawlings, and Mr Whitehouse identified the car they saw as a grey A55 or a grey A60, which was not dissimilar. It was one of six hundred cars on Cannock Chase that day, grey A55s among them. A grey A55 or grey A60 was close to the place where Christine Darby's body was found two days later. Whether the child's body was there at 4.00 to 4.20pm on that Saturday afternoon is not known. In any case, the grey A55 was not the only car parked close to the spot. Those of Mrs Rawlings and Mr Whitehouse, along with the vehicles of other innocent people, were close by.

There was only one witness who, beyond all doubt saw the car in which Christine Darby was abducted. He was young Nicholas Baldry with whom she was playing in Camden Street. He stated at first, and repeated eighteen months later, that the abductor's car was not an A55. He was shown Morris's car in the police court yard and again said it was not the one. His elders regarded this as a flaw in the child's perception. But he had the best of all reasons for his statement. He knew very well what a grey A55 looked like because his father had one. The car in Camden Street was a different shape and it was bigger. He was given pictures of grey cars to look at. Again, he did not pick out an A55. He chose a Ford Consul and a Vauxhall 101E. Perhaps it was significant that Mrs Daniel identified the car which passed Bloxwich church at 2.53pm as a Vauxhall 101E. If Nicholas Baldry was right, there was an end of the A55 and, presumably, of Morris's part in the case.

4. The Other Evidence

At whatever time he came home, Carol Morris found her husband normal in his manner. His clothes, including his underclothes, showed no evidence of the crime of which he was accused. Perhaps in itself this meant little but it was another area in which evidence of guilt was lacking.

One thing was agreed by all sides. There was not a shred of forensic evidence linking Raymond Morris with the murder.

As for the disposal of the body, Cannock Chase was by no means deserted on that August afternoon, as the police census of cars revealed. Yet the murderer of Christine Darby apparently carried the dead or unconscious child at least two hundred yards through the trees to the place where she was found. It was not something that could have been done in a dash. Would an intelligent and devious killer not have chosen some other grave on Saturday afternoon or taken the body to Cannock Chase in the lonelier hours of Saturday evening? Of course, Morris might have found it difficult to leave his wife for an hour or so on Saturday evening but that pre-supposed that Morris was the killer.

5. The Trial

At the least, it was contentious to try Morris simultaneously for indecent assault to which he pleaded guilty, and murder and attempted abduction of which he claimed to be innocent. Again the 'psychological profile' argument was that the sort of man who had committed the least of the three offences must also be the man who was guilty of the greater two. The jurors were warned by the judge not to argue that because Morris had committed one crime he must therefore have committed another. But was not that precisely what the judge's ruling and the 'psychological profile' argument of the prosecution invited them to say?

The Crown argued that Morris showed 'a perverted lust which is found only in a small percentage of the population.' In 1966, only eighty-one men in the entire country had been charged with having sexual intercourse with girls under sixteen. The argument was suspect by almost any criterion. Among the 200,000 people of the Walsall area, the police detained forty-four known sex offenders against children in the course of the murder inquiry. Morris was also on their records, reported after the 1966 incident of photographing two girls in his flat and also named by his brother. He was not even approached, let alone detained and questioned. How many more men were missed out?

As for the national figure of eighty-one men offending against under-age girls, the forty-four known offenders in Walsall would, in a national population of 50,000,000, give a figure of 10,000 not eighty-one. Some two million people in the Birmingham conurbation, from Coventry to Wolverhampton, lived within twenty miles or a half-hour drive of Walsall. The Midlands, in the words of Chief Inspector Pat Molloy, were 'crawling with such people' as those detained in the investigation. Who but such people made it worth while to publish commercially titles like *Lolita* – the pin-up magazine, not the novel – or pages of adult young women photographed as schoolgirls in uniform which appeared more widely in glamour magazines? And though it would be dangerous to judge the 1960s by the standards of the 1990s, the Brook Advisory Centre in 1992 puts the number of sex-ually-active fifteen-year-old girls at 84,000. In theory, each statistic in that survey represents a criminal offence. Was the figure of eighty-one offences for the entire country anything but a courtroom ploy?

It was argued that enticing a child into a car was rare and therefore a characteristic of Morris which made him both abductor and murderer. Using a car was apparently all too common and, indeed, the first man thought to be the killer of Christine Darby had done just that. So did another child seducer and murderer of the decade, Albert Jones, sentenced in 1961 for the murder of a Girl Guide, Barbara Nash. The car as the seducer's or the abductor's weapon was almost as old as the history of the internal combustion engine. One day there would have to be laws against so-called kerb-crawling. Meantime, the posters warned children specifically not to accept lifts from strangers.

The trial of the three offences together was, as the saying goes, throwing a skunk into the jury room and telling the jurors to ignore the smell. Added to this was the fear for their children and hatred of the killer, felt by those who had been at his mercy. The crowd outside Shire Hall shouting, 'Give him to us!' was not to be a lynch-mob. Yet there was a popular logic abroad. Someone murdered Christine Darby. Morris was the sort of man who might be guilty. If no one else could be found, he was surely the killer. On that basis he was credited with the murders of Margaret Reynolds and Diane Tift as well, though never brought to trial for the deaths of those two children.

Because one cannot prove a negative in such circum-stances, it can never be shown that Morris did not kill Christine Darby. Yet his counsel was right that the evidence against him was 'a pretty weak case', bolstered by the theory that he was the sort of man who must have done it, on the basis of his 'hallmark'. The form of the trial itself was unsatis-factory. When the judge and the prosecution acknowledged that it would be 'highly prejudicial to the accused but highly in the interests of justice', to try him in this way these words at

CHAPTER FOUR

least merited a question. How is a trial which is deliberately prejudicial to either side in the interests of justice? In the case of Raymond Morris, was not the danger that justice would be the first casualty?

His defenders suffered the disadvantage that Morris was not an attractive personality. He had clearly grown to dislike the police and seemed to behave stupidly in custody. Of course there was a conflict as to what happened during custody. Chief Superintendent Forbes said that Morris never denied the charge. Morris said that he denied it from the start and certainly said that he had never so much as seen Christine Darby. Forbes said that Morris never mentioned a solicitor. Morris said he asked for his solicitor at the beginning. If he did not ask for one, it was curious. When questioned about the attempted abduction, he had demanded to telephone John Benton. Did he really not mention a solicitor until about to be charged with the Christine Darby murder on the second day of his detention? Was not legal representation the first thing that a devious and intelligent mind would have demanded, having insisted on contact with a lawyer when detained a few days before?

Morris refused an identity parade. But he had delayed on the earlier occasion until allowed to speak to his solicitor. Then he had been willing enough. Forbes was right in saying to him that, by refusing a parade this time, he was doing himself a disservice. Had there been twenty men, Victor Whitehouse, Jeanne Rawlings, Nancy Daniel and James Deakin might well have failed to pick him out. As it was, they were presented with him alone and asked to confirm that he was the man they saw. He gave them no alternative choice. Perhaps his fear, however ill-founded, was that the police would put him on one parade after another until someone picked him out, even if at random.

Morris denied saying some of the things attributed to him by those who arrested him. Even if he did say them, few of the remarks might not have had a relatively innocent explanation. Carol Morris knew perfectly well that her husband was visited not once but three times by the police after Christine

Darby's death. She had been there. Surely she must have thought something about this. When Morris said, 'Is it my wife?' he might perhaps have meant, 'Has my wife found the photographs of the little girl and decided I might be the murderer?' When he was told she had withdrawn her alibi and he said, 'She wouldn't!' he might have meant, 'She wouldn't betray me by telling a lie,' as easily as, 'She wouldn't betray me by telling the truth.'

Courts of law are concerned with what can be proved to have happened, rather than what may actually have happened. In this case, perhaps the most satisfactory verdict, not available to an English court, would have been 'Not proven.' It would leave open the possibility of Morris's guilt but also the guilt of another man who was never brought to justice. If such a man existed, Morris was a perfect shield. Yet the most important figure in the development of the case was the customer in the bar who said on the night of 16 November 1968, 'After so long, how can they be sure they've got the right man?' It was a question as much for the court and its jurors as for the police. But the two petty criminals who threw the doubter through a plate-glass window threw justice and logic after him.

FIVE

'There Are People Who Would Die For Me': Michael X (1972)

I

The little agricultural town of Arima lies about twenty miles east of Port-of-Spain, Trinidad, with wooded hills to the north and the sea a few miles beyond them. Among its newer developments in 1972 were the ranch-style bungalows of Christina Gardens, built eight years earlier and set on individual plots of about an acre and a half. The bungalow at 26–28 Christina Gardens was owned by Mr Peter Mootoo who had leased it to a new tenant the previous year, in February 1971. It was a good sized building with a large patio, which was just as well since the present tenant had a considerable number of house guests. Some of them, like John Lennon of the Beatles, were famous names and stayed briefly. Others seemed to be in permanent residence, either in the bungalow itself or elsewhere in Christina Gardens.

With the hills and the sea to the north, the rivers and open plain to the south, Arima offered a pleasant enough setting. All that was about to change. On the night of Saturday 19 February 1972, the bungalow at 26–28 Christina Gardens was unoccupied when several of its neighbours heard a muffled explosion. The tenant was away, on a lecture-tour of Guyana, where he was a guest of the government and accompanied by Oswald McDavidson whose wife was a member of Eric Williams' cabinet in Trinidad. Guyana showed a lot of interest in its visitor. By whatever name he was known, Michael Abdul Malik, alias Michael X, born Michael de Freitas, had been a cult figure of the 1960s, as much in London as in Trinidad.

John Lennon, Yoko Ono, Sammy Davis Jnr, the world of showbiz and money had made much of him.

The Arima fire-brigade received an alarm call at 11.25pm and set out for the bungalow. By the time they arrived it was blazing and there was little chance even of saving the contents, least of all the piano which had been a present from John Lennon. A little while later, the police arrived from Port-of-Spain. This was no ordinary fire. The front door and its surroundings had been doused with kerosene, which had also been poured into the building. A trail of fuel led back across the garden.

The interest of the police was divided between arson and what they might find on the property. In general, people were divided between those who thought that Michael Abdul Malik was a crackpot and those who feared he might yet cause serious trouble. The commune which he had founded was sometimes known as the Black Liberation Army with a petty criminal, Stanley Abbott, as one of its recently appointed Lieutenant-Colonels. This army which promised one day to march on Port-of-Spain and install a people's government was a joke. Yet the police believed that it might be a joke armed to the teeth. When they arrived at Christina Gardens, they began to look for hidden weapons.

Peter Mootoo had had difficulty for some time in getting money from his tenant and this had led him to visit the property quite often. On a visit early in February, he noticed that two vegetable beds, about eight feet long and four feet wide, had been heavily manured. Lettuce had been planted in one of them. It struck him as odd that anyone should have dug so thoroughly and manured so heavily to grow lettuce. His tenant had a lot to learn about gardening. In no time, the plants grew tall, rather yellow and unappetising.

On Tuesday afternoon, the third day after the fire, Mr Mootoo apparently mentioned this to Police Inspector Osinal Lewis who was looking over the premises with Superintendent Mark and Assistant Superintendent Brewster. Inspector Lewis took a stick to see how far he could push it into the two vegetable beds in the north-west corner of the property. In the first bed, where nothing was planted, the stick would only go in six or eight inches. In the second bed, with the tall yellow lettuce, it went in easily to a depth of a foot. The soil was much looser in the second bed and it had been freshly dug. But why would anyone dig down more than a foot in order to plant lettuce?

Inspector Lewis reported this to Assistant Superintendent Brewster. That afternoon, three police station cleaners began digging up the lettuce bed. Osinal Lewis and his colleagues guessed they might find arms and ammunition buried there, the arsenal of the Black Liberation Army. Under the top soil, the loose earth was removed to show that the bed had lately been dug in the form of a trench. Then as the diggers reached a depth of about three feet without finding anything, there was a suffocating smell of decay. Inspector Lewis dismissed the cleaners and sent for grave-diggers.

Later that afternoon, at a depth of about five feet and in soil that contained large stones, the diggers found a mummified body. Inspector Lewis described the body as 'of Negro origin; had bushy hair on the head, hair on the face, a blue T-shirt and "blue-dock" trousers with the lower portion of the leg rolled up. The body was "brown skin"'. Dr Michael Healey, senior pathologist at Port-of-Spain General Hospital, examined the body when it was lifted from the grave and identified it as male. A member of the commune, Steve Yeates had been reported drowned while swimming off Sans Souci beach on 10 February. Divers had searched for a body and failed to find one. The police first concluded that Yeates, whom Malik had appointed a Colonel of the Black Liberation Army, had been murdered at Christina Gardens and buried there.

Desirée Malik, Michael Abdul Malik's wife, received a telephone call from a local journalist. 'They've found Steve Yeates' body in your garden.' 'My God!' she said, 'Steve! Are you sure?' Michael Abdul Malik had already heard of the fire and had telephoned his lawyer from Georgetown, Guyana, to get an injunction restraining the police from entering the property in his absence. But Malik could only get that injunction by returning to Trinidad and asking for it, which he declined to do. Then he heard that a body had been found in his garden. As he told his companion, Oswald McDavidson, 'This is a great mess, man. My enemies must be fixing me.' McDavidson agreed and said, 'They must have put it there.' Malik insisted that he was not going to be a 'sitting duck' for whoever came after him. He wanted to go back to Trinidad but it was important that no one should recognize him. He ordered McDavidson to shave off his beard for him and trim his hair. They went to a house where this was done and where Malik was given a nineteen-year-old girl to walk arm-in-arm with when he went out in public. A detective had already left Port-of-Spain for Guyana. But with his appearance changed and an unknown girl on his arm Malik would be safe for a while yet. He remained with McDavidson at the Park Hotel until he heard that a second body had been found at Arima.

By now the police had begun a systematic search at Arima. On Wednesday the body under the bed of lettuce was identified as being not Steve Yeates but Joseph Skerritt, a member of the commune who was also Malik's cousin. His mother, 'Tanty', was the sister of Iona Brown, mother of Michael Abdul Malik. Another day passed and the search spread beyond the garden of the bungalow to waste land on the northern side, near a sluggish stream in a ravine. There were signs that the earth had been distributed and the grave-diggers began again. Five feet down they found another body.

This time it was a young woman's body in 'a flower-print dress and a pair of rose-coloured panties'. This second victim was white. She had been buried longer than the man but was identified by her dental records in London. There had been two white women at the commune, followers of their mesmeric leader. One of them, Trina Simmonds, had gone back to London, where she was proved to be still alive and well. The body in the grave at Arima was that of Gale Benson, daughter of a former British Member of Parliament. She was twenty-seven years old, divorced, and a representative of 1960s radical chic. With her burden of white middle-class guilt over Britain's imperial past – and her money – she was the willing victim of moral, sexual and racial blackmail.

Michael Abdul Malik no longer talked of coming back from Guyana to Trinidad. He made his way along a jungle route towards the Brazilian frontier. Once across it, he would be safe from extradition. In another change of clothes and with a supply of food, he began the trek towards sanctuary in Brazil. He walked for three days. When it was almost dusk on the third day, he approached a group of men who were a government survey team. One of them gave him a lift to a farm. The farmer was friendly and told him that he could stay for the rest of the year if he wished. But at 6am next morning, while Malik was still sleeping, the man from the survey team returned with the police. The police superintendent tapped him on the shoulder and Malik opened his eyes. 'Don't shoot,' he said.

He was taken back to Georgetown and deported to Trinidad as an undesirable alien. A legend of the 1960s developed a new dimension as the drama of a murder trial began.

All his life until these last few days it seemed that Michael Abdul Malik had been lucky. Fame, if not fortune, had come to him easily. He had made most of his money lately by political imposture and trickery, before that by pimping, drug-dealing and gambling. Despite a modest prison record, he had been well rewarded for his public performances.

He was born in Trinidad in 1933, in the Belmont area of Port-of-Spain. His father, de Freitas, was a Portuguese shop-keeper: his mother, Iona Brown, lived with a taxi driver. One of the ironies of Michael de Freitas' life was that this prophet of black supremacy was not black. He was half European or 'red', as it was called in Trinidad. 'All de Freitas left you was a big cunt and a red bastard,' the taxi driver shouted at Iona Brown. But she was proud of her son's appearance. She would drag him away from black playmates in the street, scolding him with, 'I take the trouble to give you good colour and this is what you do to me.'

Onlookers sympathized with Mrs Brown. 'That child will kill his mother,' they would say, 'That boy's going to end up on the hangman's rope.' He recalled this with amusement in 1967, never guessing the fatal irony that lay in wait five years ahead.

He was educated at St Mary's College, one of the better schools in Port-of-Spain. Then, at seventeen, he became a galley boy and afterwards a merchant seaman. When he reached England, he left the ship and made his way to the British Merchant Navy Office in Cardiff, looking for work. When he reached the Cardiff dockland of Tiger Bay, however, he found other work. He became a thief, a drug pedlar and, most successfully, a pimp. Tiger Bay or Butetown, divided by the frontier of river and railway from the rest of the city, was home from home. It was a place where a self-proclaimed black man could run white women as prostitutes, perhaps in revenge for the exploitation of his own race by theirs.

After some years in Cardiff, Michael de Freitas, as he still called himself, decided the time had come for better things. He crossed the railway line and caught the London train. By now there was a sizeable population of West Indian immigrants in the area of Notting Hill Gate and along the length of Ladbroke Grove. The ghetto even called itself, 'The Grove'. He met and ultimately married Desirée de Souza. But it was other women who made his living for him.

As a pimp, Michael de Freitas was formidable. 'I ran the most successful string of gaming houses and whore houses that any black person ever did in England,' he said in 1967. In tandem with this, he tried his hand at organizing theft and robbery. His success as a robber was less assured. There was a Post Office hold-up at Reading which ended in farce when the man carrying the shotgun fainted with tension halfway to the Post Office counter. Michael de Freitas had to scoop him up, carry him to the getaway car outside and leave empty-handed.

It was at the beginning of the 1960s that he met Perec 'Peter' Rachman, a property racketeer and extortioner. Rachman was a stateless Pole who arrived in England after the end of the war in 1945. He began to build up a slum empire, buying properties whose value was depressed because the tenants' rents were controlled by law. By terror and extortion, he drove the tenants out, crowding the properties with West

Indian immigrants or letting them at very high rents to brothel-owners or club proprietors. His moment of fame came during the Profumo scandal of 1962, which threatened to bring down the Macmillan government. Christine Keeler, mistress of both the Minister of Defence and the Soviet military attaché, Captain Ivanov, had also been the mistress of Rachman. And Michael de Freitas had been one of his 'rent collectors' and eviction agents.

Rachman died of heart failure 'in the saddle' with one of his girls in 1962, after which his flat in Bryanston Street was occupied by Dr Stephen Ward whose trial for pimping brought the Profumo scandal to its conclusion. But Michael de Freitas had implemented Rachman's tactics of terror long before this. Two elderly tenants were beaten up when they refused to pay double rent, demanded on the pretext that their property had changed hands and that the new company had not received the money they had paid to its predecessor. Both companies were, of course, Rachman's. Other tenants were visited by the rent-collector and two vicious Alsatian dogs which drooled threateningly because they had not been fed. Flats were entered, while tenants were out, and dead rats left in food cupboards or in the beds. Michael de Freitas was on Rachman's side. 'I think he had rather an unfortunate deal,' he wrote later, 'If you want the true adjective for the dictionary, you can cut out Rachmanism and put in Englishism. That's a much more vicious thing.'

So began the genesis of Michael X. Half-white himself, Michael de Freitas unleashed his verbal savagery against the indigenous population of England. In comradeship with the black revolutionaries of Watts or Chicago, he promised a terrible retribution for the racist past of the white people. But he did it with great skill. Never before had the white population felt as guilty about its colonial past as in the 1960s. Of course, most people had not been born until that past was over and, in any case, there was not much to be done about it. But the white liberal middle-class had money. If they could be made to feel guilty enough, a goodly amount of that money might come the way of the conscience-prickers. Not only was it a strikingly simple idea but, for Michael de Freitas, it promised a far better income than that of a pimp or a rent-collector. He would be able to take the money while assuring those who gave it that they would be dead white meat when the revolution came.

Better still, it would give him fame in almost any field he chose. Michael de Freitas was soon to proclaim himself a painter and writer. It seems doubtful whether he ever painted at all and his only book had to be written for him, ironically by a man who under a pseudonym had written novels of black sexual savagery in books that were banned in England. Yet no one could attack Michael de Freitas as an impostor or a failure in such areas, for that would surely be racist.

He received money from millionaires and middle-class women, from pop stars and publishers. He persuaded John Lennon that the Beatles owed their fame and fortune to the fact that they had 'stolen' the rhythms of Liverpool's blacks. This guilt-therapy worked so smoothly that he was paid a £10,000 advance to write a book – which he never would or could write – about black culture. Then, after the assassination of Malcolm X in America, he knew that he must become Michael X. It was not original but it worked. Like any good revolutionary, he had a prison record. It was a short unglamorous sentence for the theft of some paint from a ship on which he worked. He laughed it off as being 'about on a par with using the office stationery for private correspondence'. And then, in 1965, he founded RAAS. To those who came forward obediently with fistfuls of bank notes, he explained that it was the Racial Adjustment Action Society. They approved of it. In the *Observer* newspaper, he was described as 'a shy, gentle and highly intelligent man'. Then it was discovered that Raas was a Jamaican slang word for 'arse' or, in America, for 'ass'.

RAAS owed its existence primarily to the money given him by a rich thirty-year-old widow, 'a beautiful woman with a lovely supple body'. But this body was nothing without money. 'From being a chick it was nice to make, Carmen became for me purely a source of money.'

In 1967, Michael X was sufficiently a cult figure to have his autobiography ghosted for a major London publisher. He was now regarded as a leading figure of extra-parliamentary politics and written about as such by correspondents of the *Observer* and the *Guardian*. However, before his autobiography, *From Michael de Freitas to Michael X*, appeared in print, he was in prison again.

A better-known figurehead of Black Power, Stokely Carmichael, visited England in the summer of 1967 under careful surveillance by Scotland Yard's Special Branch. Among his other engagements, Carmichael was to address a meeting at the Rainbow Hall in Reading. The day before this, however, he flew out of London, bound for Prague and Cuba. In order that those who attended the meeting should not be disappointed, 'Michael X' took his place. There were about seventy people in the audience, including representatives of the press.

Despite the small audience, it was an unrivalled opportunity to promote himself and his views. Such publicity required expressions of loathing for 'Whitey' so bitter that he could not be ignored. It mattered very little whether Michael de Freitas, who was half 'Whitey' himself, believed much in what he said. He need only say it. White middle-class masochism would do the rest.

So, on 24 July 1967, he treated his audience to a spectacle of intellectual clowning that would have been better dismissed for what it was. He began with the Notting Hill race riots of 1958, when white youths had attacked the black community.

'In 1958, I saw white savages kicking black women in the streets and black brothers running away. If ever you see a white laying hands on a black woman, kill him immediately.' This was what his audience wanted and the pressmen were hungry for every word of it. 'Whitey is a vicious, nasty person. Fear of this white monkey is nothing. We will deal with him, if necessary. The white man has no soul. You are dealing with a heartless sort of person, if you are talking to a white man.' As the persona of Michael X took over from that of Michael de

Freitas, he urged his audience to be prepared to kill. He himself was not only prepared to kill whites, he had actually done so. 'A book I read said I would not be able to sleep at night. But that is not true. You can sleep at night. And I sleep very well. I am no longer afraid.'

He denounced the police in England for taking innocent black people into custody, pushing their heads into police station toilets and flushing them. He denounced the white race for their violence and rape in destroying black culture. And finally he poured scorn on the white liberals who preferred to sympathize with the plight of black people rather than persuade the white community to mend its ways.

It was what his audience had come to hear. Next morning, the reports of his speech were in the national press. He had stood before their representatives and incited racial hatred, which was an offence under the Race Relations Act of 1965. He had also boasted of committing murder but there was no evidence of that apart from his own statement. He was not the only person prosecuted in 1967–68 under the provisions of the Race Relations Act. At Lewes Assizes, his white counterparts stood trial for racial incitement in their newspaper, the *Racial Preservation Society Southern News*. The white jury acquitted them. Michael de Freitas was convicted as was Roy Sawh who, speaking at Speakers' Corner in Hyde Park, said, 'If I call a white man a monkey, I am paying him a compliment. Killing whites does not count as murder. English people should be shot and you should shed blood for your freedom.'

Michael de Freitas defended himself at Reading Quarter Sessions, insisting that he would take the oath on the Koran. After the jury returned its verdict of guilty, the judge remarked that de Freitas had come to Reading 'to make trouble' and that 'you knew perfectly well what a mischievous act you were doing.' He sent the defendant to prison for a year. Before he was removed from the dock, Michael X managed to say 'You represent white justice and you have shown how it is you work out that. So my people know how to deal with you from now on.' His appeal against conviction was dismissed.

The press, which had hailed him as 'the authentic voice of black bitterness' now moved in for the kill. On 3 September 1967, the right-wing *Daily Mail* revealed his past as Rachman's rent collector, as one who had run brothels and gaming rackets. Despite his hatred for the white race, he had a white girlfriend and a child by another white girl. Perhaps the paper should have noticed that in his speech his hatred was of white men, not their women. Their women parted with money. And if a white woman was also what he called 'a chick that it was nice to make', so much the better.

He served his sentence in Swansea Prison and was released in July 1968. On his release he briefly joined a militant organization, the Black Eagles, as 'Minister of Defence'. More mundanely, his autobiography had been published while he was in prison and had been a flop. He next appeared in the press in 1969, when he was charged with possession of cannabis. Though he had been dealing in it, only a small quantity was found and he was given a conditional discharge.

The quality of a comedian, which showed in him from time to time, was evident at an earnest public meeting where the problems of racial integration were discussed. All the Labour government's efforts to engineer social acceptance of black immigrants, enforcing this by law where necessary, had been unproductive. Unlike the liberal middle class, the white working-class was more determinedly racist than it had ever been. The one institution which undoubtedly stood for racial equality and harmony was the royal family, the focus of the multi-racial British Commonwealth. A speaker at the meeting saw a way to promote social acceptance of racial tolerance.

'I'll tell you the way to get harmonious race relations in this country. You must encourage the Queen to adopt a black baby. We must petition her to do this.'

There was an awkward pause which ended with a loud and confident interjection from Michael X.

'Don't encourage her to adopt one. Let her have one!'

The sardonic suggestion annoyed a good many people, some because they thought it disrespectful, some because it confirmed that the black revolutionary was merely playing a part in which he had never truly believed.

As a political leader without a movement, he needed substantial financial backing and premises for his headquarters. From the wealthy and the well-meaning, he raised money to buy some derelict shops in north Islington which were to be an ethnic cultural centre and commercial enterprise. He proposed to develop an 'urban village' there. It came to nothing, though under the name of the Black House it was one of the most grotesque ironies of his career. To anyone who knew the British political history of the previous thirty years, the Black House was the name given by the British Union of Fascists – the Blackshirt movement of Sir Oswald Mosley – to its headquarters in the King's Road, Chelsea. Did the new leader of racial revolution not know this, or did he not care?

By now, he was the fully fledged Michael X, with a prison record for incitement to prove his credentials and a legend that involved the murder of at least one white man. White men and women of the middle classes gave him money, white middle-class women gave their bodies, presumably from the same sense of colonial and cultural guilt. The Black House never achieved its most modest ambitions but its presiding spirit now gathered new followers and associates.

One of these was an American black who called himself Hakim Jamal and described himself in a *Guardian* interview as 'excruciatingly handsome, tantalizingly brown, fiercely articulate'. As his interviewer, Jill Tweedie wrote, when Jamal referred to white people, 'No SS man could invest the word "Jew" with any more contempt.' Jamal professed to be a black American Muslim and claimed to have founded a Malcolm X Montessori school in California. In the course of a BBC radio interview, he also claimed to be God.

It was not long before God and Michael X got together. At a dinner party given by the actress Vanessa Redgrave, Jamal also met a young white woman. She was twenty-seven years old, divorced, and her family was rich. Her father had been a Conservative Member of Parliament. Her name was Gale Benson, a member of the well-heeled bourgeoisie of

Kensington and Chelsea. Jamal tested her for racial guilt and found it. He let Gale Benson, with the tight pink knee boots and the expensive clothes, lament the plight of black people a little longer at the dinner party where they met. Then he said,

'How would you know anything about it? How would you feel about having a black baby?'

'I wouldn't mind,' she said.

'Good,' Jamal said, 'Let's go find out.'

And so they did. Gale Benson became less the lover than the slave of her new master, in a reversal of colonial roles. She was to be known in her new guise as Halé Kimga, not an African name but an anagram of 'Gale' and 'Hakim', Jamal's first name. Michael X's wife was later to describe her as 'sort of a fake'. Cruel though the judgment was, in the circumstances of the young woman's death, it was hard to deny the truth of it. Gale Benson adopted African dresses, headscarves and ornaments but kept the tight pink knee boots and European underwear. Despite the simplicity of the ethnic style, money 'oozed from her clothes', as Mrs Malik described her. In fairness, her peers in the well-heeled white middle class of London were often fakes on a much grander scale. They cultivated the working class or the black community and insinuatingly regretted their own privileged backgrounds. 'I was at Eton, actually,' said one fluting voice to the horny-handed sons of Communist toil, 'but goodness, don't think I'm not ashamed of it.'

As for Gale Benson's new lover, whatever the BBC might think, Jamal was God to her. She knelt before him when she had a request and her subservience, though not her sexual submission, extended to Michael X. After her death, the pathologist Keith Simpson quoted Michael X on Gale Benson. As leader of the commune, he had power over her and, as he said, he hated her. He did 'all sorts of evil things to her'. Whenever his hatred needed violent expression, he tied her spreadeagled over a bed, took a horsewhip and 'beat her until I was tired'. As he said, 'she never complained'. Perhaps, as Michael X whipped her, Gale Benson saw herself as expiating her nation's guilt for the numbers of West Indian women flogged by the British army on such occasions as the so-called 'Jamaican Mutiny' of 1865. She evidently ignored the possibility that the deaths of black people at the hands of her own white race might also have to be avenged.

II

Michael de Freitas spent fourteen years in England, first as a petty criminal and then as a less-petty criminal and exploiter of the politically gullible. He was soon to boast that London had made him 'the best-known Black man in this entire western world'. However absurd the boast might seem, it impressed those who heard it in Trinidad. Yet the good time was not going to last much longer. Soon it became clear that the only future for Michael de Freitas was either in Trinidad or in an English prison.

The trouble came from what was almost a trivial incident to begin with. A black man, Leroy House, had gone to work for a white employer who demanded some security for giving him the job. Mr House had no money and so the white man took his ring as a pledge. But when the black man came to collect his first wages, they were not enough to redeem the ring. It was at this point that Michael X and his lieutenants arrived at the employer's offices. There was a long argument over the treatment of Leroy House. It ended with Michael X picking up the firm's books and walking out with them, telling the employer that he could come and collect them from the Black House in north Islington later on.

When the employer arrived at the Black House to collect his firm's books, he brought the police with him. Michael X demanded to know whether the police officers had a search warrant. They had not and he ordered them off the premises. Leroy House's employer was told to go away and return later still for his firm's books. When he came back, the police waited outside. Inside the building, the employer was subjected to a political harangue. This ended when he was seized by some of those present and a spiked plantation slave-collar was fastened round his neck. The spikes pointed inwards and unless the victim obeyed his handlers, the sharp tips would pierce his neck and probably his jugular vein with fatal results. The employer was terrified by this ritual. He was weeping with fright by the time that he was made to promise that he would report to the Black House annually with a week's wages. Money was also taken from his wallet, though he was given a copy of Michael X's autobiography as an exchange. He was not, of course, asked if he agreed to this arrangement.

As so often, the incident mingled menace with farce. The result was, however, that a week later Michael X and seven other men were charged with robbery. On 12 October 1971 the leader was committed for trial at the Old Bailey. Though free on bail, he was dismayed to hear that the crime for which he was to be tried might well carry a sentence of fourteen years in prison. Though the robbery had been incompetent and even absurd, he was unlikely to get much sympathy from the court on that account. Faced with the threat of a long term in prison, he decided to abscond. On 2 February 1971, some months before the case was due to be heard, he slipped out of Heathrow airport on a flight to Trinidad where he would be safe from extradition. Perhaps the British authorities were not entirely disappointed at his escape. Overwhelmingly, they felt glad to see the last of him.

Soon after his return to Trinidad, the self-styled leader of the Black Liberation Army, describing himself now more modestly as a journalist, rented the bungalow in Christina Gardens, Arima, with its acre and a half of land. Here his commune was founded and visited by John Lennon, Yoko Ono, and less famous admirers. To another house in Christina Gardens came Gale Benson and Hakim Jamal. There were other fugitives from England, including Stanley Abbott, whom Michael X, or Michael Abdul Malik as he now called himself, had left in charge of what remained of the Black House project in Islington. Trina Simmonds and Grainger Drake were among his white English followers. There was also an Indian girl, Hazra Habib. And, of course, the leader's wife and children accompanied him.

In the provincial life of Trinidad, Michael Abdul Malik with his famous friends seemed a figure of far greater stature than he had done back in London. His immediate ambition was the overthrow of the present government of the island and the establishment of his own regime. To anyone in his senses this might have seemed ridiculous. However, the government of Eric Williams had been in power for a long time and was not popular. Indeed, there had already been an attempt to unseat it by force. It might after all be opportune for the Black Liberation Army to make its bid. Like an episode from situation comedy, the future leader and commander-in-chief named members of the commune as military commanders or cabinet ministers.

The question throughout 1971 was, once again, whether terror or farce would prevail. The answer came at the turn of the year. Michael Abdul Malik despised Gale Benson. Of course, she was subservient to him but, as he later said, 'I didn't love her for this, I hated her.' It was significant that Michael Abdul Malik had spent most of his life as Michael de Freitas and that his profession had been that of a pimp. To Michael de Freitas, white women were whores who worked the streets for him. Many did. But Gale Benson with her fashionable clothes and money was another type, pretentious and irritating. She was a white slave who had got above herself.

During 1971 the leaders of the commune smuggled drugs and acquired arms. Perhaps they were consoled by the thought that the new day of revolution was about to dawn. Certainly they had little money to show for their activities. By the end of the year, they had been joined by Stanley Abbott from London and a number of others who lived in the opposite bungalow, 43 Christina Gardens. Abbott himself left England while on bail awaiting trial on charges of burglary. Another arrival from the United States, known only as Kidogo, was an underworld thug. He was a killer by choice and to kill Gale Benson was a favour he readily accepted.

It was at the end of 1971 that Malik, as he was now universally called, saw Gale Benson photographing his collection of African carvings. Some of these had been acquired by theft. He believed, or said he did, that she was actually a secret agent of M10 gathering intelligence against him. On the evening of 31 December, he called several men of the commune together, including Abbott, Steve Yeates, Kidogo, Adolphus 'Sonny' Parmassar and Edward Chadee, most of whom occupied the opposite bungalow, Malik's being reserved for his family.

Malik told this group that Gale Benson, also known as Halé, was imposing too much mental strain on Hakim Jamal. 'She must be liquidated.' Abbott suggested that they should just put her on the plane to London. 'There is no need to kill her.' But Yeates said, 'I want something definite.' And Malik said, 'I want blood. That is the only thing that will keep us together.' He announced that Gale Benson would be put to death the following morning, 1 January 1972. They would get up early and Yeates would drive her to Lorenco's farm to get milk. While she was away, they would dig her grave. Malik would take Hakim Jamal out in his car. As soon as Gale Benson came back, they would push her into the grave, kill her, and fill in the hole. Kidogo would do the killing with a cutlass. There would be no evidence anywhere but in the grave itself.

Next morning, it was Abbott who still argued against killing Gale Benson as the grave was dug. Malik was displeased. 'I don't want any of the old talk from last night about backing out,' he told Abbott. If Abbott tried backing out, he would be the one who died, 'with the knowledge that your mother will soon be as dead as you.' When Gale Benson came back from the farm with Yeates, Abbott was to grab her and jump into the grave with her. He would then hold her while Kidogo slashed her to death with a cutlass. There would be no noise or gunfire to disturb the Malik family in the bungalow. Abbott stopped arguing. On Malik's orders, he reminded Kidogo where the heart was, underneath the left breast.

Gale Benson had just got up and was standing in a pair of panties when Yeates arrived to ask her to come to the farm.

179

She slipped a dress on over her head, said 'Bye, lover' to Hakim Jamal who was still in bed, and went off in the jeep. Malik then got into his car and drove off, ostensibly to take Jamal out of the way while all this was happening. They went to see Stanley Abbott's mother, a retired school teacher. If it was possible to have an alibi, Malik had provided himself with one.

By the time the jeep returned, the hole was five feet deep. Yeates brought Gale Benson over to it and she asked what it was for. Abbott told her it was for decomposing garden refuse. He led her a little closer. Then he put an arm round her neck, a hand over her mouth and jumped into it with her, one of her arms twisted up behind her back. 'It's for you.' he said.

Gale Benson cried out to Yeates, 'Steve! What have I done to deserve this?'

Malik could have told her but he was not there. The young woman's question was ignored. In any case, she was not to die for what she had done but for what she was. Kidogo leapt in and his cutlass slashed Gale Benson's free arm as she raised it to protect her face. For several minutes he slashed at her without seeming in a hurry to kill her. Abbott shouted, 'For Christ's sake, somebody do something.' Then Yeates jumped in and took the cutlass as Gale Benson fell back against the side of the grave. Yeates brought the cutlass down vertically into the base of her throat and into her lungs. She dropped to the earth, though her legs were moving and she was not yet dead. The men scrambled out and shovelled a foot of earth on top of her. Manure was fetched and the hole filled in with that. Though still moving she was buried, Gale Benson could not have survived long after the final wound.

Malik returned, having first telephoned from Mrs Abbott's house to make sure the job was finished. The story, which Hakim Jamal also told, was that Gale Benson had left the commune. Accordingly, it was important that her possessions should disappear. Later that day, they were taken eight miles away to the bank of a stream. What could be burnt was burnt. The other items, including two suitcases and the pink knee high boots, were buried. Jamal left for the United States to raise $36,000 on behalf of the commune and, apparently, to follow Gale Benson. After three weeks or so, the professional killer Kidogo left and was never seen again. On the evening of Gale Benson's death, Malik spoke to those who had butchered the young woman.

'You are members for life and cannot resign.'

So far as Malik could see, that was the end of the matter. Jamal had gone to the United States and so, it appeared to others, had Gale Benson. Kidogo had vanished. Chadee and Parmassar had everything to gain from keeping their mouths shut. Abbott was a principal accomplice in the murder. Malik could even claim to have an alibi. The body on the northern fringe of land would be most unlikely to be discovered by accident.

But little more than a month later, Malik once again said, 'I want blood.' This time it was the blood of a member of his family, his cousin Joseph Skerritt, son of his mother's sister Edna Skerritt, 'Aunt Tanty'. Joseph Skerritt was a simple and humble contrast to Gale Benson but he was a member of the commune. As the time for the Black Liberation Army to march grew closer, there was need for more weapons. Malik hit on the idea of robbing a police-station to get guns and uniforms. Joseph Skerritt, a frightened little man, refused to have anything to do with the plan.

Skerritt was still living in his mother's house at Belmont, where Malik had been born. On 7 February, however, he was brought to the bungalow at Arima. Malik gave orders to his henchmen that another hole was to be dug next morning and that Skerritt was to be told that it was a soak-away. Indeed, why not make Skerritt dig it, since he was cause of all the trouble? As for the execution, Malik would carry out that himself.

Yeates, Chadee, Parmassar, Abbott and Samuel Brown were also present when the grave was dug. Only Abbott, Parmassar, Skerritt and Malik were still there when, at about noon, Malik jumped into the grave, cutlass in hand. 'I'm ready now,' he called to Abbott, 'Bring him.' Abbott hesitated but then clamped his arm round Skerritt's neck and jumped with him into the hole. Skerritt went sprawling. Malik grabbed his victim by the hair to steady his head, holding him face down, then chopped at the back of his neck with a cutlass.

Having inflicted a terrible wound, Malik scrambled out of the grave, only to see that Skerritt was not yet dead. Reaching for several large stones, Malik threw them in, as if to smash Skerritt's skull. But the dying victim got to his feet and began running and stumbling about the grave. His jugular vein was severed and his spinal cord was badly damaged, as he fell about, crying, 'Oh, God! Oh, God! I go tell! I go tell!' Malik ended the botched killing by taking a large stone in both hands and dropping it on Skerritt's head. The injured man fell to the earth and moved no more. The sentence of the Black Liberation Army's commander having been carried out, the grave was filled in and lettuces planted on top.

There was one more death, which was never adequately explained. Two days later there was a beach party at Sans Souci on the north coast of the island. Parmassar was there with Abbott, Yeates, and the Indian girl, Hazra Habib. Yeates swam out and got caught in the undertow. A rope was thrown to him but he failed to grasp it. He might have let the tide carry him out but he did not. As he went under, it was said that he gave the clenched fist salute. Was it possible that he had chosen to die this way? Some witnesses thought so and some did not. His body was never found.

Having misguidedly believed himself safe after the other two bodies were buried, Michael de Freitas, as the law now called him once more, faced trial for the murder of Joseph Skerritt. He was also charged with the murder of Gale Benson but not brought to trial for that. Charged with him for Skerritt's murder were Samuel Brown and Stanley Abbott. Adolphus 'Sonny' Parmassar was accepted as a prosecution witness and gave evidence of the killing. Michael de Freitas made a statement from the dock and Stanley Abbott gave evidence. But suspicion was almost conclusive in itself. Parmassar's evidence merely added the details. On 21 August 1972, it took the Port-of-Spain jury an hour and a half to find Michael de Freitas guilty of murder and Stanley Abbott guilty of manslaughter. Michael de Freitas was sentenced to death and Stanley Abbott to twenty years in prison. He lived to serve only seven of them before being executed for the murder of Gale Benson.

Hanging had been abolished in England but the Royal Gaol in Port-of-Spain still kept its gallows of English design, supplied with hangman's rope made in Birmingham. Michael de Freitas was represented by Louis Blom-Cooper QC in the Trinidad Court of Appeal. He appealed on the grounds that hanging was a cruel and unusual punishment and that this was exacerbated by the long delay between his conviction and the date proposed for execution. The appellant objected that no psychiatric examination had been made to determine if Michael de Freitas was insane and that the Mercy Committee of the Trinidad judiciary had not heard outside evidence. The appeal was dismissed. The next step was a Privy Council hearing in London, where it was argued that the sentence was unconstitutional. This too failed.

While capital punishment had been used in England, no prisoner had ever been kept waiting to die for almost three years, which was the fate of Michael de Freitas. Where there was a long judicial process after a trial in England, the condemned man was reprieved as a matter of humanity. Yet Michael X was not idle while he waited to die. In Port-of-Spain it was reported that even from the death cell the influence of the self-appointed Black Power leader could be felt. He was allowed a bed and books. His mail was not censored. When, on 2 May 1973, four men called on Hakim Jamal in Boston, Massachusetts and shot him dead, the hand of Michael X was thought to be at work. There were plans for a gaol-break in Trinidad but these came to nothing.

The world outside remembered him briefly. There were petitions and protests at the 'legitimized murder' which his sentence represented. One petition, signed by John Lennon, Yoko Ono, Kate Millett and other luminaries of the decade, described him as a political prisoner. Yet the one valid argument against executing him was that capital punishment was an evil, rather than that this one man deserved special treatment.

After all this, Michael de Freitas was hanged at last in the Royal Gaol on 16 May 1975. A carpenter had been to measure him for his coffin on the previous day, one of the more macabre rituals of justice on the island. On the morning of his death, he was reading the comic supplement from the previous Sunday's paper when the hangman, his assistant, and four warders trained in judo entered the cell.

Without the fire at Arima, on 19 February 1972, there was no reason why the two graves in the garden should ever have been discovered. It was accepted that Gale Benson had gone to Boston. Joseph Skerritt might have gone anywhere. No one would search for him. If Michael de Freitas had arranged the fire as a solution to his financial difficulties, then he put the rope round his own neck. By the time he paid that penalty, he had lost both fame and reputation.

Of course, he did not see it in that light. After his death, a letter was delivered to Patrick Chokolingo, editor of the Trinidadian magazine *The Bomb*.

> *By the time you get this letter, Patrick, I will be gone and the whole world will realize what a monumental loss they have suffered.*
>
>
> *Signed*
> *'Peace and Love'*
> *Michael Abdul Malik*
>

SIX

The Body in the Carpet
(1981–91)

I

Dusk came early to the riverside houses of Fitzhamon Embankment in Cardiff on 7 December 1989. Sunset was at 4.05pm, with a promise from the Weather Centre of freezing fog that night. Fitzhamon Embankment was a terrace of late-Victorian houses about a mile or so above the decaying dockland of Butetown's 'Tiger Bay'. It was separated from the shallow sodium-lit waters of the river Taff by the street and a wide pavement along the river bank. Despite its air of dereliction, the houses were not far removed from the brighter and more prosperous streets at the city's centre. Half a mile away across the river, that Thursday evening was sacred to late-night shopping. Page-wide Christmas advertisements in the local press warned excitedly of '15 more shopping days to go.' Howells, 'The Harrods of Wales', and its competitors offered warmly-lit seasonal plenty of a kind not much in evidence on the embankment side of the river. The display windows of St Mary Street and Queen Street shone bravely over the unemployment and recession which were felt acutely in south Wales. As an economy, these traffic-laden shopping streets were strung with Christmas lights that had hung in someone else's city the year before and would hang somewhere else next Christmas.

Solidly-built rather than handsome, the four-storey terrace houses of Fitzhamon Embankment had been designed as matching pairs. In the 1880s and 1890s they were the homes of clerks and inspectors, managers and ships' officers rather than of the shippers and coal-owners themselves. The commercial magnates who brought Edwardian prosperity to the more fortunate of Cardiff's citizens preferred the baronial style of Cathedral Road or the sea view from Penarth's Marine Parade.

Long before 1989, prosperity had withdrawn further from Fitzhamon Embankment than the receding tide from the fallen pier-head and dockland mudflats a mile downstream. In the weeks to come it was to be said repeatedly by police and the media that the Riverside area of Cardiff was occupied by a transient population in flats and bedsits. Waiters and desk-clerks, bouncers and porters, the casually and partially employed, made up much of the through traffic. They stayed a few months, weeks or days, in houses where the Edwardian clerks and managers had rooted themselves for life.

From their flats or their bedsits, the latest inhabitants of the embankment looked across the shallows of the mud-brown river to the multi-angled concrete fortress of the new grand-stand at the international rugby ground of the Arms Park. To one side was the Empire Pool, one of the latest monuments the Empire ever produced. With its plain brick walls and curved roof like an aircraft hangar, it commemorated municipal socialism's sport-for-the-masses in the austere days following World War II. Downstream were road and rail bridges, running into Cardiff Central station, whose long platforms were visible from the houses, and the tall dark smoke-stack of Welsh Brewers.

The Embankment was certainly no worse provided than the dockland streets of Butetown or Adamstown. Indeed, there was even a hint of renewal - one pair of houses in the terrace was being systematically renovated. By dusk on that December day, numbers 27 and 29 had been virtually gutted. The ground floor windows were boarded over but those on the upper floors stood open and dark, showing the premises as little more than a shell. A change of ownership had brought this about, the new landlord bent on improvement. Five months earlier, the last tenants had moved out and the houses had been handed over to the builders in the autumn.

CHAPTER SIX

The only access to the rear of the terrace was by a narrow high-walled lane that ran between the back yards of parallel streets. Here and there the rear walls were broken down. The 'gardens' behind them were not large and some were more or less filled by garages of prefabricated concrete. At 27 and 29, which formed a single unit, four workmen had already levelled the garden with an earth-mover, lowering the surface by two feet. Now they were digging a trench near the wall which divided 29 Fitzhamon Embankment from the adjoining property, 31. The trench was intended to contain a new soil-pipe from the bathroom above.

The four men had been digging with pickaxes and shovels. Fifteen minutes before sunset they were almost at the end of the task, lowering the surface a further six inches. At 3.50pm, Paul Bodenham saw a piece of orange-red material in the clay. With his three companions, he carefully scraped away the earth by hand, revealing the end of a roll of carpet which had been bound by black electric cable. As they drew the bundle clear, he sensed what was to follow.

'I had an awful feeling there was a body in there. We unwrapped the carpet and saw part of the body which was covered in polythene. There wasn't much of it left, just a lot of bones. We didn't see the head. As soon as we saw the bones, we left it alone and called the police.'

Plastic is more durable than human flesh. There was a white bag over the head of the skeleton and a black covering – a dustbin-liner – over the upper half of the body. Some of the clothes had survived as well and the skeleton was still partially clad.

There was one other piece of information that Paul Bodenham, Sidney Williams, Keith Lloyd and Bill David could offer. They agreed that the carpet in the makeshift grave seemed identical to one which they had taken up from the basement flat of 29 Fitzhamon Embankment. Unfortunately, that carpet and the rest of the material stripped from the house had gone into a refuse-skip and on to one of Cardiff's large municipal tips a month or two earlier. At this stage, the connection with the basement flat was a possibility rather than a fact. The piece of carpet in which the body had been wrapped had certainly not been taken from the floor of the basement flat, since that was fully carpeted when the workmen had stripped it. Moreover, this particular carpet was Shaw's beige-brown Kaleidoscope, a relatively common make which was sold in some quantity by South Wales Carpets at their shop in Clifton Street, off the busy Newport Road.

In the tawny sodium glare of the winter evening, the South Wales CID under Chief Superintendent John Williams moved in and erected a polythene tent over the grave and the skeleton. The first examination began as the homeward-bound commuters piled into their cars or local trains and withdrew to the middle-class comforts of hillside Cyncoed or seaside Penarth, to white-collar Llanishen or the executive ruralism of the Vale of Glamorgan. They left such areas as Riverside and Butetown to those who had nowhere else to go.

Chief Superintendent Williams and his deputy, Superintendent Neale Evans, faced several specific questions. In other circumstances, the questions would have been routine. In this case, they promised a work-load that was enough to break the collective back of CID.

What was the identity of the body in the back-garden grave?

How accurately could the date of death be determined?

Was it possible to trace and question scores or even hundreds of people who had lived at 27 and 29 Fitzhamon Embankment during any material period of time?

Had a murder taken place, rather than a death by accident or misadventure?

Chief Superintendent Williams' team set out to establish answers. Before long, the press was describing that task as 'enormous' or 'mammoth' and the thought behind this was that such answers might prove unattainable. It was a matter of chance that the body had been discovered at all. 'If it hadn't been for the renovation work going on at present, it could have remained hidden a good while longer,' Chief Superintendent Williams said that night. The truth was that it might have remained hidden indefinitely or at least until the skeleton had crumbled to dust. Renovation was still the exception rather than the rule in Fitzhamon Embankment.

As the chill of the night fog gathered, the remains of the unknown victim were removed to the Victorian workhouse-gothic of Cardiff Royal Infirmary. On the morning of the next day, Friday 8 December, the skeleton was reported as being that of a young woman in her late teens or early twenties. She had been dead 'for two months or as long as two years.' She was a white woman, five feet four inches in height, well-developed and with 'prominent front-teeth'. Her body had been wrapped in polythene within the carpet, then buried face-down. Black cable of the kind used to tie the carpet had also tied her wrists behind her back. She was semi-naked at the time of burial, wearing a grey American-made sweat-shirt and a pair of pink and white striped socks. Later, the police added 'a pair of panties' to this attire but still the suggestion was plain that sex had played some part in her downfall. Gold stud earrings had been found among her remains and also a button, made by a company called Karmen Ghia. This had apparently come from a pair of jeans.

The two houses on Fitzhamon Embankment, 27 and 29, remained behind a police barrier while soil samples and other evidence were gathered in the back garden. One possible short-cut in the investigation was to find someone who had known the missing girl. 'IF YOU LIVED HERE, CALL POLICE,' was the headline appeal on Friday, followed by 'DID YOU SEE HER A YEAR AGO?' on Saturday. The names of those living at 29 Fitzhamon Embankment had last been listed in the Electoral Register for October 1988. These names were now published in the press, three men and seven women. But each of the two houses at 27 and 29 had ten rooms. As the police admitted, they were occupied by a constantly changing population. Some tenants might stay a year, most for much less than that. 'There is also the possibility that some people stayed for a week or just a few days.' South Wales CID estimated that there could be a hundred people for a two-year period. As the possible time span extended, this figure rose to seven hundred. Worse still, tenants might have had others living with them who were not listed anywhere. This certainly proved to be so in the basement flat. The majority of those sought came forward. Others were scattered throughout the country or abroad with no idea that they were being looked for. It was not impossible that some belonged to a sub-culture which preferred not to respond to police invitations for what-ever reason. In the end, there were twenty people who had lived at 29 Fitzhamon Embankment during the preceding two years and who could be traced. As it happened, they were not needed anyway.

Of those who came forward, not one could remember see-ing a girl of the description they were given. There was, of course, another possibility. It was relatively easy to get into the back garden from the lane. The rear garden wall of the property was in a bad state of repair. Two or three people could have brought a body in and buried it in a shallow grave. Though the grave was close to the door of the basement flat, that flat was not always occupied. It was not the most likely explanation but such a burial would have diverted suspicion from someone who had killed the girl elsewhere or who hoped to conceal her death. This was a theory that was to be heard again.

On the second morning of the inquiry, the description of the victim became more precise after a dental examination of the skull by Dr David Whittaker. Though the wisdom teeth had not erupted, the development of the molar teeth made it pos-sible to determine the age at death with greater accuracy. The roots of the second molar teeth were fully developed, which would be the case at fifteen. The third molar teeth would establish their roots from the ages of fifteen to eighteen and this process was not very far advanced. At first it was pos-sible to say that the girl was between fifteen and seventeen when she died. After the weekend, the 'preferred age' at death was put at fifteen and a half. There was a further piece of dental evidence. Though none of the bones in the girl's throat appeared to have been broken, the teeth showed a pink discoloration. This indicated a strong possibility that strangulation was the cause of death. From that point, it was difficult to see the inquiry as other than a murder hunt.

What of her appearance or even her racial origin? In an area as racially mixed as Riverside and the dockland streets of Butetown, this was of some importance. The Natural History Museum in London compared the skull with a database of 2,500 others. From this the girl was identified as European or Indian. The few strands of hair still adhering to the scalp revealed her as fair-haired and determined that she was European. However, it was suggested that she was of Mediterranean rather than British origin.

'We have yet to establish the time and cause of death,' Chief Superintendent Williams added, 'but we appeal to people to think of a young girl with prominent teeth and light-coloured hair who frequented the Riverside area of Cardiff twelve months ago – or even longer.'

There was no response. That weekend, as the murder squad officers began house-to-house inquiries in the Riverside streets, a check was made on missing persons files for the south Wales area. There was no one listed who matched the girl's description. Superintendent John Williams was 'disturbed that a person as young, found under these circum-stances, is not on the missing persons list locally.' The check on files was extended nationwide, with no better result.

By the end of the first week of the investigation, no one could be found who had seen a girl of this description in the Riverside area, or anywhere else for that matter. No one had reported her missing. The cause of death was still in doubt. Though the bones of the neck were intact, she could have been strangled. A girl whose body was found in such circum-stances might have died of a drug overdose, or from the effects of glue sniffing or butane gas inhalation, perhaps even from an illegal abortion. Her companions, disinclined to face the police after the misadventure, might simply have buried her body. Murder was a more sensational explanation, of course, but it was statistically less probable.

The dental experts were called upon once more. A dental chart was 'pieced together' from the skull and this was to be shown to every dentist in Cardiff and the surrounding area. It was another 'mammoth' task. The CID team would start at the city centre and work outwards. If the girl had been the patient of a dentist elsewhere, that would be bad luck. Moreover, while it would be simple to compare a chart with that of someone already known, this chart might have to be compared with that of a good number of people. As yet, the comparisons produced nothing.

There was, understandably, a note of exasperation in police appeals as the days went by. Surely a girl of fifteen must have had parents who would know if she had left home and never returned. If she had gone missing from a school or institution of some kind, that would have been reported. Had she come from another area? By extending these inquiries throughout the country, however, the investigation had gained nothing.

Paradoxically, the national press proved to be among the most provincial in its treatment of the case. Even if this were to be the most intriguing murder mystery of the decade, it had happened outside London and was therefore of less significance. The *Independent*, which gave the most coverage to the investigation and subsequent trial, offered a four-line report on page 6 when the body was found. Nationally, those people who might have been able to help the police would simply not know that their help was required.

To put the problem in context, 4,765 people were reported missing in the south Wales area during 1989. Most were not really missing at all or were soon accounted for. At the end of that year, however, there were still twenty-two people who could not be found and who might as easily have been dead as alive. A complication in the present case was the racial origin of the dead girl. On 12 December, it had been announced that police were working on the assumption that she had been a British national. At first this seemed self-evident but the features of the skull still belied a British ancestry. Moreover, she still appeared to have no parents, no school, no dental record as yet, and no name.

Before the inquiry was over, something was to be heard about girls who prostituted themselves on foreign ships while they were in port. It was not particularly difficult to get on and off the ships that were berthed at Cardiff or the nearby ports of Barry and Newport. Could this be the case of a girl who had come from elsewhere, as an adolescent provider of comforts to a ship's crew, and had found herself adrift in Cardiff dockland? She might have come from Europe or even the United States or South America. It would explain why, though white, she showed certain non-British characteristics in her facial structure.

Such a possibility was overtaken by the results of further scientific examination. Evidence sifted from the makeshift grave proved that the South Wales CID had been unwittingly wasting their time by talking to those who were residents at 27 and 29 Fitzhamon Embankment during the previous two years. The soil samples and the skeleton had now become the province of Dr Zakaria Erzinclioglu, an entomologist from the University of Cambridge. The grave in which the skeleton had been found had supported a population of phorid fly maggots, a species of coffin fly, which had consumed the flesh of the corpse. As Dr Erzinclioglu explained to the Crown Court in Cardiff, this process would have taken about three years.

Dr Erzinclioglu also found a colony of woodlice living off the fungus of the bones. That colony would have taken a further two years to establish itself in the fungus after the flesh had been eaten away. So the police now had to look for a girl who had gone missing in 1984 rather than in 1987. More precisely, it seemed that she must have died during the summer and that her body had not been buried for several days. This was indicated when larval cases of the blow-fly were found in the remains. Their presence suggested that the body had been left long enough before burial for the blow-fly eggs to be laid and that this would have happened during the breeding season, from March to October. The most likely time of death was therefore moved back to somewhere between March and October 1984.

To trace those who had been residents in Fitzhamon Embankment in 1987 had been difficult enough. Twenty people out of a hundred seemed to have vanished completely. It was far more complicated to track down those who had left even three years further back. Some of the tenants in the houses were elderly, some might even be dead by this time. Despite all the publicity surrounding the earlier date, no one came forward to report the loss of a fifteen-year-old daughter, pupil, or inmate of an institution.

Within little more than a week from the discovery of the skeleton, the press dropped the case from its columns. Christmas was ten days away and there were topics of more immediate importance. US troops were hunting General Noriega in Panama. Romanians were hunting their ousted president, Ceausescu.

So far as the South Wales police made headlines, it was by virtue of record attacks and injuries upon them over the Christmas holiday. The season of good will left twenty-four officers, including four women, injured by members of the public and fifteen patrol cars damaged. Three of Cardiff's pubs closed down completely for New Year's Eve rather than face destruction at the hands of their customers.

The city returned slowly to life after its fortnight's hibernation. On 8 January, the local press published photographs of a face apparently fresh from a mud-pack. 'Did you know this girl?' The same pictures appeared in the national press. The South Wales CID had now won attention from London journalists by having a clay model made of the dead girl's face, based on the dimensions of the skull.

Richard Neave, a medical artist from Manchester University, had created the sculpture. He had already successfully recreated the features from a skull which survived the King's Cross station fire, in order to identify the unknown victim. He had now used a cast of the skull from Fitzhamon Embankment to work out the shape of the nose, the ears, and the other facial features. The sculpture he produced was photographed from various angles and the photographs were soon used on television appeals and on police posters, seeking information about the girl, fifteen and a half years old at the time of her death.

Chief Superintendent Williams released further information. The clothes on the skeleton had been examined and, so far as possible, dated. Most of the clothing was made in England. Though the Levi sweat shirt has been made in the United States, it had also been distributed in the United Kingdom. The earliest date for this was December 1980, so the girl must have been alive then. It was probable that she was still alive a year later and possible that she was alive between 1981 and 1984.

As for the possibility that she had come from abroad, dental examination of the skull and of fillings in the teeth showed that they had been carried out in England twelve months before her death. She had, at least, spent the last year of her life in the United Kingdom.

That was as far as the investigations had got. There was still no post mortem evidence to show beyond doubt how the girl had met her death, let alone evidence to show that this was murder rather than accident or misadventure. Though it sounded a note of desperation, the South Wales CID had nothing to lose by trying to frighten a possible culprit into the open. They urged the person who knew how the girl had met her death to come forward. 'Should that person come forward, then he or she will not have to fear for the consequences so greatly as if we come to them at the end of the day.' That scarcely sounded like a suspicion of murder.

Unfortunately for the South Wales police, two recent cases had made it less likely that anyone would come forward to them. The 1986 conviction of Paul and Wayne Darvell for the so-called 'Sex Shop Murder' in Swansea rested almost solely on the confession of Wayne Darvell. The conviction had been questioned by the campaign group Justice and five hundred South Wales police notebooks were currently being examined by the Devon and Cornwall police. In July 1992 the Court of Appeal set free the two Darvell brothers on the grounds that their convictions were unsafe. The appeal was not contested by the Crown. By then it was shown that certain entries in police notebooks could not have been made at the time claimed and there was a suggestion that an earring belonging to the murdered woman, Sandra Phillips, might have been planted in the police car in which the two accused had travelled. The 1989–90 trial of five men for the murder of Butetown prostitute Lynett White also turned on the confession of one of them, Stephen Miller, who afterwards denied his guilt. In neither case was there any convincing forensic evidence. The Lynett White murder case was being tried in Swansea even as the South Wales CID issued its appeal.

There was bad news on another front, where the police described themselves as 'disappointed' with the response to the sculpture of the dead girl and the newspaper photographs. The special incident room at Cardiff's Norbury Road Police Station had received only three or four serious calls on its confidential line. The problem with the medical sculpture was that, however accurate, its mud-coloured contours looked unlike a real person to many of those who saw it. Some leap of imagination or interpretation was also necessary.

Another week passed. The sculpture was shown on HTV's 'Crimestoppers' on Sunday 14 January. That evening, a woman claiming to be from the Riverside area of Cardiff phoned the confidential line. She recognized the face as 'very similar' to that of a girl with whom her daughter used to exchange clothes. The girl's first name was 'Sandra'. There was only a 'possible surname'. On this basis, the CID team began searching Cardiff for relatives of any girl of that possible surname – and to discover if the girl herself were still alive. It came to nothing.

After six weeks, the South Wales CID had interviewed five hundred potential witnesses in the Riverside area and had taken a hundred and thirty statements from them, all to no avail. They had traced only a minority of the residents of 27 and 29 Fitzhamon Embankment where a possible seven hundred tenants might have lived in the previous decade, most of them staying for short periods of time. An investigation which involved tracing a large proportion of them might be beyond the resources of the South Wales force. There would be more murder cases demanding their attention and, perhaps, making further expenditure of time on this one uneconomical. There was soon to be a new killer with a knife, apparently stalking the young women of the city after dark. Such peril here and now would take precedence over a mystery dating back several years.

At least the CID had made progress with the length of carpet from the makeshift grave. Detective Constable Mark Norman visited South Wales Carpets in Clifton Street, Adamstown and borrowed the shop's diary. Almost ten years earlier, in September 1980, the shop had supplied and fitted a new carpet in the basement flat and on the staircase of 29 Fitzhamon Embankment. It was Shaw's Kaleidoscope pattern, the same as the one that had been wrapped round the skeleton. There was some doubt as to whether the colours were identical, whether the off-cut of carpet round the skeleton was beige or orange, but at least the investigation had moved forward.

However, the medical sculpture was shown on television and in the press without apparent effect for days and then weeks. No parent, no teacher, no friend came forward to identify the victim. The Lynett White case was still continuing at Swansea and the press reported allegations of police intimidation and coercion. Even the two other prostitutes who told the court that they had witnessed Lynett White's murder were soon said to be telling lies for fear of being put out of business by the CID. It was not an encouragement, to those who might have committed a crime, to 'own up' or 'come forward'.

The attempt to identify the body in the carpet was saved by another telephone call on the confidential line. This time it came from a social worker who recognized the girl as Karen Wendy Price, born on 4 September 1965, last known of when she absconded from institutional care. If true, the details would fit the kind of story which the CID had in mind. It seemed ironic that after so much frustration on the part of the police, there quickly followed a second telephone call to the incident room at Norbury Road. This also came from a social worker, who recognized the sculpture as resembling Karen Wendy Price. The girl was fifteen years and ten months old when she absconded. No one had seen her since. After six weeks from the discovery of the skeleton, John Williams and his team had a name to work on.

But who was Karen Price? After all, she was not the first girl who was thought to resemble the medical sculpture. Like the mysterious 'Sandra', she might yet prove to be alive and well. Worse still, there might be no corroboration from witnesses and no trace of her. How could it be shown, beyond reasonable doubt, that the skeleton was hers?

II

One of the informants had worked at Maes-Yr-Eglwys Assessment Centre at Church Village, near Pontypridd, a dozen miles from Cardiff. Church Village was a cement-rendered linear development on the road above the valley with new dormitory estates for Cardiff. The centre held about thirty girls, either on remand awaiting court proceedings or 'beyond parental control'. It had since been closed. Such was the institution from which Karen Price absconded shortly before her death.

But Karen Price had not disappeared two years, nor even five years ago. She had last been seen in July 1981, eight and half years before the discovery of her body. If she died at fifteen and a half or thereabouts, as Dr Whittaker's evidence suggested, she had met her death very soon after that disappearance. She would have been sixteen less than two months after absconding. Small wonder that none of the five hundred people questioned in December and January had remembered her. She had been dead for more than six years before the date at which police asked witnesses if they had seen her frequenting the streets of Riverside. Her parents had not seen her since the spring of 1981, two months before she vanished from Maes-Yr-Eglwys. They assumed that she had gone away and was, by this time, married and living with a family of her own. She would, after all, have been a young woman of twenty-four in 1990.

Karen Price's childhood had been less than idyllic, despite

the haste with which she was now described as 'a happy-go-lucky' teenager. It was perhaps not surprising that photographs taken of her at the assessment centre in June 1981 showed her looking grim and moody rather than carefree. As for her ancestry, she was born of a Cypriot father and a Spanish mother, which fitted the Mediterranean characteristics of the skull. Her parents were divorced and, as a result of what Superintendent Williams called family circumstances rather than criminal activity, she had been taken into care by social services at the age of ten. Care, in Karen's case, was the Northfields Salvation Army Home, on the bleak arterial North Road running from Cardiff's city centre to its residential districts.

Mrs Price had remarried and, as Mrs Edward, was living in the westward sprawl of the Ely district of Cardiff with her new husband and a son. It was agreed, in the spring of 1981, that Karen should stay with them for a while and, if all went well, live with them. The experiment ended with what Mrs Edward called 'a heartbreaking argument' at the beginning of May. Karen came home with a cassette recorder which she had 'taken' from one of the other girls at Northfields. Her mother told her off and Karen went up to her room in a 'deep sulk'. She came down again and left the house. The argument continued down the road to Grand Avenue, Mrs Price pleading with her daughter to come home and Karen insisting that she was going to leave. The girl stopped a passing bus and got on board, Mrs Price trying in vain to hold her back. She was never to see her daughter again.

On 8 May 1981, Karen was transferred from Northfields to Maes-Yr-Eglwys. She had certainly proved to be beyond parental control. In the next two months, she absconded three times. It was not difficult. Though there was a secure unit within Maes-Yr-Eglwys, absconding from the rest of the centre involved merely walking out of the gates. On the first two occasions, she had been brought back from Cardiff by plain-clothes police who had picked her up in the city centre. As the South Wales Constabulary later described it, she was 'known to have frequented the Wales Empire Pool, Asteys

Cafe and Central Bus Terminal Area'. During one of her escapes, she had been away for three weeks. She had no money but had presumably found shelter with someone. A few weeks later she was making a living by prostitution and may have done so earlier. If this revelation shocked some of those who read her story, they were also to discover that girls younger than Karen Price survived by prostitution in the streets of Cardiff dockland, in Newport, and on ships berthed in South Wales ports.

On 2 July Karen vanished from Maes-Yr-Eglwys for the last time. The usual procedure was followed. A local search of the area was carried out. When this failed to find her after two or three hours, a missing persons form was filled out and passed to the police. A stock of these forms was kept at Maes-Yr-Eglwys for such incidents. After sending in the form, it was the policy of the centre 'to await the outcome of police investigations'. In the case of Karen Price, there had been no outcome. Maes-Yr-Eglwys was closed in 1984. Mid-Glamorgan kept its registers for two years and then destroyed them. 'We don't seem to have kept any records of this case,' said the director in January 1990, suggesting that they would probably have been returned to South Glamorgan. At the same time, nine years after the event, South Glamorgan set up 'an internal investigation into events leading up to Karen's placement in another county's assessment centre, her subsequent disappearance and steps taken to find her.' Mrs Price claimed that she had written to South Glamorgan Social Services in 1984, asking what had happened to her daughter whom she had not heard of for three years and that 'I never even received a reply'. But if something had gone wrong, would she not have been told? Believing that all must be well, her mother said, 'I really expected her one day to just knock on the door and walk right in with a family of her own.'

Neither social services nor her family could shed much light on Karen Price's fate. Yet the span of time during which she had died was now much reduced. She was alive on 2 July 1981 and, according to the evidence of the entomologists, she must have been dead by the end of October. Or, rather, this would be true if the skeleton was that of Karen Price. The death of the girl whose body had been found might lead to a trial, probably for murder. Was it certain that the skeleton found in the carpet was that of Karen Price? Or could this be another 'Sandra'?

South Wales CID invoked several new forms of forensic expertise. Peter Vanezis of Charing Cross and Westminster Medical School in London began with a recently devised video-fit technique to see whether existing photographs of Karen Price could be made to fit the shape of the skull found at Fitzhamon Embankment. The technique was one that had already been used in an Israeli court, during the trial of Ivan Demjanjuk, to identify the alleged Nazi war-criminal 'Ivan the Terrible', who had been brought to justice more than forty years after the events in question. In that case, the evidence remains in dispute. The video-fit examination in Cardiff showed that the skull could have been that of Karen Price, though it was impossible to establish beyond doubt that it was her skull. In the Demjanjuk case, despite his conviction, it seemed increasingly likely that the wrong man was on trial. The video-fit identified the features of the skull as being consistent with the photographs of Karen Price. However, as Mr Justice Rose was to remind the trial jury in Cardiff, consistency is not the same thing as proof.

At this stage, Superintendent Evans was not 'totally happy', foreseeing how easily a skilful defence counsel might argue that the identity of the body could not be proved beyond reasonable doubt. There had been a small discrepancy between the dental records of Karen Price and the teeth of the skeleton. It might be a minor 'mischarting' but what would it sound like to a jury? However, there was one further scientific proof which might yet be tried. DNA, with its so-called 'genetic fingerprinting' had produced one or two spectacular results in criminal trials, beginning with the conviction of Colin Pitchfork in 1985 for the rape and murder of two schoolgirls. In the latter half of 1989, the DNA process had been in the news several times. Yet the particular technique to be used with the skeleton was only two and half years old, perhaps, too novel to carry sufficient weight. This was not a Colin Pitchfork case, where the murder was comparatively recent. The issue was whether it would be possible to carry out a DNA test convincingly with material that had been so contaminated over such a long period as that of the skeleton found in Cardiff.

A case even more dramatic than that of Karen Price had raised this question at almost the same time. Four years earlier, the remains of a body unearthed in a Brazilian cemetery at Embu, São Paulo, were alleged to be those of Dr Josef Mengele. After forty years Mengele, responsible for 400,000 deaths in the concentration camps of World War II, was the major Nazi war criminal still thought to be at large. If the remains were his, then it seemed he had died in a swimming accident in 1979. The remains were taken first to West Germany, where a reconstruction of the face was made from the skull. There was a strong likelihood, on this basis, that the body in the Brazilian cemetery was Mengele's. But as the Karen Price investigation continued, arrangements were made to fly the other body from Germany to England for definitive tests by DNA.

These tests were to be undertaken by Dr Alec Jeffreys of the University of Leicester, a pioneer in the field of genetic fingerprinting. The identification of Mengele would depend on matching the biological code in the bone tissue of the skeleton with blood from Mengele's son, Rolf. The consent of Rolf Mengele was in doubt but there was no problem in obtaining blood samples from Karen Price's parents to match against scrapings from the skeleton in Cardiff.

To obtain a sample from the skeleton for DNA analysis, a section of bone was first sand-blasted to remove as much as possible of the fungal contamination. A sample of bone was ground into powder, containing some trace of the biological code of the victim but overlaid by the contamination from eight years of burial. In the end, using a short marker band technique, Professor Jeffreys was able to read the human biological code. It appeared on the autoradiograph as a print-out of a series of bars, in varying widths and density, very like a supermarket bar code.

The effectiveness of the DNA technique had been little challenged at the time, though Professor Jeffreys showed himself well aware of the problem of working with degraded material. In more general terms, Graham Cooke, a practising barrister, was later to express reservations over what exactly constitutes a match between two DNA samples or the formulae to be used where there is more than one match. A further point in this argument is that the same person may produce differing DNA samples at different times. These reservations were not to cloud the issue in the Karen Price case and, indeed, DNA was not to be crucial in the trial itself.

So the comparison was made between scrapings from the femur of the skeleton and blood samples from the parents of Karen Price. At the very most, in Professor Jeffreys' description, the chances were only 1 in 10,000 that the skeleton could be that of anyone but Karen Price. Eight months before her remains were found, he had estimated the chances that any two human beings might have an identical genetic code. 'Suppose we could test a million people every second. How long would it take to find one exactly the same? The answer is, the universe itself would die before we found one the same.'

The suggestion that a DNA database should be taken of the entire population filled authoritarians with enthusiasm and civil liberties watchdogs with dismay. Instant identification of rapists might have been a possibility, for example. But to what other uses might the database be put? On the side of law enforcement, Sir Richard Barratt in his *Report of HM Chief Inspector of Constabulary 1988* demanded a 'coercive power' to take DNA samples from suspects. Rape and murder were the two crimes that might be more easily detected in consequence. At this stage, however, DNA was mostly a spectacular confirmation of old-fashioned police work in South Wales. In the Karen Price investigation, the technique identified the skeleton beyond any reasonable doubt. Yet the outcome of the case still relied on evidence of the more traditional kind.

A second police poster appeared throughout South Wales and the West of England in January 1990. It included a photograph of Karen Price taken shortly before her disappearance, wearing jeans, sweat-shirt and a man's trilby hat. At the same time, in early January 1990, Superintendent Evans and his team began the next 'mammoth' task of tracing all those girls who had been at Maes-Yr-Eglwys at the same time as Karen Price, between May and July 1981, and might have known something of her fate. The centre had closed in 1984 and most of the records had been destroyed or lost. Even so, a number of the girls, now in their early twenties, were found, though they added nothing to the story. Unless their collective memory was unusually defective, it seemed odd that none of them remembered their companion. If they remembered but preferred not to say, then perhaps the fate which had overtaken Karen was more sinister than the evidence had so far indicated.

An inquest was opened in Cardiff on 1 February 1990 and was then adjourned to await the progress of the police investigation. Superintendent Evans assured the coroner that the CID were 'now following many avenues of inquiry'. The only new item of information was that the Karmen Ghia jeans which Karen was wearing in the photographs taken in June 1981 at Maes-Yr-Eglwys were the same as those belonging to the button found in the remains in the back garden grave.

Despite so much scientific ingenuity, the investigation was now stalled for want of the most humdrum information. Superintendent Williams approached the BBC and asked the monthly 'Crimewatch' programme to feature the case of Karen Price in its next transmission. Despite the popular image which it tried to cultivate, the 'Crimewatch' programme had an unfortunate involvement in South Wales murder-hunting. After the stabbing of Lynett White in Butetown, Superintendent Williams himself had appeared on 'Crimewatch' appealing for help in tracing a man whom he agreed was a 'prime suspect'. He was a white man seen outside the flat at the time of the stabbing, very distressed. 'This man was bleeding himself,' Mr Williams added, 'He's also got blood on him from the deceased.' But no more was heard of this white man with the dead girl's blood on him. After several unfruitful months, the South Wales CID had arrested five black men. Three were convicted only to be released on appeal. Channel 4's 'Black Bag' programme examined the case, though without any assistance from the BBC, who 'refused us the right to use its material' from the 'Crimewatch' programme, specifically the embarrassing assertion that a white man was the prime suspect. 'Black Bag' went ahead anyway and the BBC's attempt to prevent the righteous image of 'Crimewatch' being sullied failed when one of the solicitors in the case provided Channel 4 with the material. In the case of Karen Price, the result of the television reconstruction was to be rather more what John Williams expected.

The 'Crimewatch' programme went out at 10pm on Thursday 15 January 1990 on BBC1. It included a reconstruction of Karen Price's last days, so far as they were known, being filmed in the area of the Empire Pool and Big Asteys, with an actress, Jenni Harper, playing the part of the dead girl. About sixty people telephoned in to the programme and Superintendent Evans announced that 'firm lines of inquiry are now being followed.' Among these calls, there was one that outweighed the value of all the rest. Soon after the programme ended, the CID incident room in Cardiff received a telephone call. The caller was Meic Corcoran from Birchgrove Road in the city's northern suburbs. The message was brief and to the point.

'There's a bloke in the house that knew Karen Price.'

It seemed odd that the 'bloke' had not either telephoned the police himself or had not simply kept quiet about the events of nine summers ago. His name was Idris Ali, twenty-four years old and currently unemployed, known to the police from sentences served for burglary. There was not the least suggestion that murder or anything approaching it would have been in keeping with his character. That being so, it seemed strange that he should have felt it necessary to contact the police through an intermediary on the night of 15 January.

The two couples occupying the house in Birchgrove Road, had sat together, viewing the 'Crimewatch' programme. There was a discussion when the programme ended. Idris Ali, who never denied knowing Karen Price when they were both children of fifteen, asked his companion to telephone the police on his behalf. If he had reason to feel uneasy when he saw the images of Karen Price on the television screen, it was hard to see what he had to gain from getting someone else to telephone the police. Why not keep quiet? Was it that someone else remembered the friendship and said so in front of the rest of the household, prompting him to clear himself of any suspicion?

Mr Corcoran went to the phone and called the number at Norbury Road Police Station. He passed on the message. In what seemed like a piece of unnecessary melodrama, he was told to use the cover-name 'Garfield', if he phoned the confidential line again. As it happened, no such call was necessary. Next day, he made a witness statement and his part in the investigation was over. On the same day DC Richard Ward and DC Les Mumford visited Idris Ali at home in Birchgrove Road, near the main road out of Cardiff to the M4 motorway, Merthyr and the valleys. They questioned him between 9.30am and 3.30pm. It was a preliminary investigation and told them a good deal that they knew already.

Cardiff born and bred, Idris Ali was only a few months older than Karen Price. He had first met her when they were twelve years old, pupils at Greenhill House Special School in Rhiwbina, a suburb with golf course and garden village on the hilly north-west fringe of the city. Karen was described as 'slow' and 'slightly backward' but not in any sense retarded. By the time they were thirteen, Idris Ali had what he called in evidence a 'slight crush' on her, though he named someone else to the police as having been her boy-friend in 1981. There was nothing much remarkable in his history. Idris Ali's father was a seaman, often away from home while the brothers and sisters lived with their mother. The family had settled in Galston Street, Adamstown, an area of Victorian back-to-back housing between the Newport Road and the Cardiff to

London railway line. It was only the railway line that divided the community from the wharves and basins of Cardiff docks. In the spring of 1981, at the age of fifteen, Idris Ali had returned home to Galston Street, where his mother was living alone. His father had died while he was away.

So much for what the police already knew. On the following day Idris Ali began a statement at Norbury Road Police Station. He was understandably nervous, chain-smoking to such effect that two adjacent interview rooms on the first floor were needed, as DC Mumford described in evidence, one with its windows open to clear the smoke while the other was used to continue the questioning. It was a lengthy statement. He was allowed to go home and returned to finish it next day. The interviews which followed were tape-recorded, producing more than a dozen forty-minute tapes of his interrogations, the apparent bump of an ashtray accompanying the dialogue. In each version, his story became fuller and more melodramatic. There were contradictions. Before long, however, Idris Ali was not the only witness to the events of 1981. He prevaricated and concealed the truth, not always merely to protect himself. Then he would make new revelations which implicated him more deeply in the horrors of Karen Price's last days.

Those who brought him to justice saw in this the evidence of what Mr Justice Rose called 'the numerous lies' told to the police. Yet, if numerous, they were certainly not skilful. Instead of telling a story – true or false – and sticking to it, he responded to the scepticism of the police by incriminating himself further, little by little. He confessed to crimes which no other witness corroborated. When, on the tapes, he said to his interrogators. 'You fuckers, you caught me out there,' he did not sound as if it mattered much. It was difficult to know exactly what, and which version, to believe or whether Idris Ali reached the point of simply telling the police what he thought they wanted to hear.

During the Karen Price investigation, the Lynett White trial continued at Swansea Crown Court. The confession on which the prosecution case relied principally was that of Stephen

Miller, who said that he had told the police everything they wanted to hear in order to get the ordeal over with. Idris Ali can scarcely have believed that, after hearing his account of Karen Price's death, the police would let him go. Did he simply feel that to tell them what they wanted – and more than they wanted – would put an end to the questioning? That was Stephen Miller's explanation of his confession. Was Idris Ali a compulsive confessor, as Wayne Darvell appeared to be in the Swansea Sex-Shop murder? Darvell and his brother were released after a successful appeal against conviction. Logic was certainly not on Idris Ali's side and he made statements which seemed to defy all rationality. At one point in the subsequent trial, he was asked by the judge if he meant the court to understand that he would rather confess to a murder of which he was innocent, than let it be known that someone had unsuccessfully tried to make him commit an act of necrophilia. Was that really what he meant? 'Yes,' he said simply.

Curiosities of this kind abounded in the weeks and months to come. Yet Idris Ali told the police his general story of the summer of 1981 in terms which could largely be corroborated by other witnesses. It was at the beginning of July that two fifteen-year-olds and a thirteen-year-old companion set out on a career of crime. It was not the amiable world of Bugsy Malone but one in which self-destruction, sexual vice, violence and death acquired an almost casual acceptance.

III

So far as the midsummer of 1981 had a place in history, it witnessed the death of the IRA hunger-striker and Westminster MP, Bobby Sands, *Lemon Popsicle* at the Odeon, gang-fights round the Aneurin Bevan memorial near Ebbw Vale, and the trial of Peter Sutcliffe, 'The Yorkshire Ripper'. By July, it was also the summer of Liverpool's Toxteth riots, followed by further rioting in Brixton.

In South Wales, two fourteen-year-old girls fought one another behind a Newport fish-and-chip shop while their classmates shrieked 'Kill her!' The loser went home and took a lethal overdose of her father's blood-pressure tablets. There was a row in the press over the amount of physical punishment inflicted on boys and girls in council homes, though Maes-Yr-Eglwys was not mentioned. Motorway bridges and civic walls bore the frustration of the over-indulged middle-class young. 'Bored and blue? Nothing to do? Kill the rich! Smash their cars!' or the rampant feminism of 'Dead Men Don't Rape', to which a hopeful ghoul had added, 'They do now!' There were more proletarian exhortations too. 'Cardiff City Football Club. Fuzz is scum. Kill a jack.'

The last days of Karen Price, in July and August, were set in a central swathe of Cardiff, from the city centre in the north to the docks in the south, roughly corresponding to C Division of the city police. At the head of this area, lay the formal gardens and broad templed avenues of grey Edwardian stone which made up the civic centre of the Welsh capital. Its collection of classical, Viennese and Egyptian styles suggested the site of a long-forgotten world's fair. Adjacent to this area was the Pre-Raphaelite castle built by William Burges for the Marquess of Bute with extensive parkland stretching to the River Taff and beyond. Southwards lay the department stores and retail chains of Queen Street, High Street and St Mary Street.

At the far end of St Mary Street, the more affluent retail trade shaded into dockland and depression. In rough parallel with the river, Bute Street ran long and straight for a mile to the remains of the pier head from which Campbell's steamers once served both sides of the Bristol Channel. Bute Street consisted of a blank wall on one side and tower block estates on the other. Where the city centre and dockland met, a block to the west, was the complex of railway station, bus station, Big Asteys, Empire Pool and the river bridges within sight of Fitzhamon Embankment. To the east of the shabbier end of St Mary Street, beyond the muddy-grey walls of Cardiff prison, lay the little streets of Adamstown, divided by the main railway line and Cardiff East Moors from Roath Dock and Queen Alexandra Dock.

Beyond the Custom House Street and Bute Terrace, the dockland sky was pale blue with a few high drifts of thin cumulus, as if reflecting the sunlit waters of a summer ocean. Nearer to hand, the flat terraced streets of Adamstown had no other horizon but their rooftops and chimneys under this Atlantic blue. The area bordered land reclaimed from the sea a century before. Doors of houses opened directly on to the pale grey slabs of the pavement, long since worn smooth. Gardens of any size were rare, the spaces at the rear of the houses consisting mostly of walled yards. The brine of the sea was in the air and the soil was sand or silt.

The streets of Adamstown and the dilapidated riverside areas of station and embankment were the setting for much of the summer drama. That drama opened in Cemetery Park, one of Adamstown's few public spaces, a Victorian burial ground in a walled grass square surrounded by houses. The memorial stones of captains and stokers, dockers and donkeymen had been taken up and lined against the walls, leaving the grass as an area for pram-wheeling and football. Cemetery Park's near neighbours were Cardiff prison and the railway goods depot.

On the afternoon of 2 July, five girls in their early teens were sniffing glue from crisp packets in the park. It was a simple technique, needing a bag that was not too big to inflate. The glue went in first, then the bag was placed to the mouth and blown up, finally the air was sniffed back through the nose. Glue-sniffing became news that summer as shopkeepers were forbidden from selling the substance to children or adolescents and the robbing or burgling of D-I-Y stores became a new crime of the decade. On 3 July the South Wales press reported the case of a boy who was sniffing glue to the value of six pounds a week. On 9 July a father escaped jail for thrashing his fourteen-year-old son in an attempt to stop him sniffing glue and inhaling butane gas. This had occurred in Grangetown, just on the other side of Bute Street from Adamstown. According to the boy's mother, the family's only hope lay in moving from this part of the city. 'Sniffing is rife in our area,' she said, 'with sixteen-year-old louts forcing children as young as eight to participate.'

The desperate consequences of addiction to glue or butane

gas and the more usual substances, had been illustrated in the *South Wales Echo* and the rest of the Cardiff media throughout that summer. Arrests for drug offences in South Wales had gone up by 30 per cent in the past two years. In a dramatic initiative a former drug-user, who had lost two fingers from gangrene after using a dirty needle, set up a service to combat addiction.

There was nothing unusual about the group in Cemetery Park on 2 July. The adolescent glue-sniffers of central Cardiff were quite often girls on the run from assessment centres or special schools. Knowing what they would be sent back to, they had better reason than most 'solvent abusers' for not wanting to be seen or caught. Yet most people were still comparatively innocent in such matters and would probably not have realized at a casual glance what these adolescents were doing. Sometimes the girls sniffed glue in pairs, without interference, in the narrow approach lanes round the multi-storey car parks by the railway station. There were few pedestrians and the motorists had only a brief glimpse of a couple of schoolgirls with bags of crisps in their hands, laughing and apparently pretending to fall about. There was probably not time to see that they were drooling or stupefied or to guess the significance of the bags they held. Whatever the long-term damage, the immediate effect of sniffing glue varied. One of Idris Ali's friends claimed that she got only a momentary 'buzz' from sniffing it, unlike some of those she knew who were so far gone that they would 'hop under a bus' without knowing where they were or what they were doing.

By summer evening, the Adamstown girls and some of their boyfriends, including those who had become their pimps, progressed to the green spaces of Bute Gardens, the river bank parkland behind the long castle wall with its medieval-style Florentine clock-tower, its woodwork picked out in red and gold. In the evening of the late spring days that year, the park had been a place of joggers among the pale flowers and fallen magnolia cups. From the closed grounds of the castle itself, came the hoarse shrill cries of the peacocks. As the city grew quiet in summer, this parkland now became a haven for the more usual activities of the runaways, sex and intoxication.

The afternoon of 2 July was cool and cloudy. Indeed, it was to be a month with more rain and cloud than sun, until the weather brightened up for the royal wedding of Prince Charles and Lady Diana Spencer on 29 July. Fifteen-year-old Idris Ali, walking towards the city shops from Galston Street, saw the group of five girls sniffing glue from crisp bags in Cemetery Park. Four of the girls were Sharon, Debbie, Emma and Stacey. The fifth was Karen Price. She was wearing a dark short-sleeved Fred Perry shirt with a laurel wreath on it, Karman Ghia jeans and monkey boots. This was the day on which she had absconded for the last time from Maes-Yr-Eglwys. Idris Ali joined the group, though he was not Karen's boyfriend. Her boyfriend, or ex-boyfriend, was not involved in the events that followed. On this occasion it was Debbie, another runaway from Maes-Yr-Eglwys, who went off with Idris Ali. He described in his evidence how they tried to find shelter for the night. There was a shed with a mattress in it behind the Royal Infirmary buildings, up towards the Newport Road. They tried this but found the summer night far too cold.

Walking back into Adamstown, they made their way to South Luton Place, where Idris Ali had a friend who would let them stay the night. It was now about an hour after midnight. Idris Ali would climb a wall and then let Debbie in. As he was climbing, a police car turned the corner into the little street. He shouted a warning to Debbie and took cover but the police car was already pulling up. Though Idris Ali was concealed from the two patrolmen, a girl of Debbie's age, alone at night in this situation, was not to be overlooked. A couple of minutes later, at 1.15 am, she was in the police car, on her way back to Maes-Yr-Eglwys.

Few witnesses would recall in accurate detail the daily events of life eight and a half years before their statements were made. In Idris Ali's story, however, 2 July could be pinpointed because it was the day when Karen had absconded

212

from Maes-Yr-Eglwys and had reached Cardiff a few hours later. The next day was a blank, not so the evening. With a group of friends, including Jackie, Janice and Helen, Idris Ali and some other boys went to Waterloo Gardens, a small piece of land in the intersections of residential streets off the arterial length of the Newport Road. There was some casual outdoor sex among some of the group before they went to a friend's house, where four of them made use of a double bed.

This adolescent underworld of incidental sex and slow brain-death by intoxication had turned its back on the 'caring' professions, the scolding of middle-class evangelicalism or feminism, the vigilance of 'concerned' citizens who sought redress against the corrupting influence of 'progressive' forces. In the columns of the *South Wales Echo*, the Responsible Society urged parents to let it know if their children were receiving at school any sex education that might conflict with their own beliefs. Idris Ali and his friends, their ages between thirteen and sixteen, were regarded by the law, though not by themselves, as schoolchildren. Yet they and the concerned citizenry of the Responsible Society might have been living on different planets.

Next day, 4 July, the girls went shoplifting in Cardiff city centre. Their ambitions were modest enough. All they wanted was glue. When there was a little money, they could afford cannabis, 'a split of ganja', at £7.50 a time. When it rained, they could take cover in one of the cinemas. That week, the large shabby Prince of Wales at the lower end of St Mary Street offered *Confessions of the Campus Virgins* and *Untamed Sex*. A walk out beyond the castle to North Road brought them to the Plaza and *Emmanuelle Queen Bitch*. In retrospect, there was a chilling aptness about the offering at the ABC in Queen Street, *Strip Nude for your Killer*. Afterwards the girls were content to sniff the stolen glue along Mill Lane, running off the end of St Mary Street. In the evening, Idris Ali and a friend went to the Harlequin Ground off the Newport Road with two of the girls. In his own account, that night seems to have been the first on which he took Karen and Mandy back to his mother's house in Galston

Street. They went in through the back door which had been left unlocked.

The arrangement was simple and worked well. Mandy slept downstairs, Karen went to bed upstairs with Idris Ali. Neither of the girls was a sexual innocent, since prostitution was the quickest way out of destitution for an adolescent on the run from Maes-Yr-Eglwys. During a week or two at Galston Street, the three friends arrived back late at night, after Barbara Ali had gone to bed, and the girls left before she got up. Sometimes Karen would disappear for a few days and then return. Her possessions seemed to consist of a make-up bag and a black notebook, in which she wrote a daily account of her life and her impressions of people. According to his evidence, Idris Ali said to the two girls, 'We could make a lot of money. It's down to you two.'

By his own account, he was generous to Karen before this, giving her money for cigarettes and personal needs. Yet he boasted that he was soon doing well as a fifteen-year-old pimp, when Karen, Mandy, and another girl, Jane, were working for him. Jane's speciality in her fourteenth summer was a blond 'Mohican' hair-cut. There were other adolescent runaways in his team but after almost ten years he could not remember their names. It seems unlikely that many of them had reached the age of consent at sixteen. However, indignation at the sale of juvenile bodies was less widespread than the middle class and its media might have claimed. It was certainly a thriving business in Cardiff city centre, aided by those adult males who, for example, watched for likely punters leaving the Central Station and then propositioned them on behalf of the girls.

The square before Cardiff Central Station was a specimen of post-war reconstruction in brick and concrete. On the far side, beyond the lines of parked buses in their bays was a row of bus company offices and a cafeteria, known as Big Astey's. According to Mandy, it was on 5 July that she and Karen began soliciting on the pavement outside Big Asteys. It was safer than the station foyer, where there was always danger from the railway police. The greatest problem for the girls was that they had nowhere to take their clients. Most of these clients had nowhere to take them and would be unlikely to try booking a room of any sort accompanied by a girl who was suspiciously young in appearance. There were references during the case to a back room in central Cardiff, specializing in the schoolgirl trade, but that was unlikely to be of much help.

Even so, Karen and Mandy made £40 between them on 5 July and gave some of it to Idris Ali. On 6 July, they made £50, giving him £20 and keeping £15 each. Trade began to pick up rapidly and on 8 July Karen alone had made £60 from three punters and given half of it to Idris Ali, according to trial evidence. With these two girls and Jane working for him, he was scarcely poor any longer. As their confidence increased, the girls left the comparative respectability of the station area and began to solicit men in the shabbier streets towards the docks.

The next day was almost the beginning of the weekend. July sunshine came at last when Karen and Mandy set off to spend their money in a few days at Barry Island, eight miles away. The town of Barry was built very much in the style of the South Wales valleys but, across its causeway, Barry Island seemed like a small part of Southend or Blackpool attached to the last seaward stretch of the industrial spine. The centre of the island was its busy and boisterous funfair with the metallic din of music and blazing lights. It was a good place for a day or two. The neon rippled and flashed and faded for the Lucky Penny machines. Above the park at dusk, the neon-studded chariots whirled like hammers. The Flitzer Thunderbird chair-ride swirled and clashed against the steam-organ blasts. Across the road from the amusement park were pale twilit sands and a dark violet sea. On the sands, Karen, Mandy and other runaways slept safely at night, either by the headland of Friar's Point or under the pillared shelter that ran along the top of the beach. The 'emergency action team' of the Social Services department would have more immediate problems than scouring the dark length of coastline for fugitives from its care.

For those few days in July, Barry Island offered what was easily recognized as a good time with its tang of shell-crusted sand, a scent of warm vinegar from the cafés, a clash of cutlery and shouted orders from open kitchen doors. The special attraction that weekend was a free concert at the Pleasure Park by Emperor Rosko and his Road Show on the night of 9 July. If necessary, Barry Island was also a place where the girls could make money. On the calm glitter of the sea, the heartbeat of the coasters' engines throbbed and faded. Across the railway line was Barry Dock and the crews of ships from all over the world. But still the two girls remained loyal to Idris Ali as their fifteen-year-old protector.

While Karen and Mandy were away, Idris Ali's lifestyle changed little. It was a time of year when the city turned to holidays and entertainment. The drab length of Grand Avenue in working-class Ely became a festival ground for a week and a circus for a day with musicians, actors, acrobats and puppets. By August, the lawns of Cardiff castle drew crowds to the searchlight tattoo. In his statement to the police, Idris Ali said that he spent these summer days of mid-July at the Empire Pool or in Sophia Gardens and the castle grounds, where he could smoke 'a split of ganja' without being disturbed. A friend of his, a Cardiff City football supporter, took him to a house on Fitzhamon Embankment to buy marijuana at the going rate of £7.50 a time. He could not recall which house it was. He also remembered going to a 'Teardrop Explodes' rock concert at the Student's Union in Cathays Park, buying the tickets from Spillers Records in the Hayes. He may have gone to the concert but it was not held until the following spring, in March 1982.

After several days at Barry Island, Karen reappeared in Cardiff. She had had her hair done and was more smartly dressed than when she had left Maes-Yr-Eglwys. It seems that she and her companion now set about making money in earnest. The areas chosen for soliciting were Despenser Gardens, just behind Fitzhamon Embankment on Riverside, and the upper length of Bute Street, where it began its long drab mile to the pier head. Despite the money they had made, the girls still had no premises of their own. For that they would have needed an adult protector. Soliciting was still a matter of flagging down men driving on their own and using the client's car as a bedroom or as transport to somewhere more secluded.

Going off with a man whose sole moral qualification was his sexual desire was a risk of the trade. Once the car drove off, the girl was beyond even the help of her adolescent pimp. As Mandy said, 'I couldn't very well take Idris in the car with me.' Sooner or later, one of the girls might flag down an unmarked police car or a Social Services posse but this was less likely if they stuck to men driving alone. In any case, the hazards seemed unavoidable and the money infinitely desirable.

On their working days, the girls waited near the corner of Tyndall Street and Bute Street, under the plate-iron grey of the railway bridge where the road dipped down between high pavements. Had they known something of the past or future of prostitution in that area, they might have been less encouraged. It was what one policeman called 'an upside down world', where people lived as much at night as by day. The mortality rate was traditionally high. Mary Kelly, the last victim of Jack the Ripper, had begun her career on Bute Street before moving to London. By the time that a search began for Karen Price, Lynett White had also died of multiple stab wounds in the centre of Butetown.

For the time being, the girls catered for the carriage trade without interference or mishap. There was even a convenient cafe by the railway bridge. To either side were long streets of Victorian dockers' houses with tall, narrow pubs at many corners. All the same, a more desolate or unerotic tableau would have been hard to devise. Down the length of Bute Street, a fortress-like public convenience in grey concrete stood padlocked and derelict beside the long black concrete of the railway wall. This concealed the branch line to the pier head, custom house and commercial banks. Here and there on the wall, patches of tall garish lettering advertising theatres and cinemas long since closed were still just visible.

Idris Ali's account of this summer, as he described it to the police, offered the most plausible date for what happened next. It seems to have been on Wednesday 15 July, in the evening, that he took Karen to the Adamstown pub, 'where the gipsies go'. They were playing pool when he noticed a young man sitting by the table and got into conversation with him. The man was very large with a square-set head, close-cropped hair, a Fu-Manchu moustache and a well-trimmed beard. He wore evening dress with a gold medallion on his white shirt-front and rings on his fingers. Idris Ali thought he looked like 'Jack the Lad'. The man's name was Alan Charlton and he was twenty-one years old. To say that he was power-fully built was an understatement. He was in training as a weight-lifter and had developed a fifty-three-inch chest.

When asked by the stranger what he did for a living, Idris Ali said that he 'lived off other people's immoral earnings'. Charlton seemed neither impressed nor shocked by this, though he gave the boy what Ali called 'a funny look'. Presently Charlton got up and said that it was time for him to go to work. His work, he explained, was acting as bouncer or 'doorman' in the rougher part of town, at the Excel restaurant and a nearby pub, the Philharmonic at the lower end of St Mary Street. He was earning £20 or £25 a night. Idris Ali sug-gested that he ought to get better paid for facing the risk of injuries from difficult customers. Charlton was more than a match for one at a time but sooner or later he might confront a gang of them.

Both establishments that had been mentioned were in an area where a doorman of Alan Charlton's powerful build and well-protected knuckles would be a useful deterrent. The Excel Restaurant was in Caroline Street, known locally as 'Greasy Lane'. It was no wider than a lane, connecting St Mary Street with the opposite façades of department stores on the Hayes. On one side of Caroline Street was the yard of Brains Brewery. For the rest, it consisted of century-old, two-storey terraced houses. These had long since been turned into fish and chip shops, inexpensive restaurants, or exchange counters for 'Books and Mags'.

CHAPTER SIX

The Philharmonic was almost opposite the point where Caroline Street came out into St Mary Street, a double-fronted pub with bare boards, bar snacks and an air of austerity. It stood close to the railway station in a block of decaying cinemas and little shops. This was the end of the city centre nearer the docks where, fifty years earlier, the police waited to turn back evening trouble-makers trying to cross the social frontier from Butetown and the waterfront.

Alan Charlton, in a new and smartly-cut dinner suit, the white shirt tight across his broad chest, was soon working for a group of enterprises. He stood guard first at the Excel and the Philharmonic, then went on to act as doorman at the Xanadu night club in nearby Wood Street. It was his job to be on public view and natural that he became quite a familiar figure in the summer of 1981. There were no complaints of his conduct. The fact that he was seen so much and so frequently by people whom he had no cause to notice or remember was important in the inquiry that followed. He might later be described and identified by those who were strangers to him. There must have been many people to whom he had only spoken a few casual words. It would be unreasonable to expect that he should recognize all of them or remember every exchange of conversation.

Later on in the evening of their meeting at the Adamstown pub, Idris Ali and Karen Price walked into town and went for a meal at the Excel. By this time, Alan Charlton was apparently off-duty, sitting at a table, and he asked them to join him. Reverting to the topic of conversation in the pub, he asked Idris Ali if the girls on whose immoral earnings he lived ever went to sex parties. It seemed that such a party might involve lesbian performances, oral sex, even whipping and bondage. Ali said that they did not. Indeed, they had scarcely had the opportunity. On the other hand, organized parties were worth thinking about as a means of making money. They would pay better and be more agreeable than soliciting unknown motorists on the pavements of Bute Street or Riverside.

Nothing came of the suggestion at this meeting, perhaps

219

because Idris Ali sensed that once his girls were at one of these parties, Alan Charlton might take control of them. In Ali's version of events, it was apparently on the following day that Charlton saw Karen Price and her fifteen-year-old protector drinking tea or coffee at an outdoor table of the Hayes cafe, under the trees between the department stores and St David's Hall. He asked whether they had thought any more about going to the sex parties. They had not.

The next meeting was at the Excel Restaurant probably on the Friday evening, 17 July. This time, Charlton invited Idris Ali and Karen Price to a party at 29 Fitzhamon Embankment on the following night. His own basement flat, where he had been living since the previous month, was to be used for this and the party may have spilled over into other parts of the house. Another witness remembered a couple of dozen guests there, most of them in their twenties. Some, including Idris Ali who also described the occasion, smoked cannabis. So far as the sex was concerned, he was an observer rather than a participant. For the other guests, inhibitions were at a discount. There was oral sex, some of the women performed as lesbians and blue movies were projected on the wall. The bondage and whipping referred to may have been on the blue movies rather than in reality. There was a reference during the subsequent trial to a girl being driven round the floor on all fours with a dog-leash, which may have happened at one of the parties or on a more private occasion, or perhaps not at all. However, no specialist in sexual aberration could have taught much to the revellers of Fitzhamon Embankment, not even to those in their teens.

In 1981 video recorders were not at all commonplace and blue films were still projected in the traditional manner. The Super 8 projector to be brought out for these entertainments was kept in a ground floor flat at Fitzhamon Embankment, perhaps because the tenant of that flat was away in the United States at the time. The first blue movie show had been some time before, at a curry party in the basement flat, possibly when it was vacant before Alan Charlton's arrival. On the night of 18 July, the projector was operated by an SAS soldier, a holder of the Northern Ireland medal, who happened to be living in the house. Eight years later, he remembered Alan Charlton sitting on the bed and a girl he identified from memory as Karen Price in a trilby hat and dark coat sitting on the floor, her face illuminated by the sidelight of the projector as she watched the films.

Idris Ali's reaction was that blue movies didn't 'do much' for him. At about 10pm, he left the party and walked home the short distance to Galston Street to have a meal and 'a wash and brush-up'. An hour and a half later he went back to the party to collect Karen. There was a second party at Fitzhamon Embankment a week later and, after the lapse of years, memories of the two occasions became hard to differentiate. However, it seems to have been on the second occasion that Idris Ali claimed to have taken both Karen and Mandy to the flat, though no one else remembered Mandy being there. This time, there were about sixty people, many of them hotel employees. It was no longer just a matter of going to a party but having a financial arrangement with Alan Charlton. The two girls made £155 by their services to the guests. The agreement was that the host should get £45 and his choice of a girl for the night. He chose Karen.

There was another occasion, possibly after the first blue movie party, when the chef from a city pub was a guest. He and Charlton took two girls to the basement flat for the night while Karen, this time, spent the night with another man upstairs. According to the chef's evidence, Charlton suggested in the morning that they might swap girls for a while, but the chef refused.

So far as Idris Ali and Alan Charlton were concerned, the amiability of their first meetings was short-lived. Eclipsing the casual trade in such girls as Karen and Mandy or Jane the Mohican blonde was the growing threat of Alan Charlton to Idris Ali's position. Idris Ali at fifteen was earning more than Alan Charlton as a bouncer at twenty-one. Idris Ali was still legally a child. He had no job in a club or restaurant which might enable him to introduce his girls to clients. He had no bedroom to which the girls could take their clients. If, as witnesses alleged, Charlton was a threat to Ali's ascendancy, it would have been an unequal match. According to her evidence, Charlton was soon to make such a move with Jane, Idris Ali's fourteen-year-old Mohican blonde from Maes-Yr-Eglwys. In the meantime, as Mandy described it, he remained a paying customer.

Mandy testified that when she visited Alan Charlton alone for the first time, he gave her £10 which she divided with Idris Ali. Then there was a second visit, which might well have been the last. They were sitting on the bed when, according to her testimony, Alan Charlton told her to get down naked on all fours and bark like a dog while he made love to her. The idea repelled her. It was later suggested that it had come from one of the blue films or possibly the incident of the girl and the dog-leash. When Mandy refused to obey, the easy-going and joking Alan Charlton coloured with anger. According to her evidence, he seized a small penknife and cut her bare thigh with its blade, midway between her knee and hip. She could not believe that a man who had been so amiable a moment before would do her such an injury. The scar was still there ten years later, she insisted, but if the attack occurred as she described it, then it was an omen of far worse things to come.

IV

By 1990 the sequence of events in July 1981 had grown uncertain in the memories of many of the witnesses. Yet, apart from Karen's disappearance from Maes-Yr-Eglwys on 2 July, there was one other date that served as a landmark. On 29 July there had been a public holiday to celebrate the royal wedding of the heir to the throne, Prince Charles, to Lady Diana Spencer. Even nine or ten years later, everyone seemed to know where he or she was on that day and whether certain incidents had happened before or after. The SAS projectionist remembered that he had left Cardiff to be home for the celebrations and the blue movie shows had been abandoned. The occupant of the ground floor flat had been in the United States. Idris Ali, in a burst of patriotic high spirits, had shinned up a flagpole and purloined a Union Jack for a street party in Adamstown. Alan Charlton had been keeping the peace outside the Excel, the Philharmonic and the Xanadu night club.

According to the best recollections of those concerned, the two blue movie parties appear to have been on 18 and 25 July. Mandy's second visit alone to Alan Charlton had been soon after the second party. There was nothing inconsistent about her having gone to the second party, even if she was in care at the time. It was on a Saturday evening and the girls of Maes-Yr-Eglwys were allowed weekend home-leave from Friday afternoon until Sunday evening where this was thought desirable by their social workers. There had been a social services conference on 7 July at which it was decided that, despite her habit of absconding or overstaying weekend leave and having to be brought back by her social worker, every effort should be made to maintain Mandy's relationship with her home. Though she had absconded early in the month, she had certainly been returned to council care by the royal wedding day when there was a party for the inmates of Maes-Yr-Eglwys. It was a public holiday and 'South Wales took to the streets as thousands of people ate, danced, sang, and drank in longed-for sunshine.' Idris Ali was at the Augusta Street street party, just opposite Cemetery Park in Adamstown. On the following day, Thursday 30 July, the girls of Maes-Yr-Eglwys were taken by minibus on an outing to the seaside at Porthcawl, twenty-five miles west of Cardiff. Their destination was Coney Beach funfair near the old harbour. When the time came to return, it was found that Mandy and one of the other girls had gone missing.

Mandy's social workers assumed that she had 'met up with boys from Porthcawl'. But the little seaside town was not where they expected her to remain. The reports on her noted that she was 'thought to have been associating with prostitutes' in the dockland area of Cardiff and had presumably returned to them. In fact, the two runaways disagreed in their memories of the escape, as to whether they had gone to Newport or to Barry where they solicited and went on board a ship in the docks. Her companion thought they had been together for four days but this seems likely to have been when Mandy absconded again in September. In Mandy's evidence they were together only for a day after 30 July, which would probably have brought her back to Cardiff on Saturday 1 August or perhaps on the Sunday.

A further date that could be established was 22 July. Alan Charlton phoned the police on that day to report a robbery in his basement flat. His camera had been stolen and the gas meter had been rifled. It might have been thought that he had made this story up to cover his own theft from the gas meter, since he certainly had a camera after 22 July. All the same, a man who had committed murder in his flat just before that date and possibly had a body concealed there, would scarcely draw the attention of the police to the premises in this way. It seems likely, therefore, that Karen Price was still alive when Mandy returned to Cardiff at the beginning of August.

Mandy was not picked up again until Saturday 8 August. Though she recalled her first meeting with Alan Charlton as having been either outside Big Asteys near the station or while he was on duty outside the Excel Restaurant, her two visits to him may both have occurred after 30 July. The week of 1–8 August 1981 was also the one in which Karen Price probably died. Unless the social services records were radically inaccurate, Mandy did not abscond again until 5 September. She was positive in evidence that Karen was dead before that. The only time when she could have made three closely-spaced visits to Fitzhamon Embankment was apparently in the week of 1–8 August.

There was to be more than one version of the death of Karen Price – more than one version from Idris Ali alone in his witness statements. Yet so far as there could be an independent witness, it was surely Mandy. Her account of what happened best fits the forensic evidence, though it still leaves discrepancies. She was not on trial herself and, in that respect at least, had nothing to gain or lose by telling the truth in detail. What follows is her account, supplemented by details from the evidence of Idris Ali, where there is no apparent conflict.

It is only fair to add that when this version of events was put to Alan Charlton almost nine years later, he denied any part in it. He repeated that he did not know Mandy nor Idris Ali. He 'categorically' did not know Karen Price. Idris Ali and Mandy admitted being present when Karen died. He knew nothing about it. If they admitted being there, he insisted that they were surely guilty of the murder. He was not.

From Porthcawl, Mandy came to Cardiff, back to the territory she shared with Idris Ali and Karen Price. They wandered round St Mary Street, Asteys, the Empire Pool, and the station, sometimes through Bute Gardens and the elegant avenues of Cathays Park. The civic centre was half-deserted in its August calm, the clerks and secretaries of city hall and its neighbours gone to Ibiza or St Ives. For those who stayed at home, the searchlight tattoo brought the 1st Battalion of the Welsh Guards to the castle grounds with sixteen bands, pipes, a corps of drums, and the Royal Military Police display team. In Queen Street and St Mary Street, the department stores were quiet and business was slack. But the shabbier cinemas showing luridly-titled and feebly produced sex-films were open for business as usual, an oasis of darkness in the summer afternoons. Such places offered a refuge. For all their success on the streets and at the parties, neither Idris Ali nor the girls had anywhere that they could call their own.

According to Idris Ali's evidence, it was the end of a summer afternoon when the fifteen-year-old boy and the two girls walked down to Big Asteys and began playing the machines. Aztec Gold and Silver Chest were popular at the time, a waterfall of coins about to spill over at the drop of a punter's penny but never quite seeming to do so. Wary notices were pasted on them by the managements. 'Do not bang. Alarm fitted.' And there were the one-armed bandits. Idris Ali recalled that they were playing the one-armed bandits at Big Asteys in the early evening. Then, like a shadow across the sun, a large man stopped outside the plate glass window of the cafe, staring in. It was Alan Charlton. The time was just before seven o'clock.

He came in and began talking to the three of them. Presently he suggested that they might like to go back to his basement flat with him to smoke dope or sniff glue and have a party. Idris Ali and the two girls agreed. It was somewhere to go and something to do. Despite her story of an incident with a penknife on the last visit to Fitzhamon Embankment, Mandy presumably felt reassured by the presence of her two friends.

The basement flat, with its door opening into the back garden by Fitzhamon Lane, consisted of a living room, bedroom, kitchen and shower. Among its other contents was a set of weights which Alan Charlton used for training. When they got back there, Idris Ali built himself a split of cannabis and the others began to smoke as well. There was a record player, probably borrowed from the ground floor flat while its tenant was in America. They put some records on and danced but there was no 'smooching or anything like that' in Mandy's recollection. She thought they were in the ground floor flat but this may simply have been because the door leading into the basement was at ground level in the back garden. The dancing ended and then they drank lager for a while. Idris Ali recalled that he was not paying much attention to the others when he heard the beginning of the quarrel.

Mandy described how Alan Charlton had told the girls to take their clothes off, lie on the bed, and put on a lesbian performance while he photographed them. Among other forms of merchandise, there was still a good trade in such photographs before the age of universal video and, of course, they might be useful to show to potential customers if Charlton ever took over the girls. His attitude may have suggested that the time had come when he was prepared to take them over from Idris Ali. Charlton was to take over Jane by the girl's own account and, in Idris Ali's version, had made a bid for Karen. If such evidence was correct, perhaps this was to be the evening of the decisive move.

But the girls both refused to undress or to put on a lesbian performance for Alan Charlton's camera. Mandy later said that she 'never had any inclination that way'. It was suggested that some of the older women had put on displays of this kind in the basement flat at the end of the parties but not that either of the two runaways had been involved.

Mandy recalled that Alan Charlton's response to her refusal was to hit her hard across the face, though not hard enough to knock her to the floor. Karen shouted angrily, 'Leave her alone!' and tried to pull him off. The reaction of his companions, as they described it in court almost ten years later, was astonishment that Charlton's amiable and hospitable mood could have changed so suddenly to viciousness and aggression. He then turned round and hit Karen a powerful blow, knocking her to the floor. If anything, she was more slightly built than Mandy and no match for Alan Charlton. Ignoring the other two, he stood over the fifteen-year-old girl, beating her with his clenched fist, as if for defying his commands. But would he not realize that a man of his physique was likely to do appalling damage to an adolescent girl of relatively slight build? Both Mandy and Idris Ali swore that they tried to stop him but they later saw themselves as two children against this powerfully built adult. Idris Ali remembered Alan Charlton at one point picking up Karen by the throat and slapping her. Mandy pulled at his clothes while Idris Ali still tried to drag him off, receiving an incidental back-hander which knocked him out of the way.

Neither of the two witnesses saw any apparent cause or explanation for the savagery of the attack. Alan Charlton simply 'lost his rag' in Idris Ali's account or 'went berserk', as Mandy put it. He stood a little to one side of Karen, 'punching and slapping' the fallen girl. Idris Ali also replied during questioning that he remembered Charlton kicking her and saw Karen lying curled up in attempt to protect herself from the blows. Mandy heard Karen uttering 'loud cries' at first but there were apparently no words attached to them.

Not surprisingly, for a girl who was short of fourteen years old, Mandy was terrified and instinctively looked away. 'I was standing in the corner crying,' she said. The attack on Karen seemed to go on for 'ages' but when the younger girl looked back, it had stopped. Alan Charlton, still standing over his victim, said, 'God, she's dead!' Mandy, unable to believe that her companion was dead, went across to Karen and shook her but failed to rouse her. She had still no idea whether her friend really was dead or not. 'I'd never seen a dead person before.' Karen was lying on her side with her knees drawn up and a trickle of blood coming from her mouth. Alan Charlton 'just walked away from her,' Mandy said. 'He did not seem upset or bothered at what he had done.'

Almost ten years later, when Mandy recalled the sequel, she remembered standing terrified in the corner of the room. 'I was too scared to bloody move,' she said, 'You know what I mean?' Anyone who heard her account would know just what she meant. At the same time she felt 'mesmerized' by what she saw and 'couldn't believe it was happening.' She had alleged that Alan Charlton had then lifted Karen Price and laid her face-down on the bed, her jeans and pants pulled off. He also pushed her knees up so that, in Mandy's words, Karen's position was 'like when you've got your bum in the air.'

According to her version of events, Mandy knew rather than saw what followed as Alan Charlton stood behind Karen. She thought he was 'enjoying' himself and seemed 'relaxed'. Presently he turned away and said to Idris Ali, 'It's your turn' or 'You've got to do it now.' In Idris Ali's account, he stood where Alan Charlton made him stand but did nothing. Alan Charlton, according to Mandy, pulled her across and said, 'Watch. You might get to enjoy having it like this.' Her evidence, if she was accurate, was a horrific account of a man whom she described as Jekyll and Hyde and as a psychopath. One minute he was laughing and joking, then unpredictably he would become violent. She swore that she had the scar on her thigh to prove it.

Mandy's description of the death of Karen Price, taken on its own, cleared Idris Ali of any part in the assault or in what happened immediately afterwards. 'He was just as scared as me,' she said. He had tried to pull Alan Charlton off during the assault but being, as he described himself, 'a puny git' at fifteen, he failed. He later claimed that he had held a cheap mirror under Karen's nose as she lay there and had seen breath upon it, also that he had tried to make Alan Charlton call an ambulance. After nine years, Mandy did not remember these things but they may still have happened.

At some point after she was lifted on to the bed, a plastic carrier bag was drawn over Karen's head and the other two witnesses insisted that it was Alan Charlton who had tied her wrists behind her back. Mandy thought that he had used curtain wire to do this but it was probably the electric cable with which Karen's wrists were still tied behind her when she was found more than eight years later. When Alan Charlton went out of the basement flat to fetch the cable, Mandy could not remember whether he left the door open or closed it. She was so terrified by him that she could not even make an attempt to escape. 'I was bloody shaking,' she said simply.

No attempt was made to dispose of Karen's body that night but either Alan Charlton discussed it with Idris Ali or, at least, decided in his own mind what was to happen. There was a spare length of the carpet with which the floor of the basement flat had been covered. It was kept in a cupboard outside but he may have brought it in at this point. Mandy testified that she was sitting silent on the floor when he pulled her to her feet and said, 'If you say anything about this, you'll go the same way . . . You'll end up in the carpet.'

Idris Ali insisted that he had received a similar warning. 'I was fucking terrified,' he said, and then, 'He was a big guy. I was fifteen. I was scared.' Nine years later, when confronted with the crime, his response was much the same. 'I'm still scared of that guy. I'm not fucking saying anything.' There was no reason to doubt him.

On the night of her death, the two witnesses said, Alan Charlton lifted Karen Price's body 'in a crouching position' and put it into a built-in cupboard in the basement flat. Idris Ali said that he was told to come back in two days and help bury the girl. If not, he added, Alan Charlton promised to 'drop me in the shit'. He understood that, if there was any trouble, the murder would be put on himself and Mandy. Both had cause to believe this and to be scared of what might happen to them. There was nothing to suggest that Alan Charlton had a criminal record. But Idris Ali described himself as 'just out of prison', and living as a pimp. He was in no position to go to the police. If he admitted to them that he had been in the room with Alan Charlton when Karen Price was killed, he claimed that they would say, 'Bang! That's it! You're away with him.' As for Mandy, she insisted that she had been too terrified of Alan Charlton to pick him out on an identity parade even as an adult woman nine years later. Her best course was surely to keep the secret of the murder to herself. There is no evidence that she ever spoke of it to anyone.

Mandy left the basement flat first on the evening of Karen's death. Idris Ali hurried after her and caught her up. He told her to say nothing of what had happened. If she did, Alan Charlton would 'come after them'. In any case, telling the police would do Karen no good. In the horror of what they had witnessed and the terror of what might lie ahead, they parted company and assumed that neither would see the other again.

Mandy was soon back in council care. She remained there for almost a month before vanishing again. The social services failed to find her and thought that perhaps she was somehow being harboured by her mother, perhaps once again making her living on the streets. At fourteen, her part in the story seemed to be at an end.

Four days later, after trying to 'sort out' his mind, Idris Ali described how he went back to Fitzhamon Embankment. Though he swore to the truth of what followed, Alan Charlton denied that it ever happened. Once again, in Idris Ali's version, it was late in the afternoon. Alan Charlton was at home and in a bad mood. 'Where the fuck have you been?' he demanded, 'You were supposed to be here two days ago.'

Idris Ali's testimony described how, outside the back door, Alan Charlton had already begun to dig the grave, using a pickaxe and a shovel. The grave was about three feet deep, four feet wide and five feet long. They finished the work, Idris Ali using the shovel. In the flat itself there was what he described as a 'fowsty' smell, which made him 'heave a few times'. Karen's body was still in the cupboard and her skin had changed to a mottled colouring. Her body fluids had escaped and, when she had been lifted out, Alan Charlton gave Idris Ali the job of cleaning out the cupboard with rags. Idris Ali claimed that the body was stiff and that they had to break some of the bones to lift it out. This certainly goes against the forensic evidence which revealed no broken bones. Indeed, the body was buried face-down, when it was discovered in 1989, in much the position that it had been on the bed, at the time of death, in Mandy's testimony.

According to Idris Ali, it was Alan Charlton who cleaned up the body, which was covered only by the Fred Perry shirt while it was in the cupboard. Somehow, they managed to get the rest of the clothes on and then wrapped the corpse in dustbin-liners. The roll of carpet was brought in and the body covered by it, except the head and feet which protruded. At last the dead girl was carried out into the summer twilight of the shabby little garden at the back of the Riverside terrace.

This was the moment of greatest risk, increased by the discovery that the grave was too small for the body. There was nothing for it but to carry the corpse back into the flat and enlarge the excavation. Alan Charlton had pretended to be working on the area as a garden and subsequently planted a few flowers but he and Idris Ali were fortunate that no one happened to see them at that moment. They finished work in the dusk and buried Karen Price about three feet under the back garden. There seemed no reason why they should ever be brought to account. Each of the three witnesses to her death had strong motives for remaining silent. If ever the body was discovered, they would surely be far away. It might lie there for ten years, twenty years or for ever. Perhaps the houses of Fitzhamon Embankment would be demolished one day in the cause of urban renewal. By then there would be nothing but fragments of bone, unnoticed as the earth-movers gouged up the clay soil by the ton. The body of Karen Price was perhaps not the only one lying undiscovered in Riverside or Butetown.

So the three participants in the drama went their separate ways. Alan Charlton, who had been born in County Durham, left Cardiff the following year and became a roofer in Somerset. Idris Ali lived as he had done. He claimed that the death of Karen Price preyed on his mind but it could not do so to much effect. If his story was true and he had gone to the police with it, might they not have looked at that story and charged him with the murder? It was, after all, very much his word against Alan Charlton's. As for Mandy, she escaped the world of casual prostitution and the caring professions which had alternately ruled her at thirteen. She did unexpectedly well in her next few years, thanks to her own exertions and strength of character, and married happily. That she had been on the streets as a child was a matter of circumstance, not of personality.

No one else outside her immediate family seemed to have any further interest in Karen Price's disappearance. She was by no means the only girl of her age who had passed beyond the scope of a 'concerned' society. When the police failed to find her, she became one more statistic among other missing persons. Maes-Yr-Eglwys sent her papers back to South Glamorgan. South Glamorgan filed them. Then Maes-Yr-Eglwys closed down and its registers were destroyed. There seemed to be very little more that anyone could have done.

For other people the future was to be bright. The Cardiff Bay project promised to throw a barrage across the mouth of the docks. Blue water would sparkle where once the mud-banks had risen above the dredged channels at low tide. There would be leisure and money and youth. Promotional posters showed how it would happen. Where runaways had solicited by the drab railway wall, female mannequins would sit at computer terminals, their work made perpetual holiday by a view of a sunlit and well-paved waterside, lined by expensive cars and cafe tables that might have graced Palm Beach or Rapallo. The cocoa-brown estuary of the Bristol Channel would be transformed. Some of the more agreeable aspects of the past would be packaged as 'heritage', a world where nostalgia replaced history. Or so it seemed. Meanwhile, real history lay under the garden soil of Fitzhamon Embankment, waiting to be discovered.

V

Such was the ostensible story of the last weeks and days of Karen Price, drawn from Mandy's evidence and corroborated in part by Idris Ali. According to its chronology, Karen had absconded from Maes-Yr-Eglwys on 2 July 1981 and met Idris Ali in Cemetery Park, Adamstown, on the same day. By 5 July she was soliciting and on 8 or 9 July she went to Barry Island for several days. She and Idris Ali met Alan Charlton on 15 July, attending the 'Blue Movie Parties' on 18 and 25 July. On 30 July, Mandy had absconded from the outing at Porthcawl and came to Cardiff, probably via Newport or Barry, on 31 July or 1 August. Within a week, Karen Price was dead. By 12 August, she had been buried in the back garden of 29 Fitzhamon Embankment. So far as conflicting details of evidence could be reconciled a decade later, that was the story, told by Alan Charlton's accusers.

But much depended on how the story was told. Without Idris Ali's admission to his fellow lodger that he had known Karen, it might never have been told at all. In the first witness statement taken over two days in February 1990 he again admitted his association with Karen but not that he was connected with her murder. He never concealed the fact that at fifteen years old he had been a pimp or that Karen Price was one of his girls. The police were naturally interested to know who the others might have been. At some point he said enough for them to pick up Mandy's identity. With two suspects under interrogation, the South Wales CID set about finding the truth.

Idris Ali was picked up at 1.15 on the afternoon of Thursday 22 February and again taken to Norbury Road for questioning. The interview began at 2.15pm, with Detective Constable Les Mumford asking most of the questions. Idris Ali was later to suggest that he had been bullied into making certain statements, yet DC Mumford had both the appearance and the manner of a sympathetic therapist rather than an inquisitor. It was a long afternoon and an even longer night. At 4.03 on the morning of 23 February, the questioning over and breaks having been allowed, Idris Ali began a witness statement. By this time he had implicated Alan Charlton.

The police already knew that Alan Charlton had once occupied the basement flat at 29 Fitzhamon Embankment and that he was now working as a roofer on the other side of the Bristol Channel, at Bridgwater in Somerset. He had made a witness statement on 16 December 1989, at a time when the identity of the dead girl was not known and when, in any case, the police still assumed that she had died three years after Charlton had left Fitzhamon Embankment. Now Inspector George Lewis of the South Wales CID set out from Cardiff for Bridgwater to collect him.

Idris Ali's story of Karen's life followed Mandy's account, until the point where they had met Alan Charlton and attended two parties. It was after the parties, according to Idris Ali, that Karen had disappeared. Under further questioning, he admitted that he had seen her again and that he had been present, alone with Alan Charlton, when she was killed. After her initial disappearance, he had heard it rumoured among the other girls that Alan Charlton was keeping her tied to a bed in his flat, for his own use and that of his friends or customers. If this was so, then none of the other tenants at 29 Fitzhamon Embankment heard any sound of screams or disturbance. Until 22 July, Alan Charlton had a girlfriend, Sian, a nurse, who used to visit him. Then there had been the party on 25 July. After that, the ground floor flat was empty until 1 August, when its tenant came back from the United States.

In Idris Ali's chronology, it was in the afternoon, a few days after the second party, that he decided to go to Charlton's flat and demand the truth about what had happened to Karen Price. By then, it was alleged, Ali's third girl Jane was reporting stories of Karen being kept tied to the bed. Concerned at this, fifteen-year-old Idris Ali set off to see what had happened and to confront Charlton.

'Christ,' said DC Mumford with gentle scepticism, 'He's a big boy to go down and see on your own.'

When Alan Charlton opened the door, Idris Ali pushed his

way in. This hardly sounded like the 'puny git' of fifteen who said, 'He was a big guy . I was scared.' Karen was lying on the bed, her feet tied with bootlaces.

'Did she have bruises?' DC Mumford asked. Idris Ali replied that she did not. Nor did she have cuts or black eyes. She merely looked scruffy or as if Alan Charlton had been 'scruffing her up'. She began shouting and screaming, 'Get me out of here!' She said, in Idris Ali's version, 'They're all having me! They're all abusing me!' This sounded very much like a witness statement euphemism. DC Mumford asked Ali to repeat what it was she said 'in street language'. The witness obliged. Karen had shouted, 'They're all fucking me.'

Nine years had passed since these events and it was understandable, if the story were true, that there might be inconsistencies in the details. In one version Karen's feet were tied to the bed with bootlaces, then her legs were tied together. At one moment Idris Ali remembered her hands were tied behind her, then in front of her. In one version, they were not tied at all, which was why he had to hold them while Charlton strangled her. In this version, he recalled Karen screaming, 'Get me out of here!' and Alan Charlton saying, 'Get over here and hold her fucking hands!' Charlton himself was now kneeling astride her. Idris Ali refused to have anything to do with this until Charlton told him to hold the girl's hands, 'or you'll go the same way.' Then, said Idris Ali, 'I was fucking terrified.'

He later suggested that he might have had reason to fear what Karen would do, since she was 'ranting and raving . . . threatening to grass everybody up.' In her shouts, 'She wanted to get out of there. She wanted to go back to the home. She was going to get the police on to me.' Was this enough to turn her rescuer into an accessory?

While this interrogation of Idris Ali was in progress, two other CID officers had brought in Mandy for questioning soon after 6pm on 22 February. Like the other inmates who had been at Maes-Yr-Eglwys in 1981, she had already made witness statements, on 24 January and 3 February. In neither of these had she mentioned either Alan Charlton or Idris Ali. When allowed home after questioning, she had told her husband that the police were investigating the death of Karen Price and that she had given them 'a load of bull'. Her husband warned her that she had been silly to do so and advised her to get in touch with a solicitor. Before she could do that, the police called for her again.

On the evening of 22 February, she had been questioned at Norbury Road Police Station by DC Taylor and PCW Cullen. With surprisingly little persuasion, she told the story of having been with Idris Ali and Karen Price in Big Astey's on the afternoon when Charlton met them there. They had gone back to his flat, where there had been an argument about nude photographs. He had beaten Karen with his fists until she was dead. Then she had been lifted on to the bed. It seemed that she was then dead and that what Charlton did to her was an act of necrophilia. He had tried to make Idris Ali follow his example. Mandy herself had never been back to the house since the evening of Karen's death. She had been 'on the game' a few times as a child runaway but Idris Ali had never been her pimp. 'Idris wasn't my pimp. I never had a pimp.' Nor was Alan Charlton. She had never again seen either Alan Charlton or Idris Ali after the evening of Karen Price's death.

It seemed that the murder squad of South Wales CID had got the evidence it needed almost overnight. But several things were about to go wrong. Mandy discovered that, having told the police her story, she was not yet to be allowed to go home. Indeed, she had been brought to Norbury Road under arrest. They now locked her in a cell at Norbury Road. As she was being locked up, she alleged, 'people' said to her, 'You're going in for a long time. Twenty-five years may be.'

Only then did the danger of her situation appear plain. She was not there as an innocent witness but as a murder suspect. After all, the truth she now told, if it was the truth, had been kept from the police in her earlier witness statements. She had, at the least, concealed a murder. There were other matters to think over, alone in the cell. In 1981, she seemed to have little to lose but in the nine years since the death of Karen Price, Mandy's life had changed considerably for the better, largely through her own efforts. She had passed her GCE exams and got a job. She had made a success of her marriage. Perhaps unwisely, she had said nothing to her husband of her early years on the streets, though he knew of the dismal background to her childhood. Now, out of the blue, came the threat of publicity, criminal charges and the destruction of all that she had built up. If someone really had told her that she might go away for twenty-five years, it had been an extremely foolish threat. She was terrified by it. 'I wasn't going from here for something I never did,' she said plaintively. Few people would not have sought a way out of this at any cost.

The way she chose was ill-advised. Next morning, facing PCW Cullen and DC Taylor in the interview room at Norbury Road, Mandy withdrew her previous story and denied all knowledge of the death of Karen Price. She claimed that she hardly knew Idris Ali and he had certainly never been her pimp. She knew Karen Price while in care but had spent very little time with her. The stone-walling continued throughout the day. With understandable irritation, her interrogators asked her why on the previous evening she had told the story of Karen Price's death, if it was untrue. Mandy's reply was that she had been told by the police that if she made a statement, she could go home. So she made her statement.

But her position was already hopeless. Both she and Idris Ali confirmed that Karen's wrists had been tied behind her back with wire of some kind. When the skeleton was found the wrists were still tied behind the back with cable. But this detail had not been included in the 'Crimewatch' broadcast. How could a witness know of it unless he – or she – had been present at Karen's death? Despite this, Mandy held out for almost twelve hours under police questioning on 23 February. The questioning began at 11.10am and ended, after a long interval at 9.15pm, at 10.49pm. She was interviewed in a ground floor room while Idris Ali was questioned in two rooms on the floor above. To begin with neither knew the other was there.

Mandy's interrogators were gentle with her, they could afford to be. She had gone too far the evening before to pull back now.

'What's going to happen at the end of the day?' DC Taylor asked patiently, 'What do you think?'

'I don't know,' she said miserably.

'Give us a guess.'

It reduced her to silence. Two days before, her life had been settled and reasonably secure, the nightmare of another girl's death almost nine years in the past, perhaps almost forgotten. Now it threatened all that she had worked for, suddenly and completely. It was not hard to understand the impulse to run from the threat in a moment of panic that came too late. Yet the weakness of Mandy's denials, as the day dragged by in a sequence of inconclusive interviews, was put to her by DC Taylor.

'Who's to say – if you keep telling lies – who's to say that you and Ali didn't do it?'

This produced no response, perhaps because she was reflecting that it was a similar threat to the one she said Alan Charlton had made almost nine years before. DC Taylor returned to the point a little more forcefully.

'The more it goes on, the more it seems you might have taken part in the murder.'

Still nothing. The time came for DC Taylor to say something about Idris Ali and his questioning in the other room.

'Idris is upstairs. He's saying – I won't say he's giving you the out – he's saying you took no part in it.'

'Of course I took no part in it. I wasn't there.'

To explain her account of the murder, which she had given on the previous evening, she insisted rather feebly that DC Taylor had pressurized her. She had said it all to get the police 'off my back'.

'How long was I there?' she asked of that interview, 'You kept on at me . . . Idris said this, Idris said that . . . . If I made a statement, I could go home.'

Was she yet another witness who told the police what she thought they wanted to hear just to get the ordeal over with?

That was too good to be true. But the second day of questioning passed without any further progress. Mandy was told that
her husband had been shown the files of her record as a
juvenile. He had already known of the wretched circumstances of her childhood and, though it had never been
discussed between them, he now told the police that he had
privately accepted the possibility that she had been on the
streets at that age. The more credit to her for having pulled
herself up from such squalor. In the interview room at
Norbury Road, her interrogators mingled persistence with
humanity. At 9.15 on the evening of 23 February, with the
questioning suspended for an hour and a half, she was
allowed to talk privately with her husband and her solicitor.
Her worst fears for her marriage and personal life were without foundation. So far as the case was concerned, she would
be given anonymity, protection if necessary. The last point
was important. Two days later she repeated that she was still
'petrified' of Alan Charlton. She knew what he was capable
of. He would know where to find her. Perhaps her evidence
against him might cost her her life.

'We'll protect you,' DC Taylor said, 'It isn't like that. This is
England. This is 1990.'

In the light of such promises, she once again told the story
of Karen's murder and swore that it was true.

Idris Ali had been loyal to her, whatever his motive may
have been. He told several versions of a story in which he had
gone alone to Fitzhamon Embankment on the occasion of
Karen's death, the plucky lad of fifteen who had gone to res-
cue a girl of the same age from the hands of a brutish adult
bully. When DC Les Mumford told him, 'Mandy's playing ball
with us now,' there was no point in maintaining this pretence.
Yet it was merely the end of a period of questioning during
which Idris Ali had tried to leave Mandy out of it.

'You fuckers, you caught me out there,' he said.

'You caught yourself out, Idris,' Mumford said quietly. His
interrogation had been in just that tone, 'You've been bopping
and diving. Your arms and your feet have been going. We
know you're scared. We're sympathetic.'

When told that his statements did not match one another, Idris Ali said,

'I'm trying to get myself out of the shit, plus cover Mandy . . . . It's not nice for her to go through a thing like that. What she seen and what I seen, you know, in the years gone by.'

From Mandy's evidence, the officers questioning the pair knew that a sexual act after the victim's death was part of the insane scenario alleged at Fitzhamon Embankment. During the questioning of Idris Ali, Les Mumford went downstairs and read a photocopy of Mandy's statement. He went back and suggested that Ali had not 'told the truth'. Ali admitted 'messing you about'. Next day he added, 'I've been making up a lot of it as we go along.'

Why? In Idris Ali's own account it was because there was one thing, worse than murder, that he could not bring himself to mention. It was an act of necrophilia which, he alleged, Charlton had committed and which, despite Charlton's orders, he had managed to avoid himself. Mandy had at first said nothing of this in her statement because, as she later explained, the memory of it sickened her. There was no doubt of that. On the interview tape, when she at length referred to it, she was in tears and DC Taylor asked her,

'Are you going to be sick?'

When the alleged act of necrophilia was put to Idris Ali, he refused to discuss it.

'I don't want to get involved. I don't want to fucking know because it sickens me . . . . There's things I'm not telling anyone.'

There was of course, no evidence that he himself had committed such an act, only his allegation that Alan Charlton had tried unsuccessfully to make him do so. Idris Ali's fear was that his family would hear of this. What would his wife's reaction be?

'Shock-horror, isn't it?' he said plaintively.

At 12pm on 23 February, there was a lull in the questioning during which several events took place. First of all, Idris Ali asked the duty inspector what was going to happen to him.

He was told that he would be detained during further inquiries. For the first time, according to police evidence, there was an outburst in the presence of Detective Inspector Graham Mouncher.

'This is fucking shit, man!' Ali was reported as saying, 'I've told you all I know . . . I've got a wife and a family out there . . . I'm retracting all I said . . . I was kept against my will. When I tried to leave the interview room, the police officers barred my way.'

He insisted that neither he nor Mandy had committed any crime. Mandy had been allowed home after four hours in the cells. Why should he not be allowed to go as well?

Though the South Wales CID had a story, a temporary retraction of evidence by both the principal witnesses would not help matters in court. As if to smooth the way a little, Idris Ali was allowed a supervised visit from his wife. She was innocent of any connection with the alleged crimes, not having met him until long after 1981. The supervising officer, DC Mitchell, a tall Scotsman, heard Ali tell his wife the story of Karen's death and burial. His wife began to cry and urged him to tell the truth, if not for her sake then for the baby's. Both were soon in tears.

After the noon interlude, there were two other confrontations, one intended and one accidental. A 'confrontation' was staged between Idris Ali and Mandy, police officers bringing them both into the same room. Despite the lapse of nine years, Idris Ali recognized her immediately. As he was being led away to the interview room once more, Inspector George Lewis arrived from Bridgwater and brought Alan Charlton to the custody desk.

'That's him,' Idris Ali said, 'That's Charlton.'

Nothing of all this appeared in the press until a banner headline in the *South Wales Echo* for 24 February announced:

Body in Carpet – 2 men, woman quizzed

KAREN : THREE ARRESTED

The report added that 'A 29-year-old unmarried man from Bridgwater in Somerset was picked up at 6pm last night from his work.' That was the first news of the arrest of Alan Charlton.

It was some time later when an identity parade was held for Mandy and the other girl, Jane, to whom Alan Charlton had allegedly become a pimp to see if they could recognize the man they had known almost nine years before. Idris Ali was, of course, disqualified by virtue of having seen Charlton at the custody desk. The parade was held with a row of volunteers from a Cardiff weight-lifting club. Given Charlton's fifty-three-inch chest and powerful build he would have stood out far too conspicuously among any other group. The young women viewed him through a one-way glass panel to shield their own identities. Mandy, when asked if she saw the man who had killed Karen Price, said he was not in the line-up. Worse still, so did Jane, the other witness.

By contrast with Idris Ali and Mandy, Alan Charlton behaved reasonably and sensibly at the time of his arrest. He agreed that he had lived in the basement flat of 29 Fitzhamon Embankment from June 1981 until February 1982. He worked as a doorman at the Excel, the Philharmonic, and the Xanadu. He was a conspicuous figure, known by sight to a great many people who were not personally known to him. He had never known Idris Ali, nor Mandy nor Karen Price. At first he was asked whether he had known Karen Price nine years ago.

'Not that I remember,' he said. After all it was a long time.

He was then shown Karen's photograph.

'I categorically do not know this girl,' he said.

He was pressed further, as to whether he had ever seen her, nine years before. It was an almost impossible question to answer without qualification. Of course he could not swear that he had never set eyes on her and then forgotten but he was certain he had never known her 'personally'. When shown photographs of several other residents at Fitzhamon Embankment, he said that they were 'vaguely familiar'. He really had not known them very well.

Everything in this was, more or less, what an innocent man

might say. He also denied categorically ever having known Idris Ali or Mandy. Their account of the murder was 'a fairy story'. Indeed, as he said to his interrogators, if Idris Ali and the girl admitted being present when Karen Price died, 'It seems to me that you have the man you want for this murder and his accomplice.'

Alan Charlton's defence was all or nothing. Yet it was an absolute defence. There was no forensic evidence to connect him with the killing and, perhaps, no reliable circumstantial evidence. The two principal witnesses both had previous convictions of one sort or another. Both, according to the police, had lied with some energy during the present investigation. Apart from their allegations against Alan Charlton, there might be little that could not be explained, however, implausibly. Those allegations were to be regarded with some caution. Suppose, for example, that the two witnesses had been able to get into the ground floor flat at Fitzhamon Embankment while the tenant was in the United States. There might have been drug-taking, glue-sniffing or some other pastime which ended in the death of Karen Price. Was it impossible that they might have been able to bury her body while Alan Charlton was at work? Surely, living so much on the streets of central Cardiff, they might know something of him and his movements.

There could be no further progress without independent evidence or witnesses. On 27 February Cardiff magistrates received a bail application on Alan Charlton's behalf. They refused it and remanded him in custody until 5 March. He was then put on an identity parade, where two witnesses failed to pick him out. Mandy later said that she could have picked him out but was too frightened of him to do so. It would sound like a rather lame answer under cross-examination. The murder squad began to spread its net wider.

VI

It would not do simply to show that Alan Charlton had been well known at Fitzhamon Embankment. There had to be links connecting him with either Mandy or Idris Ali or Karen Price, preferably all three. As the questioning of witnesses continued South Wales CID found a number of people whose memories associated Alan Charlton with Idris Ali or either of the men with Karen Price. Unfortunately, after nine years, none of these witnesses gave evidence which was conclusive.

Arthur Wells, who had been the handyman at Fitzhamon Embankment in 1981, was shown the photograph of Karen in a trilby hat. He remembered seeing Alan Charlton talking to a 'very similar' fair-haired girl outside the house. Karen, if it was she, had been sitting on the low garden wall facing the river accompanied by a woman of about thirty when Charlton spoke to her. Mr Wells was pressed on the similarity. After all, a girl wearing a trilby hat was less easy to identify in any case. Judging by the photograph, Mr Wells said that if this was not the girl he had seen at Fitzhamon Embankment, it was 'very, very like her'.

What else could he remember about Alan Charlton? He recalled that Charlton had done some decorating at Fitzhamon Embankment. Then there had been a time when Charlton told him that his training as a weightlifter would benefit from a vegetarian diet. Charlton had even tried a little gardening, scattering lettuce seeds on the earth, at the rear of 29 Fitzhamon Embankment but Mr Wells was of the opinion that he had little idea how to go about it. Was this a further cause for suspicion or not? The training was certainly genuine, since Charlton had a set of weights in his flat. Finally, Mr Wells recalled that blue films had been shown during parties held in the basement flat. While Mr Wells was telling his story, Charlton was shown a photograph of him. He said again that the face was 'vaguely familiar'. Perhaps that was not unreasonable after eight or nine years, since Mr Wells had not lived at 29 Fitzhamon Embankment but in the adjoining house.

One other memory of Fitzhamon Embankment came from Mr Glyndwr Pethers, who had also known Alan Charlton by sight. Mr Pethers recalled seeing a youth, whom he described as 'a skinny half-caste', leaving the house one day. Charlton had called out to him, 'Idris!' Mr Pethers remembered this because one of his own names was Idris and he thought that the call was directed at him. Unfortunately, Mr Pethers in his statement remembered this as happening in 1980, which it could not have done, if Charlton was calling to Idris Ali. Charlton was not in Cardiff in 1980. Yet Mr Pethers remembered him and, like Mr Wells, recalled the unsuccessful attempts at gardening at the rear of the house.

When Charlton was questioned about this, he denied that he had made any attempt at gardening. He and his girlfriend Sian had acquired a puppy in July 1981, an Alsatian-Doberman cross. He was merely trying to fence off part of the back garden so that he could safely leave the dog there. That he had bought the puppy was corroborated by Sian and by other witnesses. He kept it for three weeks and then got rid of it because the basement flat was an unsuitable place to keep a dog. It may also have been against the terms of the tenancy. Again, the presence of the puppy would surely have been incompatible with that of a dead body. Was this another sign that Alan Charlton might be telling the truth, when he said he knew nothing of the murder nor of those involved? His performance on the interview tapes was certainly impressive in this respect.

The Excel Restaurant provided one or two tenuous links between Alan Charlton and Karen Price. Beverley Cavanagh had been a waitress at the Excel and recalled seeing Alan Charlton and Idris Ali there. Helen Cowland, another waitress, saw Idris Ali talking to a girl in a doorway sometime during the summer of 1981. Though so many years had elapsed and Mrs Cowland had never known Karen Price, she remembered the girl as looking like Karen's photographs. Yet these sightings were somewhat less than a firm link in the chain of evidence. How many weak links could there be before that chain snapped?

Prince Mottram made a statement in which he said that he had seen Idris Ali and Alan Charlton together outside Astey's cafe, in Wood Street. But in his statement he dated the year as 1982. If that were so, it could only have happened in January or February, before Alan Charlton left Cardiff. In any case, the evidence did not indicate whether Charlton and Ali had known one another well or had encountered each other in the street as comparative strangers. It also raised again the question of whether Alan Charlton was to be thought guilty merely because he could not remember every person whom he had met casually nine years earlier.

There were, of course, witnesses who might link the two men beyond question. The third girl, Jane, for whom Idris Ali was said in evidence to have acted as pimp, alleged that she had then been acquired by Alan Charlton and that, on three occasions, she had taken a man back to the basement flat of 29 Fitzhamon Embankment. She had also had the name 'Alan' tattooed on her hand by another girl at Maes-Yr-Eglwys, though this tattoo had been surgically removed before 1989. However, the court ruled that her evidence must be approached 'with caution'. Much of it was uncorroborated and it appeared that 'Alan' might have been a boyfriend other than Alan Charlton.

Apart from Arthur Wells, there were others who remembered something of what went on at Fitzhamon Embankment that summer. David Harries, the former SAS soldier, had identified Karen Price as the girl who was sitting on the floor while the films were shown. But the girl was wearing a trilby hat, like another of the girls present, and the light was poor. As in the case of almost every witness, after nine years of fading memory, there were inconsistencies in his successive statements. He maintained that Karen Price was the girl sitting on the floor. Yet having picked out Mandy from a set of photographs shown him by the police, he gave evidence that she was not at the party. Had he simply picked her out by chance? It was possible. Of the two men, he recognized Alan Charlton from a set of photographs but failed to remember Idris Ali.

Matters were not helped by the fact that David Harries volunteered three later statements to the police which went missing. They were not seen by either the prosecution or the defence. He said, reasonably enough, that he tended to remember further details of these events nine summers ago as he thought about them more carefully. He made his first statement in January 1990 and the final ones, which were not revealed to either side in the case, at the end of the year.

Finally, there was the evidence of the chef who had gone back to Fitzhamon Embankment when three girls were in attendance. He and Charlton were downstairs with two of the girls, the third girl was upstairs with someone else. He now thought that the girl upstairs had been Karen Price. It was another fragment of the story, if the story had been remembered accurately. There was virtually nothing connecting Mandy with Alan Charlton in the statements of the witnesses. This was of considerable significance, since the investigation relied upon her account of having been present when Karen Price was killed. When further evidence was examined in detail, there was doubt as to whether it was physically possible for her to have been at Fitzhamon Embankment or even in Cardiff. That would leave only the word of Idris Ali, who had contradicted himself in the course of police inquiries.

In his defence, it was said that Alan Charlton's lifestyle was not an issue. Yet the evidence of his life after he had left Cardiff was unlikely to enhance his claim to innocence. This was, perhaps, unfair since he had no relevant criminal convictions during that period. Much of what happened between 1981 and 1984 was related in the testimony of Peggy Pesticcio, who had been his companion from the autumn of 1981 and was with him when he left Cardiff in February 1982. They made their way to Taunton and then, after some years, the 'stormy relationship' of 'on-off' living together, as she called it, broke up.

During this time, the couple had both been CB radio enthusiasts. Peggy Pesticcio's call-sign had been 'Misty Blue'. Alan Charlton's, she recalled, was 'The Executioner'. That now seemed an unfortunate choice, even as a joke. After they had parted company and Mrs Pesticcio was living with her husband at Tilbury in Essex, Charlton drove there to take some of her clothes back. He had a four-inch penknife tucked into his sock and when she asked why, she alleged that he said simply, 'To do your old man with.'

Then he said that he was going to leave her all his effects before driving the car 'into a brick wall'.

Yet the most potentially damaging evidence from Mrs. Pesticcio concerned a photograph which Alan Charlton kept in his wallet. It showed a girl lying full-length and naked on a bed. When the first photographs of Karen Price appeared in the press, Mrs Pesticcio at once identified her as the girl in this photograph. Alan Charlton had never denied having had a photograph in his wallet but he insisted that it was not of Karen Price. It was of another girl, Diane. When Diane was questioned by the police, she agreed that there had been such a photograph of her lying on a bed but that it showed her wearing a pair of knickers rather than completely naked. Which girl was in the photograph was never to be determined. Would Alan Charlton really carry around a photograph of a girl whom he had murdered? Either he was innocent of this or, if guilty, perhaps he regarded it as a trophy of some kind. In the end, it could not be proved to be a photograph of Karen Price.

The evidence which Peggy Pesticcio gave to the police might do little for Alan Charlton's character but neither did it much strengthen the case against him. The photograph in his wallet might have been Karen Price or not. However, since Mrs. Pesticcio had recognized it by first seeing Karen's photograph in the *South Wales Echo*, that identification was 'contaminated' as evidence in court.

From this evidence, the South Wales CID were to build their case. The final taped interviews with the suspects were on the evening of Saturday 24 February. However, by no means all the exchanges occurred during the official taped interviews. On that Saturday morning at 10am, DC Les Mumford had entered Idris Ali's cell, where the prisoner had allegedly confessed to him both strangling Karen and the occurrence of necrophilia. He would never admit in evidence to being present during the latter crime because his family wouldn't 'accept' it. When the interviews resumed with the tape recorder on, he denied committing either crime. Why, in that case, had he made the admissions in his cell, where there were no other witnesses? He complained that it was first thing in the morning and Mumford 'just came in', adding, 'My defences were down.'

On the final tape, that evening, Idris Ali repeated that he had been making up much of the story as he went along and was now ready to compile a tape about 'How Karen Price died.' DC Les Mumford said gently, 'Let this be that tape.' The details changed again. In this version, after Karen had been beaten but not killed by Alan Charlton, Idris Ali was holding her hands while she lay on her back. Mandy was holding her feet, crying as she did so. Charlton was sitting on Karen's stomach as he strangled her. At one point, he indicated that Charlton had stopped before the girl was dead and made Ali himself finish off the act of strangling her. By this admission, Ali now also implicated Mandy specifically in the crime. The two had obeyed Charlton under duress, if this story were true. Perhaps Idris Ali believed that this would clear them in court. He certainly showed no sign of knowing that duress is not a defence to a charge of murder.

As if for good measure, he added another chapter to the story. After Karen was dead, Charlton went out of the room and returned with a knife, apparently a kitchen knife of some kind. He made both Ali and Mandy cut the dead girl's face with it. Then Charlton cut her back, her arms and her legs. The cuts were deep, 'like cutting a fish'. The press reports were more melodramatic and translate this into a vision of 'gutting' Karen, which was certainly not the suggestion. Presumably the story, which was not supported in any way, was intended to show that Alan Charlton shut the mouths of the two witnesses by making them accomplices in this manner. It was perhaps coincidence that something similar had been alleged in the Lynett White trial at Swansea, where two prosecution witnesses claimed that they had been made by the accused men to stab the murdered girl.

On the evening of Sunday 25 February 1990, Alan Charlton

was charged with the murder of Karen Price. He maintained his story that he knew nothing about the people or events of July and August 1981. The accusation against him was 'well out of order'. Idris Ali had been talking to the police officers about Saturday's England versus Wales rugby international at Twickenham just before he was charged. While he was exercising in the yard of Norbury Road police station, under the supervision of PC John Davies, he asked where Alan Charlton was being held. PC Davies indicated the room. Idris Ali asked if the door was securely locked, saying that Charlton would kill him if he got out. 'He's a fucking psycho,' he added.

After he was charged, Ali allegedly said to Sergeant Warwick, 'I had to do it. How long do you think I'll get?'

This was the last of his admissions to the police. However, a police officer who was on duty in the Norbury Road detention suite gave evidence of a conversation overheard in the showers, when Idris Ali was talking to another prisoner, and telling once again the story that no one else had told against him.

'What have they got you for, mate?' the other man asked.

'That girl Karen down Riverside. The one that was murdered.'

'Fuck me, that's a bit heavy! What's the score with that, then?'

'There were two of us there. If I hadn't done it, I'd have been topped. Charlton made me do it. He's a psycho. He'd have done me, if I hadn't done her.'

Though there was no evidence of bones being broken in the dead girl's throat, the dental evidence of Dr Whittaker had shown a pink discoloration of the teeth in the skull, which indicated strangulation. Was it possible, despite Mandy's evidence, that Karen had merely been knocked unconscious by Alan Charlton and that either he or Idris Ali had strangled her on the bed when she came round? Had Mandy, in her statements to the police, been protecting Idris Ali from this, as he had tried to protect her by saying that he went to see Charlton alone? On the day after he had been charged, Monday 26 February, he and Charlton appeared at Cardiff magistrates court and were remanded in custody. But that was also the day on which Idris Ali allegedly added the medical officer of Cardiff prison to the list of those whom he told that he had strangled Karen Price. What purpose he thought it would serve was never clear. When asked in court why he had made the confession to the doctor, if he was innocent, Idris Ali said, 'My head had gone, boss.'

Was this the effect of several days of questioning or of a teenage decade of soft drugs? As an afterthought, he added, 'I never liked doctors, anyhow.'

Without his off-the-cuff confessions, might not Idris Ali have avoided implication in the worst of the crime? Mandy insisted that Charlton had killed Karen before she was lifted on to the bed. Nothing had been done to kill her while she was on the bed. She had not been cut nor stabbed. Alan Charlton maintained that he knew nothing of Ali. It must have seemed that Ali was hell-bent on involving himself in the crime. Once during the recorded interviews he accused his questioners of 'fucking with my mind', but that seemed scarcely enough to explain his progressive self-incrimination. He complained of being pressurized but the voice of DC Mumford on the tapes said gently, 'We know you're scared. . . . We're sympathetic.'

The events preceding the trial were by no means over. The mud-grey walls of Cardiff prison enclosed some of the most wretched remand accommodation that could have been imagined. On the other hand, they did not exclude cannabis nor pornography of one sort or another. The spring of 1990 was to be a season of riot in the prison as the staff continued to struggle against overcrowding and dereliction. Even prisoners remanded on a murder charge seemed to mix more freely than might have been supposed.

Alan Charlton, a Category 'A' prisoner, fraternized quite freely with others if their evidence is to be believed. Philip Ashon, serving a sentence of twenty-one months, informed the police that Alan Charlton had visited his cell to smoke cannabis or borrow a soft-porn magazine.

'He came into my cell and we had a smoke of cannabis. He

started talking about his case. He said that he was in for murder but that they didn't have any evidence on him. They couldn't prove anything. He just carried on talking, saying he met these two people in a pub and went back to a flat. They had a smoke and he wanted sex with this girl but she wouldn't agree. Charlton said he put her on the floor, tied her up, and raped her.'

This was not quite the story Mandy had told. Indeed, Charlton's alleged account of the murder matched the strangling version rather too neatly.

'He said he wanted Mr Ali to top her because she wouldn't have sex with him and she threatened to go to the police. Ali wouldn't do it, so Charlton slapped him. He still wouldn't do it, so Charlton said he strangled her himself. He said they then wrapped her in a carpet and buried her.'

In this version, the events were telescoped so that it sounded as if Karen's death had followed soon after the meeting in the pub, rather than a few weeks later. But that was not all. According to Philip Ashon, he and another prisoner, Kelvin Childs subsequently visited Charlton in his cell. Charlton told the same story about the killing and 'inscribed' the word 'Death' on his hand.

It was suggested that Ashon had told the story because he was a friend of Idris Ali's brother. In whatever version, it made nonsense of the legend that men accused of sex crimes – especially when the victim was under-age – were the pariahs of the prison system. Apart from the suggestion in the showers that the death of Karen Price was 'a bit heavy', there was no indication that either Charlton or Ali stood in any danger. Indeed, if the evidence of the other prisoners was right, there was a certain cachet in having committed the ultimate crime against the girl. Power or prestige attached to the man who had killed.

Like Alan Charlton, Idris Ali spent a year on remand in Cardiff prison. In his version, Charlton approached him on a prison landing and said, 'You shouldn't have made statements against me. We'll fight this case together, if you write down things and say the police pressurized you into giving false confessions.'

Charlton, according to Ali, repeated this suggestion several times. In the end, he wrote an account in a note book of how the investigating officers had shouted at him and bullied him into making statements. He gave the note book to Charlton.

Whether or not this was true, Ali certainly wrote letters from prison to a friend in Shepton Mallet prison, the first written on 21 April 1990. These were intercepted and the contents noted. 'Well, guy, so you heard I am in here . . . . The police stitched me up.' A second letter referred to his having been 'stitched up' by the police and said of Mandy, 'She could have come forward nine years ago.' Of Alan Charlton, he wrote, 'I don't know the man.'

Alan Charlton, of course, still maintained that he had never known Ali until they were arrested and that none of the alleged prison conversations had taken place. Certainly, evidence offered by other prisoners was likely to be regarded with something more than 'caution' in a murder trial. Once again, it was a point upon which the Lynett White case had turned and was, therefore, vulnerable to particular scepticism.

From all this, once again, Ali emerged with his prospects worse than they had been. The taped evidence of police interviews suggested that the officers questioning him had been anything but bullying or hectoring. They did not shout at him, they talked quietly and persuasively. If the bullying happened elsewhere, he never produced convincing evidence of it. The friendly testimony of Philip Ashon and the letters to Shepton Mallet cancelled one another out. In the Ashon version of events, Idris Ali had been present when Karen Price was strangled by Charlton. In the letters, Idris Ali had never set eyes on Charlton before. One or other account must be false. To make matters worse, he withdrew the allegations in the letters and explained that he had first thought of defending himself by 'dragging the police's name through the mud'. As the time for this trial approached, he decided against this, presumably on legal advice. But this retraction, made publicly in court, cast further doubt on the truth of any evidence that he gave.

But why had he ever given any evidence at all?

The troubles of Cardiff prison were to play a part in the months before the trial. By 1991 its prison officers were taking industrial action, refusing to accept any more detainees. The breakdown of the system had reached a point which sounded farcical when detailed in the press. 'Cardiff prisoner given rail pass and told: "Go to jail on your own," on 30 May 1991 was an account of how a prisoner at Cardiff who was being transferred to another prison 'was today given a rail pass – and told to surrender himself at the gate.' A few weeks later on 14 June came news of a prison escape by two inmates. They were on remand and therefore entitled to wear civilian clothes. They waited until visiting hours and then simply 'walked out through the front door', without a question or a challenge.

During the ten months when Alan Charlton and Idris Ali were remand prisoners, conditions were such that it seems not at all impossible for Charlton to have fraternized with other inmates who were not Category 'A' or top security. Yet the history of those ten months was dominated by news of a prison riot which involved Idris Ali. If the story reached the jurors, then Idris Ali could scarcely be an unknown name as his trial began.

At first it was not clear how or why the riot had started, though it caused 'mass destruction' to 'A' wing of Cardiff prison and major damage which took a year to repair. According to the evidence at a subsequent trial, Principal Prison Officer Owen Williams reported a fight at breakfast time on 8 April 1990 between Idris Ali and Patrick McCann. He said that he saw another prisoner, Desmond Preedy, pick up a tea bucket and throw it at the prison staff, 'Ali threw a metal tray and the leg of a table. It was terrifying. The inmates charged forward – they started smashing everything in sight. It was mayhem. We then began to evacuate those prisoners who did not wish to be involved.' Steel bars were used as battering rams, the canteen was looted, there was an attempt to break out on to the roof of the prison, and a two-inch thick steel door was battered in.

Another of the prison officers on duty, Clifford Cox,

described negotiations with Idris Ali after fires had been started in 'A' wing. He said that Ali told him that firemen would be allowed in to deal with the fires. 'He said that if they found any prison staff among them, there would be dead bodies.' Another officer 'nearly died' in the riot when he was choked to unconsciousness as his keys were taken.

To make matters worse for Idris Ali, Patrick McCann alleged the cause of the fight. He walked into his cell where, he claimed, he found Ali going through his private possessions. 'I gave Ali a dig in the ribs and he started shouting, getting aggressive. He threw a tray at me and I threw him out of the cell.' McCann then locked himself in with his cell-mate.

If there was such a threat, by a man on a murder charge, that there would be 'dead bodies' in the prison, it was at the least ill-judged. Idris Ali and nine other prisoners were charged with riot and, in the sentences eventually imposed, he was marked as one of the ringleaders. The case of prison riot was tried after the murder charge. During the murder trial, no reference was permitted to any other charge than the one being tried. Yet Idris Ali had put himself in the news through the riot, nine months before the murder trial. It would have taken only one or two members of the murder jury to know this in order to challenge the image of the gentle misled adolescent who never meant harm to anyone.

After the riot, a number of those involved were put into solitary confinement, pending police investigations and disciplinary proceedings. Several of them then went on hunger strike. This became a major news item in South Wales. On 19 April, eleven days after the riot, the *South Wales Echo* reported that Mrs Ali 'said her husband Idris Ali is refusing food in sympathy with other prisoners held in solitary following the riots in "A" wing on 8 April.' He had 'united with the other prisoners in protest at conditions in the jail and alleged assaults by warders.' Both the newspaper and Mrs Ali referred to the charge in the 'Body in the Carpet' case, of which Idris Ali maintained his innocence. The report did not specify that Idris Ali had been one of the rioters but the implication could easily be read into it. He was 'in sympathy with other prisoners held in solitary.' If one of the murder trial jury remembered that a defendant in the Karen Price murder was an alleged rioter, the gentle figure in the witness-box might be seen in another light.

There was no doubt that conditions in Cardiff prison were appalling, though the previous evening's correspondence column, on 18 April, contained a lady's demand to 'Bring back the rope, the birch, and above all hard labour – then they would be too tired to have time on their hands or the opportunity to riot.' There was, in truth, very little sympathy for the rioters.

On the other hand, the more deeply Idris Ali incriminated himself, the better the chances for Alan Charlton. There was no reference to any criminal conviction against Alan Charlton. Idris Ali admitted his record as a burglar and a pimp, in order to explain why he had been reluctant to report Karen Price's death to the police. By now there was also the untried charge of prison riot and the evidence of the 'dead bodies' threat. He had told contradictory stories to the police and as a witness in court he did not improve matters. The only other person to corroborate his innocence of murder – though he had admitted it himself – was Mandy, who had also told more than one story to the police.

Against this, Alan Charlton maintained calmly and rationally that he had never known either Idris Ali or Mandy, and that he 'categorically' had never known Karen Price. It was already clear that Karen Price was almost sixteen rather than fifteen and a half when she died. If the extreme age-limit suggested for the girl at death were invoked, it might have stretched to seventeen, long after Alan Charlton had left Cardiff. It was at least arguable that he was an innocent man, 'stitched up' not by the police but by the other two who were truly and exclusively responsible for the death of Karen Price.

Given what the jurors might already know of Idris Ali from public events, the defence which Alan Charlton offered was by no means hopeless.

According to Idris Ali, when they first encountered one

another as remand prisoners at Cardiff, Alan Charlton said to him, 'You shouldn't have opened your mouth. They wouldn't have anything on us.'

Whether or not this was said and whether or not Alan Charlton had any part in the death of Karen Price, the thought behind this remark surely preoccupied both men during their year of remand in the shabby Victorian prison. Until the 'Crimewatch' broadcast of February 1990, the police had no interest in Idris Ali as a possible figure in the case. It was apparently he who said to a fellow lodger that he was probably one of the last people to have seen Karen Price alive. As Alan Charlton allegedly pointed out, he could as easily have kept his mouth shut. If anything was said by his acquaintances, he might simply have said that he knew Karen when they were at school together but hadn't seen her for some time before her death. This could have saved him from the police and prevented the questioning of Mandy.

With these two witnesses out of it, the case against Alan Charlton must have been further weakened. Access to the back garden of 29 Fitzhamon Embankment was not difficult. True, there were witnesses who offered evidence of glimpses and memories that might link him with Karen. Yet each memory was so fragmentary in itself, that it might well not have withstood a vigorous defence in a murder trial. Despite the marvels of technology, there was not a scrap of forensic evidence connecting Alan Charlton with the girl's death. He was perhaps right to think that if Idris Ali had kept his mouth shut, 'They wouldn't have anything on us.' Or rather, they might have had something only on Alan Charlton. And whether that would have sustained a murder charge was open to question.

If Idris Ali was right, it was only his conscience and his sleepless nights, the thought of Karen 'playing' on his mind, which determined him to come forward. To that extent, it had been a close-run thing. But then, so was the discovery of the skeleton in the carpet. Had the builders at Fitzhamon Embankment not decided to dig down an extra six inches on that December afternoon in 1989, no crime would have been discovered. Karen Price would have disappeared and neither the caring professions nor anyone else would have taken any further steps to find her. In those circumstances, perhaps Idris Ali's urge to confess might have been appeased.

VII

The trial of Alan Charlton and Idris Ali opened in No. 1 Court at Cardiff Crown Court on Monday 21 January 1991, almost ten years after the murder with which the two men were charged. The proceedings were to last for just over five weeks. If they were less reported than they might have been, this was because the bulk of the national press was occupied by the final stages of hostilities in the Gulf War. 'Home news' was reduced to a page or two. Panelled in pale oak and hung with portraits of nineteenth-century jurists above the doors to the judge's room and the jury room, the Cardiff courtroom was a building within a building, its high-set viewless windows making it seem physically remote from the wide avenues and civic offices of Cathays Park. The oval space of the raised dock with its brass guard-rails stood between the stepped benches of the public seats and those of the court itself.

Alan Charlton and Idris Ali were brought before the Honourable Mr Justice Rose and pleaded not guilty. The judge looked a good deal younger than the popular image of his profession. His manner was one of brisk courtesy, intervening as little as possible, like one who knew that this particular trial was to be a long haul.

John Griffith Williams QC, leading for the Crown, recapitulated the story of Karen Price's death as told in the statements of Idris Ali and Mandy. Of the two accused, Alan Charlton was 'the dominant party'. 'We allege that he bears the greater responsibility for her death. He determined that she was die and he with the help of Ali strangled her to death. After you have heard the evidence, you may come to the conclusion that she died because these men were worried she would go to the police and expose them as pimps, and in

Charlton's case make allegations of sexual abuse.'

This was the first indication that the prosecution case relied on Idris Ali's story of Karen having been strangled rather than on Mandy's version of Charlton beating her to death with his fists. Strangulation was certainly suggested by the pink discoloration of the teeth. Professor Bernard Knight, the pathologist in the case, could not confirm that Karen Price had been strangled but found 'nothing inconsistent with strangulation as a cause of death.' This, of course, cast doubt on Mandy's account of Karen having been killed by Charlton's beating and being dead when lifted on to the bed. Of the two versions of Karen's death, Mr Griffith Williams said reassuringly, 'It would be very surprising if there were not some inconsistencies.' As to the motive, it was now suggested that Ali and Charlton had murdered Karen as a matter of policy, to silence her. Was it, then, a calculated and cold-blooded killing by two pimps, rather than the result of Charlton's brief but uncontrollable rage?

Mr Griffith Williams followed his argument with energy and tenacity, though the real battle was to be between the two accused. The young and young-middle-aged jury of six men and six women glanced from time to time at the two figures in the dock. Alan Charlton, his grey flannel suit tight on his shoulders, was a large thick-set man with a darkish crew-cut and a slight beard. Idris Ali talked and joked with the warders in the dock as he waited for each session to start. By contrast with Charlton's visible tension, he seemed self-confident in his grey-green suit, his dark hair now worn longer than in his newspaper photographs. Yet even if he were acquitted of murder, there was another trial to follow for prison riot.

The first week of the trial was occupied by the opening address for the Crown and the presentation of subsidiary evidence, whether the colour of carpets sold in Clifton Street or the gruesome career of the coffin-fly. Then, on Monday 28 January, after lunch, came the first hitch. Alan Charlton was unwell. In the absence of the jury on Tuesday morning, a consultant explained that the defendant was suffering from the strain and pressure of the case. Specifically, Alan Charlton showed signs of stress because he was being held in prison and was not free to consult his legal advisers. The trial was also going too fast for him to consult them as often as he wished.

Mr Justice Rose remarked that the trial was going no faster than legal proceedings normally do. He ordered it to continue. Next morning, Wednesday 30 January, Idris Ali was absent. He too was unwell, though in his case it was a matter of vomiting. In his absence and that of the jury, Gerard Elias QC submitted a plea on behalf of Charlton. He asked that it should be made clear that Mandy did not say she recognized Charlton at the identity parade of 5 March 1990. She failed to pick him out. Later that day, in a statement, she said that she thought the man whose position was No. 11 in the line-up was Charlton – which was right – but that she couldn't be sure after more than eight years. Later still on that day, she said that she had recognized him on the parade but had been too frightened of him to pick him out. None of this altered the fact that she had failed to identify him when asked, for whatever reason. Even had she done so, Mr Elias added, it would not necessarily incriminate Alan Charlton. He was a conspicuous figure and often on public display in the summer of 1981. She might easily have recognized him from seeing him on duty at the Excel Restaurant.

The true combat in the case began on that afternoon of Wednesday 30 January when Mandy, having given evidence the previous day, was cross-examined by Gerard Elias. This cross-examination lasted into the next day, by which time overnight snow had turned Cardiff Civic Centre into a winter landscape.

It was hard for those in court to see this married woman as the thirteen-year-old child who had stood in the corner of the room and watched or heard her young friend put to death. She was, understandably, a most reluctant witness who entered and left the court with her two plain clothes police protectors. Her voice had a distinctive Cardiff intonation and was so quiet that Mr Elias, a few feet away, failed to catch some of her answers. The judge repeated them for him.

CHAPTER SIX

Gerard Elias was deliberate but never hectoring. Yet the jury was not permitted to forget that this witness, by her own admission, must have given false evidence to the police on one occasion or the other. As to her evidence against Alan Charlton, 'This is a pack of lies, isn't it?' 'No,' she said quietly. Later he asked whether she had ever been examined by a psychiatrist? She could not remember. Was she an accomplished liar? Mandy was not sure what that meant. 'Someone who lies easily and convincingly,' Mr Elias said helpfully. She denied it.

Her explanations for lying to the police were surely not convincing, Mr Elias suggested. She claimed that she had denied her involvement for fear that her husband would find out that she had been on the streets as a child, 'I didn't want him to know about my past.' But she had been told during the police interview that her husband had already been shown the files, that he had said he had thought she might have been on the streets then and that he had come to terms with the possibility.

The cross-examination continued. Sometimes the questions merely reduced her to silence. 'Can't remember?' Gerard Elias suggested gently. The point was not lost on the jury. At other moments when there was no answer, he asked, 'You want to help us if you can?'

Mandy was to be recalled, but for the moment, Gerard Elias concluded by two rhetorical questions to fix his client's explanation in the minds of the jurors,

'Is it the case that Karen died from inhaling glue or some other substance?'

'Is it the case that you and Ali and perhaps others killed Karen and tried to put the blame on Charlton?'

As he sat down, Roger Backhouse QC rose to cross-examine Mandy on behalf of Idris Ali. By now there was an extra warder in the dock, sitting between the two defendants. Mr Backhouse treated Mandy as though she were his own witness, since she was the one who might save Idris Ali. Gerard Elias had cited her as a liar. Roger Backhouse went through certain crucial answers that she had given to the police, adding 'And that was true, wasn't it? . . . And that was right, wasn't it?' Little by little, something of her credibility was re-established.

'I want to ask you a few questions about yourself,' he said encouragingly. In the next ten or fifteen minutes he elicited a self portrait of Mandy as a young woman struggling against childhood deprivation, passing examinations, getting a job, making a stable marriage at sixteen. So far as there was a success story during the case, it was hers. Was it beyond the comprehension of the jurors that, faced with the ruin of all this by a dark secret from her childhood, she should have given way to panic, evasion or untruth?

Yet again she gave her version of the last moments of Karen Price. From time to time, Mr Backhouse dwelt on the truth that Mandy and Idris Ali were two children trying to save their friend from a powerfully built adult. Once again, Mandy appeared as the little girl sheltering and crying in the corner of the room, afraid even to look at the horror a few feet away. 'I couldn't believe she was dead. I'd never seen a dead person . . . . I was too bloody scared to move, do you know what I mean?' Then there was the act of necrophilia which she alleged Alan Charlton committed and which had made her feel physically sick so many years later.

It was now about 3.20 on the afternoon of Wednesday 21 January, the press benches empty but for one journalist. Alan Charlton rose in the dock, putting his hand up like a school-boy in class.

'Yes?' said Mr Justice Rose.

Alan Charlton asked to be allowed to go into the witness-box and answer Mandy's perjury.

'You'll have your chance, Mr Charlton,' the judge said equably.

'I just want to say that I shall arrive here tomorrow morning in possession of all my faculties to go into that box.'

'I don't think you'll be giving evidence tomorrow,' said Mr Justice Rose, no doubt estimating a further week of the prosecution case.

'After what's been said, I won't be allowed in that box.'

There were murmurs between judge and counsel and something was said by Gerard Elias about Charlton's wish to leave the dock. The judge looked at him.

'You may go down, Mr Charlton, but the case will continue in your absence.'

Alan Charlton with two of the three warders close to him was near the steps of the dock.

'This will be all over the news tonight. I've already had threats from some of the other prisoners because of the lies told in that box.'

Mandy turned to face him from the witness-box.

'It's the truth,' she said, more loudly than she had given the rest of her evidence.

'It ought to be on your conscience, Mandy!' he said, just as loudly.

'It ought to be on yours!'

Mr Justice Rose tried to wave the witness and defendant to silence. At this point, however, Idris Ali also rose and began saying something to Alan Charlton. A woman's voice from the public benches shouted.

'Idris! Calm down!'

The court adjourned for fifteen minutes with sounds of shouting from the steps leading down from the dock. Charlton had gone down, Idris Ali remained and then, presently, went down as well. When the hearing resumed he was alone in the dock with the warders, standing up and saying to the judge, 'I apologize for the outburst.' Charlton reappeared and apologized through his counsel at the end of the afternoon. Yet perhaps in the exchanges which had just taken place there was one word spoken in the presence of the jury which was to decide the outcome of his case.

The court rose early, at 4pm, to enable those present to make an early start homewards through the snow. Proceedings were delayed in the next few days by the illness of a juror and on Thursday 7 February, Alan Charlton was again missing from the dock, through ill health. He did not wish the trial to go ahead in his absence. By this time a

number of witnesses had been examined who offered tenta-
tive sightings of Alan Charlton with Idris Ali or Karen Price in
1981. The most consistent of these was Jane, the Mohican
blonde, who claimed that she had had both men as her pimps
at fourteen. Unfortunately, as Inspector Nicholas Reville
explained, Jane had also failed to pick out Alan Charlton on
the identity parade. When questioned by police about a tattoo
mark 'Alan', she claimed it referred to a different man. Later
she withdrew all this evidence and confessed that she had
been too 'frightened' of Alan Charlton to tell the truth. She
also alleged that she had had sex with Charlton himself when
she was fourteen but it had not been of her own free will.

With Charlton absent from the trial on 7 February, Mr
Justice Rose pointed out that the principal objection to continuing with the hearing would be that an accused is entitled
to hear the case that he must answer. However, the court was
now to hear tapes of Idris Ali's questioning by the police.
These did not concern Charlton. In law, they might be
evidence against Ali but could not be evidence against anyone
else. Therefore the hearing of the Idris Ali tapes would go
ahead. There were a dozen of these, each about forty minutes
long, occupying the next two days. Shortly before the end
of each tape, there was a raucous klaxon sound on the
recording, as if to warn the interrogators that their time was
almost up. The court was also to hear police tapes of Alan
Charlton being questioned and to be shown a video of the
BBC 'Crimewatch' programme which had appealed for
information about Karen Price and had prompted Idris Ali's
indirect response to the police. DC Les Mumford then gave
evidence of the uncorroborated confession made by Idris Ali
in his cell, which was not on tape.

According to this confession, Ali said that he had had a
sleepless night. When asked why, he said, 'You don't understand. It was a bad thing that went down . . . . I strangled her,
man.'

When asked how he had done it, he was alleged to have
said, 'With my hands, man . . . I didn't want to do it. He made
me.'

CHAPTER SIX

When he was asked if anything else had happened, something which Mandy had already suggested, DC Mumford said that Ali replied,

'I can't say. You don't understand, it's my life. Listen, that guy is a psycho. He made me have sex with her when she was dead.'

In fairness, the only admission that Ali had made elsewhere was that Charlton had tried to make him do this but that he had avoided it. On the next tape he had insisted there was 'no way' he had committed an act of necrophilia. The fact that Charlton had done so 'sickened' him.

So far, the trial had been dominated by the prosecution account of Karen's death. It was not to remain so. At the beginning of the following week, on Monday 18 February, Gerard Elias began to build an alternative sequence of events, casting doubt on the possibility that Alan Charlton could have had anything to do with the murder of Karen Price.

To this point it had been assumed that the carpet in which the skeleton was found, though it could not have been taken from the floor at Fitzhamon Embankment, was an off-cut from the work done in 1980. Though Alan Charlton was not the only person who might have had access to this surplus piece of carpet, he would have been one of the most likely.

Gerard Elias now called an architect as witness. Mr Roy Barker appeared firm, professional, competent and impartial. The point at issue was whether the lounge, stairs, and lobby of the basement flat at Fitzhamon Embankment could have been carpeted with two rolls measuring twelve feet by fifteen and a half feet, leaving an off-cut five by seven feet. It was a question of mathematics. Though Mr Barker had based his calculations on a scale model of the house rather than on measurements taken there, he calculated that it was impossible to carpet such an area and leave an off-cut of the size used to wrap the body. The off-cut would be four feet nine inches long. At its widest it would be a mere two feet eleven inches and at its narrowest only two feet two inches. In theory, at least, it seemed out of the question that the carpet in which the body was wrapped should have come from the same rolls as those used on the floor of the basement flat. As Mr Elias later pointed out, no one remembered there being an off-cut of any kind kept at 29 Fitzhamon Embankment. The pattern of the carpet round the skeleton might be the same but there was no evidence from Mr Barker's calculations linking it to the carpet in the house, let alone to Alan Charlton.

This was the beginning of the new version of events. Mandy was now recalled and cross-examined by Mr Elias on the secure unit at Maes-Yr-Eglwys, also known as 'the cell', where girls could be confined with no access to the outside world. She could neither remember it nor whether she was ever confined in it. 'Can't remember?' he asked sympathetically. When she absconded at the end of July 1981, did she not spend four nights with another girl, Sharon, and possibly a boy, David, sleeping on the beach at Barry? She could not remember that either. Had she been with them, it would have reduced to three days the time in which she could have witnessed Karen's death. When she spoke of 'Alan' as her boyfriend in 1981, was this not Alan Jones rather than Alan Charlton? She could only say that Alan Jones and Sharon were 'vaguely familiar' as names. Did she not visit 29 Fitzhamon Embankment to buy drugs from a flat other than Charlton's? Did she not know tenants in an upper flat and was that not how she was familiar with the house? She denied all this. After this final cross-examination, her part in the trial was over. The jury might have been uneasy at the amount she could not remember and the diminishing time during which she could possibly have witnessed the murder.

When Gerard Elias rose to present the case for his client on the afternoon of Monday 18 February, he told the jury that 'Mr Charlton exercises his right to remain silent in this court.' Alan Charlton, he explained, maintained that he was innocent and that there was no case for him to answer. He had never known Idris Ali nor Mandy. He had 'categorically' never known Karen Price, let alone murdered her. He was saying to the Crown, if they still thought him guilty, 'You prove it.' As a defendant, he was certainly not required to prove his own innocence.

Mr Elias's next witness was a tall bearded social worker who had had Mandy as part of his case-load. A good deal of his evidence was matter of fact. In the autumn of 1978, at eleven years old, she was arrested for shoplifting. She was made a ward of court and was then the subject of a police report when caught glue-sniffing in St Mary Street and its arcades. In February 1981, she had attacked her social worker in the kitchen of her mother's home and hit him over the head with a broom handle. She was sent to Maes-Yr-Eglwys as being beyond parental control but absconded on 9 June. She was picked up in Barry on 24 June and spent three days in the secure unit. She now said that she could not even remember that the unit existed. Because of her threats of running away, she was returned to the secure unit on 6 July. Would she really not have remembered that such a place existed? From 7 July until she absconded from Porthcawl on 30 July, there was no report of her either running away or being allowed home leave. If that were so, then she could not have gone with Karen Price to Barry on 8 and 9 July. She could not have solicited on the streets of Cardiff, nor had Idris Ali as her pimp, nor met Alan Charlton in July. A whole swathe of her evidence must be false. Moreover, all the evidence which Idris Ali had given about the events of July 1981 became unreliable, since they involved her. It was already proved that his dating of events by the Teardrop Explodes rock concert was wrong. The group had only appeared once in Cardiff, at the Students Union on 21 March 1982. He could not have been Mandy's pimp in July nor taken her to Galston Street, nor been with her at the blue movie party, since the last of these had been before 29 July. What was left for the jury to believe?

Moreover, Alan Charlton had been visited constantly in his flat by his girlfriend Sian until late July. He had kept a dog there. He had phoned the police to report a robbery on 22 July. Unlike Idris Ali, Mandy had given evidence that the dancing and the murder had taken place in the ground floor flat rather than Charlton's basement flat. But if she was securely at Maes-Yr-Eglwys until 30 July and not in Cardiff until a day or two later, perhaps several days, this was impossible. On 1 August, the tenant of the ground floor flat returned from the United States and was himself in residence.

In opening the case for the Crown, Mr Griffith Williams had said that it would be 'very surprising' if there were not inconsistencies in the evidence after all this time. At what point might inconsistencies become impossibilities? If the two principal witnesses had been wrong about so much, what was left? If the evidence given by her social worker was confirmed by documents at Maes-Yr-Eglwys, it seemed that Mandy could only have witnessed the murder sometime in the period of 1 to 8 August, at the end of which she was picked up and taken back to Maes-Yr-Eglwys. But the events of that week were now in doubt, after her failure to remember them under cross-examination. She could no longer be sure that she had not been with Sharon and David at Barry during the first four days of that week. How reliable was her recollection, then, let alone her evidence?

Yet the balance swung the other way when measured against the testimony of Anthony Hurd, summed up later by Mr Justice Rose. Mr Hurd, now retired, had been third in command of Maes-Yr-Eglwys during 1981. Mandy's social worker spoke of what South Glamorgan knew but Mr Hurd and Maes-Yr-Eglwys belonged to Mid-Glamorgan. The counties were different authorities and operated independently without a great deal of liaison between their social services departments. In his answers to Mr Griffith Williams, Mr Hurd had been positive that he had never known a girl kept in the security unit for longer than seventy-two hours. Twenty-four hours was the norm and had become the official maximum soon after 1981.

Moreover, the policy at Maes-Yr-Eglwys was to maintain a girl's link with her family, usually allowing her home leave at weekends, whether she absconded or not. Sometimes this weekend leave was supervised but that seemed to be a rarity. Mandy was an habitual absconder, in that she would go on weekend leave on Friday and not bother to come back on Sunday. She would be collected from home by social services a day or two later, unless she had also vanished from there.

In addition, Maes-Yr-Eglwys even had a system of home leave for the day. According to Mr Hurd, Mandy might easily have been in Cardiff for several days with leave, at a time when her local social services department of South Glamorgan thought she was at Maes-Yr-Eglwys, apparently under lock and key. If Mid-Glamorgan was right, she could certainly have been with Karen Price at Barry sometime during the weekend of 9 July. She could have been at either or both of the blue movie parties on any Saturday night in July. Idris Ali might well have sheltered her at his home and been her pimp during that month, even though she might have spent some of the time back at Maes-Yr-Eglwys.

Yet this in itself did not convict Alan Charlton of murder. He kept silent and exercised his right not to give evidence, a fact upon which the prosecution is not permitted to comment. Counsel for Idris Ali, however, was entirely free to comment on this and Mr Roger Backhouse soon did so.

Inspector George Lewis was called as a defence witness to give details of Idris Ali's previous convictions and sentences served for burglary. After all, it was his case that he had not reported Karen's death to the police in 1981 or subsequently because of his criminal record. That record was now before the jury. As he put it in court and as the press reported him, 'I'm a burglar, and whenever I've appeared in court I've nodded my head. But when it comes to murder, and having sex with dead bodies, that goes way beyond all things.'

On the morning of Tuesday 19 February, Idris Ali was called as the principal witness for his own defence. A Bible was produced for him to take the oath but he shook his head. 'It's not my religion,' he said quietly. Though he swore on the Koran, his manner was Cardiff born and bred, frequently and familiarly addressing counsel as 'boss'. In a moment of measured drama, Roger Backhouse asked him, 'Did you kill Karen Price?'

'No.'

'Who did?'

'He did,' Ali said, pointing at Alan Charlton in the dock.

It was a dramatic enough opening to make the evening headlines but after that there was little to do beyond go through the story again. Idris Ali in the witness-box appeared a gentle and quietly-spoken man. Indeed, Mr Backhouse several times asked him to speak up so that the jury could hear him. Mr Justice Rose added more curtly, 'If the jury can't hear you, you're wasting your time.' The defendant also smiled a good deal in the witness-box, perhaps from nervousness or else in an attempt to be pleasant. The expressions of the jurors suggested that they were unmoved by a man on trial for Karen's death smiling in the witness-box.

Then, as he described the murder of Karen Price, whom he now called 'my best friend', Idris Ali appeared to weep, his elbows on the edge of the witness-box and his face covered by his hands. Mr Backhouse asked him why he had confessed to this murder, if he had not committed it. Several times, in similar phrases, Idris Ali insisted that he had confessed to the police and to his wife in order to prevent his family from hearing that Alan Charlton had tried to make him commit an act of necrophilia. It was not clear how or why he thought a confession would prevent this, since his wife heard of it anyway in May 1990. But would he really rather confess to a killing of which he was innocent – and for which he might go to prison for life – than let it be known that someone had tried unsuccessfully to make him commit an act of necrophilia? This reasoning seemed so bizarre that Mr Justice Rose tried to get it straight for the benefit of the jurors.

'You would rather admit to killing someone than to someone having attempted to make you have sex with a dead body?'

'Yes,' he said simply.

Gerard Elias began his cross-examination of Idris Ali that afternoon. In the face of contradictions and evasions, he remained cool and precise. As this continued, he would say for the benefit of the jury, 'I see. We're back to where we were two or three minutes ago.' Throughout the cross-examination, which lasted into the next day, Idris Ali appeared buoyant and self-confident, as if he could not see that his defence was crumbling all about him. In answer to one question, he insisted that he had 'nothing to hide, not like Charlton.'

'Is that an answer to my question?' Mr Elias asked.

'It's a good answer,' Idris Ali said, spreading out his hands as if to appeal to the court.

'I see. It's a good answer, is it?'

Back came the question of why he had confessed to a murder of which he was innocent. Why had he confessed to the prison doctor, for example? He could only say that his head 'had gone' and then that he did not like doctors.

At last came the question of why he had changed course and decided to say that he had been 'stitched up' by the police. The letters written from Cardiff prison to a friend in Shepton Mallet prison were produced and Mr Justice Rose ordered that they should be copied for the jury.

'Your honour,' said Idris Ali, 'I thought letters were private.'

'Yes,' said Mr Justice Rose, 'I accept that you thought that. This, however, is a murder trial.'

It was almost the only occasion in the proceedings when there was a discernible murmur of approval from the public benches.

In the closing addresses to the jury, there was little for counsel to do but recapitulate the evidence. The Crown had made its case and Gerard Elias stuck to the inconsistencies in that case so far as Alan Charlton was concerned. Alan Charlton had no knowledge of the crime, let alone any connection with it. He had 'categorically' never known Karen Price, nor Idris Ali nor Mandy. A good deal had been heard about drugs and blue movie parties but Alan Charlton's lifestyle was not on trial. There was no case for him to answer and no reason why he need give evidence. If the Crown still though him guilty, then the law required the Crown to prove that guilt. In general, Mr Elias likened the case to a jigsaw puzzle. If a piece did not fit, it must be discarded. This would certainly have made a good deal of the evidence against Charlton questionable.

Roger Backhouse reminded the jury that Idris Ali had at least 'had the grace' to give evidence, unlike Charlton. Yet that in itself presented a problem, since his performance in the witness-box had shown such confusion. Mr Backhouse conceded that Idris Ali might not seem to them an attractive personality, he might not be what his counsel called 'prisoner of the month' at Cardiff Crown Court. Yet on Ali's behalf, he also asked them to remember that they were, in effect, trying a sixteen-year-old, puny for his age and four feet eleven inches tall. What chance would he have had to save Karen from the burly adult Charlton? What risks might he have run by going to the police in the summer of 1981 – with or without Mandy? Yet it was Idris Ali who showed conscience and remorse. Might not the crime still have been unexplained, if he had said nothing after the 'Crimewatch' programme in February 1990?

In the wake of this, Mr Justice Rose summed up. He began by warning the jury of the lapse of time since the alleged crime was committed and the difficulty of clear recollection by the witnesses. He also warned them not to be overawed by experts. They may have assumed that questions of mental stability were at stake during the trial. 'Put that from your mind.' It might also be suggested that some evidence could be affected by drink, cannabis, or glue-sniffing. 'Put drugs from your mind.' Nor was it for them to wonder why girls of thirteen who had absconded from an assessment centre should be on the streets of Cardiff earning a living by prostitution.

So far as the evidence was concerned, Mr Justice Rose accepted that it might be a jigsaw with pieces missing. The question was whether there were enough pieces to make a picture. As for Idris Ali's appearance in the witness-box and his evidence elsewhere, 'Even if he told you it was twelve o'clock, you might prefer not to believe him unless you heard the chimes striking through the window.'

On matters of law, which are the concern of the judge rather than the jury, Mr Justice Rose none the less reminded the jurors that duress is no defence to a charge of murder. As for statements made by Idris Ali and Mandy, these could only be evidence against the person making the statement. No one can be convicted on evidence given 'behind his back', when he is not there to challenge or answer the accusations. In the case of Mandy and Idris Ali, the jury was to accept their evidence where it was corroborated.

The summing up of the evidence, which had begun on the morning of Monday 25 February, continued throughout the rest of the day and was concluded on Tuesday morning. It was just after 12pm when the jurors retired to consider their verdict. Mr Justice Rose instructed them to return such a verdict unanimously.

One way or another, it might have seemed a straightforward matter. Yet those waiting for the verdict in the marble-paved lobby of the Crown Court building, a mock-Renaissance memorial to Edwardian prosperity, were still waiting there as the February afternoon turned to evening. The view on the public benches of the courtroom was that one or two of the CID officers had begun to look worried. The jury had been out for several hours with no sign of their return as yet. Unless they were going through the evidence with great thorough-ness, it seemed that there might have been a disagreement of some kind. As one of the pressmen in the lobby remarked, Alan Charlton had been impressive on the tapes. He had answered confidently under questioning and had said nothing that would convict him of the crime. To deny all knowledge of the crime and those associated with it was, in one respect, 'a dodgy defence', but was it not the answer that an innocent man would give?

At this point, the low winter sunlight was shining from a bleak and colourless Channel sky on the green blinds of the half-moon windows high in the courtroom wall. Another half-hour passed and the sky was dark. It was at 5.45, almost five hours after the retirement, that the court began to fill again and there was a message that the jury was coming back. As counsel and prisoners took their places, a burly and agile prison warder was positioned at the courtroom door, another at the gate of the dock leading into the courtroom. Two uniformed policemen were also posted near the main door, in case a guilty verdict inspired one or both defendants to leap the brass rails of the dock and bolt for freedom.

The jurors filed in and sat down. For whatever reason, they looked uneasy and self-conscious. One of the youngest women had been chosen as 'madam foreman'. When Mr Justice Rose had resumed his seat on the bench, the clerk asked Madam Foreman if a unanimous verdict had been reached. It had. Did the jurors find Alan Charlton guilty or not guilty of the murder of Karen Price?

'Guilty.'

There was a single quick and muffled cry from the public benches. Charlton himself sat in the dock with his head bowed, showing no other response.

Did the jurors find Idris Ali guilty or not guilty of the murder of Karen Price?

'Guilty.'

This time the gasps and cries came from the womenfolk of the Ali family.

Inspector Lewis entered the witness-box to give the antecedents of the accused. Idris Ali's previous convictions were already known. Now the law's protection was removed from Alan Charlton. The police had allegedly described Charlton to Ali as 'a nasty piece of work', apparently with good reason. When he met Karen Price with Idris Ali in the Adamstown pub, he had only been out of prison six months after serving a sentence for an attack on a fifty-five-year-old woman in west Wales. He had tricked his way into her house, ordered her to go upstairs and undress, then gripped her by the throat until she lost consciousness, so that he could take the clothes off himself. As he did so, he saw that she had had a mastectomy and he backed away. The woman, having recovered consciousness, asked him why he was doing this. 'I don't know,' he said, 'It just comes over me at times.'

Perhaps the relief on the faces of the jurors came from the knowledge that they had not convicted a man without a previous criminal record, one who might have been falsely incriminated by the two principal witnesses in the trial. It seems that their reading of Alan Charlton's character was correct.

On behalf of Alan Charlton, Gerard Elias submitted two medical reports. He also pointed out that since the crimes of 1979–81, his client had lived in the community for ten years without repeating such behaviour. For Ali, Roger Backhouse repeated that this was the offence of a boy of no more than sixteen at the time of the murder. In Alan Charlton's case, nothing more was said in court about the nature of what it was that 'came over' him. His co-defendant referred to him frequently as 'a psycho'. Was he?

During 1981, Charlton had been in training as a weightlifter with a set of weights in his flat. Did he also take anabolic steroids to help him in his training? Though these were not officially available except on a medical prescription, they were unofficially available from many gymnasiums. Was his sudden violence in wounding Mandy with his knife, as she claimed, and killing Karen the consequence of so-called 'steroid rage', which had reduced other men's murder convictions to manslaughter on appeal? To take anabolic steroids without medical supervision was inviting trouble. It was certainly a characteristic of steroid rage that, under the influence of such medication, a man who was normal or amiable at one moment would lose all control without warning. In just this way, Alan Charlton had 'lost his rag' or 'gone berserk', as his two companions described it when Karen Price was killed.

Mr Justice Rose, addressing the two men standing in the dock before him, informed them that they had been convicted on 'overwhelming evidence'.

'Because of the passage of years and the numerous lies both of you told the police, it will probably never be known precisely what the sequence of events was which led to this girl's murder. Clearly you both took part in it, and I am sure that you, Charlton, played the major role.'

The mandatory sentences were passed. Alan Charlton was

to go to prison for life. Idris Ali was sentenced, as though he was still sixteen, to be detained during Her Majesty's pleasure, an indefinite sentence. He was soon to receive a further four-year sentence at Merthyr Tydfil Crown Court in July 1991 for his part in the April 1990 riot at Cardiff prison. As the two men were taken down, Ali appeared tearful and Charlton unmoved.

The judge called up Inspector Lewis and thanked him for hours of police time spent on a 'complex' case. Turning to the jury, Mr Justice Rose thanked them, remarking that the trial had begun on the first day of hostilities in the Gulf War and seemed about to end on the day those hostilities ceased. The process of justice provided 'some indication of the purpose for which our troops are fighting . . . . I doubt whether the defendants would have enjoyed the same privileges, which they have had during this trial, under Saddam Hussein.'

For the last time in five and a half weeks, the court heard the usher's 'All rise!' as the judge left the bench. A young reporter ran to a white radio car parked outside in King Edward VII Avenue. A group of women stood in tears in the court's marble vestibule. Karen Price's father, tall, thin and walking with the aid of a stick, left the court after seeing justice done to the daughter whom he had imagined now living with a family of her own. The press were waiting to photograph and interview him on the wide tree-lined pavement. News of the verdict spread from the civic centre to the busier streets, though too late for the evening editions. A newspaper-seller among the homeward tide of commuters in the entrance of the Royal Arcade said, 'Why don't they hang 'em?'

After so much trouble with the case of the Darvells in the 'Swansea Sex Shop' killing and the murder of Lynett White, the South Wales CID seemed to have won against the odds. Detective Superintendent Neale Evans drew the veil from Alan Charlton's past, describing him as 'a devious and intelligent man who ruled by fear . . . . He has an impressive personality and there is no doubt he influenced the teenagers in more ways than one. He is a stranger to the truth and I do not know if he has any conscience. He is a perverted individual and he has got his just reward.' As for Idris Ali, Superintendent Evans allowed the possibility that 'his conscience got the better of him.'

For most of those who witnessed the legal process, it was the web of circumstances rather than the characters of the two men which exercised the greater fascination. Did Alan Charlton give himself away, before the jury, as they watched his outburst when Mandy was giving evidence. He called her by her Christian name. While he might have called her a liar or worse, would he have used the first name of someone who was a total stranger? And then there were the things that might so easily have not happened. If only the spades of four workmen had not gone down an extra six inches through riverside soil on a December afternoon . . . . If only Idris Ali had said nothing at the end of the 'Crimewatch' programme . . . . The thread of discovery and retribution had been tenuous in the extreme. Yet after almost ten years it had held firm. All the same, how easily Karen Price might have been another Mamie Stuart, found forty years later in the third decade of the twenty-first century. Would anyone have connected her with two men, by that time in their fifties and sixties, whom the dead girl had known in the summer of her sixteenth year?